Network Your Computers & Devices

Step by Step

Ciprian Adrian Rusen
and 7 Tutorials

Published with the authorization of Microsoft Corporation by:
O'Reilly Media, Inc.
1005 Gravenstein Highway North
Sebastopol, California 95472

Printed and bound in Canada.

1 2 3 4 5 6 7 8 9   TG   5 4 3 2 1 0

Microsoft Press titles may be purchased for educational, business or sales promotional use. Online editions are also available for most titles (*http://my.safaribooksonline.com*). For more information, contact our corporate/institutional sales department: (800) 998-9938 or *corporate@oreilly.com*. Visit our website at *microsoftpress.oreilly.com*. Send comments to *mspinput@ microsoft.com*.

Acquisitions and Development Editor: Kenyon Brown
Production Editor: Holly Bauer
Editorial Production: Octal Publishing, Inc.
Technical Reviewer: Chuck Houghton
Indexing: Ron Strauss
Cover: Karen Montgomery
Illustrator: Robert Romano

978-0-735-65216-3

To the people who enlighten my life with their candid smiles.

Also, to Seth Godin and Ed Bott for being subtle but important influences in my decision to write and publish this book, thus making one of my biggest dreams come true.

Contents

What do you think of this book? We want to hear from you!

Microsoft is interested in hearing your feedback so we can continually improve our books and learning resources for you. To participate in a brief online survey, please visit:

microsoft.com/learning/booksurvey

What do you think of this book? We want to hear from you!

Microsoft is interested in hearing your feedback so we can continually improve our books and learning resources for you. To participate in a brief online survey, please visit:

microsoft.com/learning/booksurvey

Acknowledgments

I would like to thank all of my friends who helped in the writing of this book through their patience, moral support, and sometimes, even technical support. It was great to hear their "You can do it!" encouragements whenever I was in need of hearing such words.

A Romanian *"Multumesc!"* goes to Alexandru Muntean, Alexandru Orbescu, and the 7 Tutorials team. They all have been very active helpers and true friends. Without them, some of the pages in this book would have been finished at a much slower pace.

A French *"Merci!"* goes to both my sister and my girlfriend. Their love and subtle support did wonders for keeping my energy levels up as I worked on the book.

Last but not least, I would like to thank Ken Brown, the senior editor on this project. He's been a really great guy to work with. We had an outstanding collaboration, and I can't wait for us to hopefully work together on future projects.

Introducing Home Networking

In a modern home, it is no longer unusual for family members to own multiple computers and network devices. In most houses, you can find at least a desktop computer, which is generally used for more performance-intensive tasks such as gaming or professional work of any kind. Parents bring home their work laptops or notebooks, which they use to connect to their business network and do a bit of work outside the office, when needed. Children also have their own systems, usually a mobile computer that they can easily take to school or university. All of these computers probably have different operating systems, depending on the year when they were purchased and the preference of each person. Some family members might be Windows users, while others might prefer the Mac computers from Apple. Some people who are very fond of free software might use the latest version of Ubuntu Linux. In addition to computers, a family may own other devices such as printers, scanners, consoles, mobile phones with network connectivity via Bluetooth wireless, and so on.

With the help of a router and a few network cables, you can create your own home network and connect all these computers and devices together. The list of advantages for doing so is very long and includes:

- The possibility to easily exchange data between all computers and devices.
- Sharing devices between all the computers on the home network. For example, you can share the home's printer or an external hard disk drive that everyone can use to back up their most important data, and so on.
- Media streaming between computers.
- Paying for only one Internet connection and sharing it with all the computers and devices on your network.
- Wireless access to the network and the Internet throughout your entire house.
- Playing multiplayer games via your home network.

This book covers all you need to know about setting up your home network and taking advantage of all its capabilities. Included in the book are chapters about setting up and using the networking features in Windows 7, making different operating systems work together on the network, and streaming your media over the network and the Internet. It also covers sharing devices in the network, the tools and features you need to use to keep your network secure, and setting up parental controls for your children. Last but not least, it also provides guidance on how to troubleshoot network and Internet problems by yourself.

Operating Systems Covered in the Book

This book is focused mostly on Windows 7 and shows how to use the network-related features included in this operating system. However, there are dedicated sections that cover network interoperability between Windows 7 and the following operating systems: Windows XP Service Pack 3, Windows Vista Service Pack 2, Mac OS X v10.6 (Snow Leopard), and Ubuntu Linux v10.10 (Maverick Meerkat).

Assumptions

The exercises in this book assume that you know the basics of computing and that some of your computers have Windows 7 already installed and configured. The exercises do not cover Windows 7 installation and personalization tasks. They dive directly into networking features and configuration settings.

This book explains how to install, configure, and manage a home network setup similar to the one shown in the following diagram.

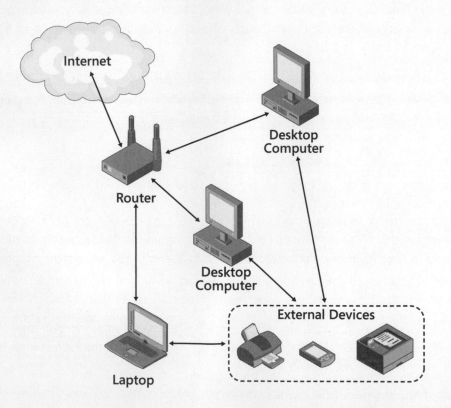

In your home, there are several computers (desktops and laptops or notebooks), each with an operating system installed and all connected to the router. Also, there are several external devices (such as printers, scanners, and so on) connected to any of the computers in your network that you would like to share with the network.

Minimum System Requirements

To run Windows 7 and work your way through the exercises in this book, your computer must meet certain specifications.

Windows 7

To run Windows 7, including the Aero desktop experience features, your computer needs to meet the following minimum requirements:

- 1 gigahertz (GHz) or faster 32-bit (x86) or 64-bit (x64) processor
- 1 gigabyte (GB) of system memory (RAM) for 32-bit systems; 2 GB for 64-bit systems
- 16 GB of available hard disk drive space for 32-bit systems; 20 GB for 64-bit systems
- Support for DirectX 9 graphics with Windows Display Driver Model (WDDM) 1.0 or higher driver and 128 megabytes (MB) memory (to enable the Aero theme)
- Internal or external DVD drive
- Monitor with a minimum of 1024 × 768 screen resolution
- Keyboard and mouse or compatible pointing device
- Internet connection for product activation, accessing online Help topics, and any other Internet-dependent processes

Some features of Windows 7 work only if you have the hardware or network connections to support them. For descriptions of the system requirements for specific features of Windows 7, visit *windows.microsoft.com/en-us/windows7/products/system-requirements/*.

Completing the Exercises

In addition to the hardware and Internet connection required to run Windows 7 and the other operating systems in your home network, you will need the following to successfully complete the exercises in this book:

- A home router with wireless capabilities.
- Ethernet network cable.

- Any version of the Windows 7 operating system.
- Access to the following peripheral devices:
  - Printer
  - Speakers
  - External storage device: USB memory stick or external hard disk drive
- Your own practice files and folders. Simply choose what you want to use from your own computer to complete the exercises and back them up before starting the exercises.

Some exercises cover operating systems other than Windows 7. However, it is not mandatory to have them in your home network. The exercises simply show what you would need to do in case the computers in your home network have a wide variety of operating systems installed.

How to Access Your Online Edition Hosted by Safari

The voucher bound in to the back of this book gives you access to an online edition of the book. (You can also download the online edition of the book to your own computer; see the next section.)

To access your online edition, do the following:

1. Locate your voucher inside the back cover, and scratch off the metallic foil to reveal your access code.

2. Go to http://microsoftpress.oreilly.com/safarienabled.

3. Enter your 24-character access code in the Coupon Code field under Step 1:

Step ❶

Coupon Code: 95QX-TEZQ-MHK2-F8QZ-N15R

CONFIRM COUPON

(Please note that the access code in this image is for illustration purposes only.)

4. Click the CONFIRM COUPON button.

   A message will appear to let you know that the code was entered correctly. If the code was not entered correctly, you will be prompted to re-enter the code.

> ✔ **Coupons Confirmed.**
>
> Coupon Code **9KQX-TEZQ-MHK2-F8QZ-N1SR**
> provides FREE access for 99999 days to
> **Microsoft® Office 2010 Inside Out**

5. In this step, you'll be asked whether you're a new or existing user of Safari Books Online. Proceed either with Step 5A or Step 5B.

    5A. If you already have a Safari account, click the EXISTING USER – SIGN IN button under Step 2.

    5B. If you are a new user, click the NEW USER – FREE ACCOUNT button under Step 2.

    You'll be taken to the "Register a New Account" page.

    This will require filling out a registration form and accepting an End User Agreement.

    When complete, click the CONTINUE button.

6. On the Coupon Confirmation page, click the My Safari button.

7. On the My Safari page, look at the Bookshelf area and click the title of the book you want to access.

0-Slot Bookshelf

You are using **0** out of **0** available Bookshelf slots.

You have full access to the content of the titles you place in your Bookshelf Folder. Any title placed in your Bookshelf Folder must remain on your Bookshelf for 30 days.

1-1 of **1 Items**   < Prev | **1** | Next >

	Title	Published	Added To Folder ▼		
1.	**Microsoft® Office 2010 Inside Out** Ed Bott; Carl Siechert Slots: **0** [ADD TO FOLDER]	29-SEP-2010	27-OCT-2010	0 Notes 0 Bookmarks	May Remove On 10-AUG-2284

How to Download the Online Edition to Your Computer

In addition to reading the online edition of this book, you can also download it to your computer. First, follow the steps in the preceding section. After Step 7, do the following:

1. On the page that appears after Step 7 in the previous section, click the Extras tab.

2. Find "Download the complete PDF of this book," and click the book title:

Overview	Table of Contents	Extras	Notes & Tags	Bookmarks	Search This Book

Extras

The publisher has provided additional content related to this title.

Description	Content
Visit the catalog page for Microsoft® Office 2010 Inside Out	**Catalog Page**
Visit the errata page for Microsoft® Office 2010 Inside Out	**Errata**
Download the complete PDF of this book.	**Microsoft® Office 2010 Inside Out**

A new browser window or tab will open, followed by the File Download dialog box:

3. Click Save.

4. Choose Desktop and click Save.

5. Locate the .zip file on your desktop. Right-click the file, click Extract All, and then follow the instructions.

Note If you have a problem with your voucher or access code, please contact *mspbooksupport@oreilly.com*, or call 800-889-8969, where you'll reach O'Reilly Media, distributor of Microsoft Press books.

Features and Conventions of This Book

This book has been designed to lead you step by step through all the tasks that you're most likely going to perform while networking your computers and devices. If you start at the beginning and work your way through all the exercises, you'll gain enough proficiency to be able to work with all the common types of network devices. However, each topic is self-contained. If you've set up a network previously, or if you completed all the exercises and later need help remembering how to perform a procedure, the following features of this book will help you locate specific information:

- **Detailed table of contents** Search the listing of the topics and sidebars within each chapter.
- **Chapter thumb tabs** Easily locate the beginning of the chapter you want.
- **Topic-specific running heads** Within a chapter, quickly locate the topic you want by looking at the running heads at the top of odd-numbered pages.
- **Glossary** Look up the meaning of a word or the definition of a concept.
- **Detailed index** Look up specific tasks and features in the index, which has been carefully crafted with the reader in mind.

You can save time when reading this book by understanding how the *Step by Step* series shows exercise instructions, keys to press, buttons to click, and other information.

Convention	Meaning
➡ SET UP	This paragraph preceding a step-by-step exercise indicates the practice files that you will use when working through the exercise. It also indicates any requirements you should attend to or actions you should take before beginning the exercise.
✖ CLEAN UP	This paragraph following a step-by-step exercise provides instructions for saving and closing open files or programs before moving on to another topic. It also suggests ways to reverse any changes you made to your computer while working through the exercise.
1. 2.	Blue numbered steps guide you through hands-on exercises in each topic.
1. 2.	Black numbered steps guide you through procedures in sidebars and expository text.

Convention	Meaning
See Also	This paragraph directs you to more information about a topic in this book or elsewhere.
Troubleshooting	This paragraph alerts you to a common problem and provides guidance for fixing it.
Tip	This paragraph provides a helpful hint or shortcut that makes working through a task easier.
Important	This paragraph points out information that you need to know to complete a procedure.
Menu and Command Shortcut	Information that simplifies the steps for selecting menus and commands to perform a task.
Bluetooth -> My devices -> New device	An arrow (->) between a menu and commands means that you should select the menu and command(s) in the order they appear. For example, "Bluetooth -> My devices -> New device" means go to the Bluetooth menu, then select the My devices command, then select the New device command."
Keyboard Shortcut	This paragraph provides information about an available keyboard shortcut for the preceding task.
Ctrl+B	A plus sign (+) between two keys means that you must press those keys at the same time. For example, "Press Ctrl+B" means that you should hold down the Ctrl key while you press the B key.
	Pictures of buttons appear in the margin the first time the button is used in a chapter.
Black bold	In exercises that begin with SET UP information, the names of program elements, such as buttons, commands, windows, and dialog boxes, as well as files, folders, or text that you interact with in the steps, are shown in black, bold type.
Blue bold	In exercises that begin with SET UP information, text that you should type is shown in blue bold type.

Getting Help

Every effort has been made to ensure the accuracy of this book. If you do run into problems, please contact the sources listed in the following topics.

Getting Help with This Book

If your question or issue concerns the content of this book or its practice files, please first
consult the book's errata page, which can be accessed at:

oreilly.com/catalog/errata.csp?isbn=0790145314765

This page provides information about known errors and corrections to the book. If you
do not find your answer on the errata page, send your question or comment to O'Reilly
Media Customer Service at:

mspbooksupport@oreilly.com

Getting Help with Windows 7 and Homegroup

If your question is about Windows 7, networking, and Homegroup, and not about the
content of this book, your first recourse is the Windows 7 Help & How-to system. This
system is a combination of tools and files stored on your computer when you installed
Windows and, if your computer is connected to the Internet, information available from
windows.microsoft.com/en-US/windows7/help. You can find general or specific Help
information in the following ways:

- To find out about an item on the screen, you can display a ScreenTip. For example,
  to display a ScreenTip for a button, point to the button without clicking it. The
  ScreenTip gives the button's name, the associated keyboard shortcut if there is one,
  and unless you specify otherwise, a description of what the button does when you
  click it.

- You can also display help information when you select the Homegroup Control
  Panel. For example, after you open the Homegroup window, you'll see a list of
  topics, as shown in the illustration that follows.

Click a topic to open the Windows Help and Support window.

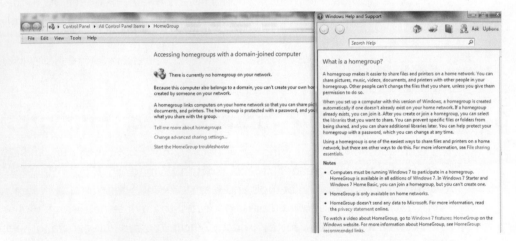

You'll also see a question mark (?) in the taskbar. This indicates that you have opened a Help window. Sometimes, videos and recommended links are available.

The following resources can provide you with more in-depth help and support information. For additional Windows 7 support and Homegroup help, go to:

windows.microsoft.com/en-US/windows/help/contact-support

and

windows.microsoft.com/en-US/windows7/products/features/Homegroup

To practice getting help, you can work through the following exercise.

SET UP You don't need any practice files to complete this exercise. Start Windows 7 and then follow the steps.

1. Click the **Start** menu. Choose **Control Panel** -> **All Control Panel Items** -> **Network and Sharing Center**.

   The Network and Sharing Center window opens (the basic network information and setup connections for your computer will look different).

2. Click the **question mark (?)** on the far right side of the screen.

   The Windows Help and Support window opens.

Tip You can maximize the window or adjust its size by dragging the handle in the lower-right corner. You can change the size of the font by clicking Options -> Text Size on the toolbar.

3. Below **Networking and sharing: recommended links**, you'll see a bulleted list of topics. Click **What you need to set up a home network**.

What you need to set up a home network

The variety of options for home networking can make buying decisions difficult. Before you decide what hardware to get, you should decide what type of network technology (the way computers in a network connect to or communicate with one another) to use. This article describes and compares the most common network technologies and lists hardware requirements for each.

Network technologies

The most common types of network technology are wireless, Ethernet, HomePNA, and Powerline. When choosing a network technology, consider the location of your computers and the desired speed of your network. The costs of these technologies are similar. The sections below compare these four technologies.

  ▸ Wireless

  ▸ Ethernet

  ▸ HomePNA

  ▸ Powerline

Hardware requirements

There are several kinds of hardware used in home networks:

  • **Network adapters.** These adapters (also called network interface cards, or NICs) connect computers to a network so that they can communicate. A network adapter can be connected to the USB or Ethernet port on your computer or installed inside your computer in an available Peripheral Component Interconnect (PCI) expansion slot.

  • **Network hubs and switches.** Hubs and switches connect two or more computers to an Ethernet network. A switch costs a little more than a hub, but it's faster.

Windows Help and Support displays information that is related to setting up a home network. You'll also see a list of network technologies. You can click any network technology to display the corresponding information.

4. Click **Show all** to display all the information. Click **Hide all** to hide the information.

5. When you return to the **Network and Sharing Center**, below **Control Panel Home**, you'll see a few topics. Click one of them to display additional information.

Control Panel Home

Manage wireless networks

Change adapter settings

Change advanced sharing
settings

See also

HomeGroup

6. Click the **Back** and **Forward** buttons to move among the topics you have already viewed.

7. At the upper-right corner of the **Control Panel** window, click the **Search Control Panel** box, type **Homegroup**, and then press the **Enter** key.

The Windows 7 Help window displays categories and topics that are related to the word that you typed.

8. In the results list, click the **Find and fix problems with Homegroup** topic.

The selected topic appears in the Windows 7 Help window.

9. Click **Next** to start the process of detecting the problem, or click **Cancel**.

✖ **CLEAN UP** Return to the Network and Sharing Center. Click the Close button in the upper-right corner of the Windows 7 window.

More Information

If your question is about Windows 7, networking, Homegroup, or another Microsoft software product and you cannot find the answer in the product's Help system, please search Microsoft Support at:

support.microsoft.com

In the United States, Microsoft software product support issues are addressed by Microsoft Product Support Services. Location-specific software support options are available at:

support.microsoft.com/gp/selfoverview/

Chapter at a Glance

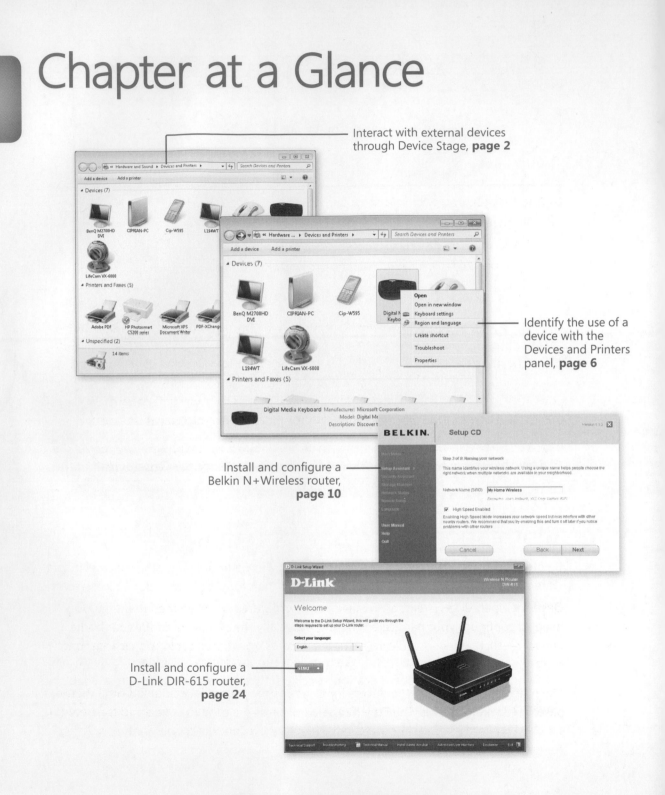

Interact with external devices through Device Stage, **page 2**

Identify the use of a device with the Devices and Printers panel, **page 6**

Install and configure a Belkin N+Wireless router, **page 10**

Install and configure a D-Link DIR-615 router, **page 24**

1 Setting Up a Router and Devices

In this chapter, you will learn how to

✔ Prepare to install and configure a router.

✔ Install and configure a Belkin N+ Wireless router.

✔ Install and configure a D-Link DIR-615 router.

As soon as you have Windows 7 installed and personalized on your computers, it's time to install the appropriate software and drivers for the hardware devices that you'll need to use: printers, network cards, keyboards and mice, mobile phones that you want to connect to your computers, and so on. Once this is all done, it is time to begin setting up your home network. The first step is to install and configure your router so that all your home computers can access each other and also share the same Internet connection.

In this chapter, you will learn how to manage and interact with hardware devices via the Device Stage feature in Windows 7 and how to install and configure your router.

> **Practice Files** You won't need any practice files to complete the exercises in this chapter.

Installing Hardware and Drivers

Once the operating systems are installed and configured on all your computers, you need to configure your hardware properly, especially the devices used for your home network—such as wired and wireless network cards, the router, cable connections, printers, and so on.

Make sure that you install the drivers for all your network cards, including both Ethernet-based and wireless cards. The Ethernet network cards are used to connect to the network via cable while the wireless network cards are used on your notebooks (or netbooks) to connect to the network via wireless signals.

In most cases, Windows 7 will automatically detect the network cards and install drivers for them. However, it is best to install the latest driver version, either from the media provided by the manufacturer of the network card (as part of the packaging) or from the manufacturer's Web site.

If the correct drivers are installed, Windows 7 should be able to connect properly both via cable and wireless.

See Also If you experienced problems connecting to the network or the Internet, refer to Chapter 15, "Troubleshooting Network and Internet Problems."

If you have other devices such as printers, scanners, phones, webcams, and so on, ensure that you connect them to the appropriate computers and install the correct drivers. Again, search the media provided by the manufacturer or the manufacturer's Web site for the latest driver versions.

Important You should only install drivers that are specifically designated for the operating system you are using. For example, don't install Windows XP drivers on computers that are running Windows 7, or vice-versa. This will surely crash your computer and cause further problems. Also, be careful to install 32-bit drivers for 32-bit operating systems and 64-bit drivers for 64-bit operating systems.

Interacting with External Devices Through Device Stage

Device Stage is a feature that aims to provide a friendly way of interacting with external devices connected to your computer. It can be accessed through the Devices And Printers panel in Windows 7 and provides a single location for managing your external devices.

Unfortunately, this feature depends a lot on the drivers and support that are available for each device. Most new devices are compatible with Windows 7 and their drivers take advantage of Device Stage, providing benefits such as allowing you to completely manage them from the Devices and Printers panel. You can do everything you need from within one convenient window: see the status of devices, view information about them, share devices over the network, change their settings, synchronize them with your PC (for example, mobile phones), configure or use features of the device, perform trouble-shooting, etc.

For older devices that cannot take advantage of this feature, Windows 7 still allows you to modify a basic set of configuration options and troubleshoot problems that might arise. While you might not enjoy all the benefits of a device that is fully compatible with Windows 7, it's still better than searching for hidden administrative tools and guessing where to go to change the device settings.

Finding the Device Stage

Device Stage is the official name of the feature but cannot be found under this name in Windows 7. In the operating system, it is actually named Devices and Printers, and by default, its shortcut can be found on the right side of the Start Menu.

Alternatively, you can go to Control Panel -> Hardware And Sound -> Devices And Printers.

Devices Included in Device Stage

Device Stage shows your own computer plus the external devices connected to it. The list of devices includes mobile phones, portable music players, digital cameras, webcams, monitors, keyboards, mice, printers, scanners, Bluetooth adapters, external hard drives, media extenders, and network devices connected to your computer.

Devices Excluded from Device Stage

Device Stage will not show devices that are a part of the base components of your computer (those that are inside your computer case). This means that you will not see internal hard disk drives, CD/DVD/Blu-ray drives, sound cards, video cards, memory, processors, internal modems, internal network cards, and so on.

Some external devices are not included, as well. A couple of common examples include your speakers or an older mouse and keyboard.

Examples of Device Stage Usage Scenarios

What exactly you can do with a device that's listed in Devices and Printers depends on the level of support for Windows 7 that the manufacturer of the device provides. For example, when I access my Microsoft Digital Media Keyboard, I can quickly configure it, get support for issues, register it, or even access a guide for healthy computing practices.

If I right-click the same keyboard, I quickly have access to configuration options such as the Region and Language used when typing.

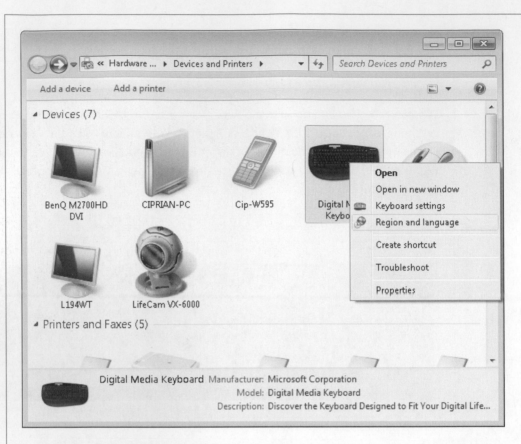

For my old HP Photosmart C5200 printer, I have a small but useful set of options. From within its Devices and Printers window, I can quickly see how many files there are in the printing queue, if the printer is ready or not, and what the default setting for page size and orientation is.

I also have options for changing the printing properties and getting support for my device.

For newer models of printers, you have more options available.

Preparing to Install and Configure a Router

Installing and configuring your router is the most complex and important activity in setting up your home network. This device is used to connect the entire home network to your Internet service provider. Therefore, it must have the correct settings if it is to connect without problems. Once the router setup is complete, you must configure the settings of your home network so that all computers can connect to the router and the Internet. Lastly, you need to enable the wireless capability and configure it so that all notebooks and netbooks can connect to the home network.

Configuring the router depends a lot on the manufacturer and the specific model you have. There is no universal method for configuring a router, as each producer uses a different approach. Therefore, carefully read the user manual while going through this procedure. While you progress through the configuration, pay attention to the following details:

- **Internet WAN (Wide Area Network) settings**   All of these settings are obtained from your Internet service provider (ISP) and are used to connect your home network to the Internet. You might need to contact your ISP to gather information you need to configure your router's connection to the Internet.

- **Connection type**   What kind of connection will you be using? The most common connection types are the following:

  - *Dynamic*   Your ISP will automatically assign an IP address to the router. This IP address is based on the Media Access Control (MAC) address of your router. A MAC address is a unique identifier used by most network adapters for identification. The MAC address can be found in the configuration screens of your router; it is composed using following format: XX-XX-XX-XX-XX-XX. The MAC address can be formed only with letters and numbers. One example is: 0A-19-5B-BC-D2-E1.

  - *Static IP address*   The ISP will assign a static IP (Internet Protocol) address to your router. An IP Address is composed using the following format: XXX-XXX-XXX-XXX. The address is comprised only of numbers (for example, 86-34-233-84). When such a connection is used, you need to know the values for the IP Address, Subnet Mask, and Gateway Address. All these details share the format of the IP Address—they are formed only from numbers and can be given to you only by your ISP.

  - *Point-to-Point Protocol over Ethernet (PPPoE)*   This is generally used by telephone companies that also provide Internet connections. PPPoE requires the ISP to create a user name and password for you. You need to enter these details into the router's configuration screens. This information is used to "dial" the connection to the servers of your ISP.

  - *Point-to-Point Tunneling Protocol (PPTP)*   Mostly used in Europe, this is another type of connection that requires authentication through a user name and password. It provides similar levels of security to typical virtual private network products.

- *Domain Name Server (DNS)*   A DNS has the function of translating the human-readable domain names we use for Web sites—for example, *www.google.com* or *www.7tutorials.com*—into the corresponding IP addresses that are used by network devices. You will need two DNS addresses: a primary and secondary. These addresses are the IP Addresses of two servers and you will obtain this information only from your ISP.

- **Local Area Network (LAN) Settings**   These settings are applied to your home network. Most routers come with a predefined set of configurations. If this is the case with your router, go ahead and use them. There is no need to change them, as they will work properly right out of the box. The LAN settings define what kind of IP Addresses are assigned to your home computers and whether they are assigned dynamically or statically. For more information, consult the manual of your router and follow the recommendations of the manufacturer.

- **Wireless Settings**   These settings are applied to all laptops or netbooks that access your home network via a wireless connection. First, you need to enable the wireless capability. Here there are a couple of details you should configure:

  - **Service Set Identifier (SSID)**   This is the name that will be displayed when a laptop searches for wireless networks in your area. Here, it is best to give it a recognizable name so that people in your home know that it is your network. The name can contain letters, numbers, and underscores.

  - **Security Type**   This setting defines the authentication and encryption methods (or lack of it) that are used to protect your network. Your options include WPA2-PSK (best protection method, highly recommended), WPA-PSK, WEP (very poor protection, easily cracked), or no security, which means everybody can freely connect to your network. If you select to enable any type of security, you must also type an access key (or password). Make sure this key combines letters, numbers, and special characters such as #, &, +, etc. Write this access key down, as you will need to know it in order to establish a wireless connection to your home network.

Once the router is configured correctly, make sure that all desktops are connected via cable and check if your drivers are installed correctly.

To help you understand how to configure your router, we also have two installation and configuration exercises, based on two different models: one from Belkin, and one from D-Link. If you look through both exercises, you will notice that the important elements are the same, irrespective of the router model. The number of steps might vary based on the approach the manufacturer uses, but the important aspects you need to pay attention to are the same.

Installing and Configuring a Belkin N+ Wireless Router

The first router we are using to demonstrate the installation and configuration process is a popular model: the Belkin N+ Wireless. This particular device has a good reputation for its reliable wireless coverage and signal strength.

In this exercise, you will learn how to set up your router so that all computers on your home network can connect to it and access the Internet. The steps in this exercise apply to most Belkin routers.

SET UP Be sure that you know the details you need to use for connecting your router to the Internet. Ask your ISP to provide them to you. Also, inform them that you are about to install a home router; the ISP might need to make some changes on their end in order for your router to connect to the Internet successfully. Once this is done, unpack your router carefully and identify the instruction manual and installation CD or DVD. Plug in the power adapter of your router and connect your computer to the router via the network cable provided in the package. Connect the router to the Internet using the cable from your Internet provider or from the modem your Internet provider has installed. Finally, insert the router's installation CD or DVD into your computer's CD/DVD-ROM drive and run the *SetupAssistant.exe* file.

1. Once the Belkin Setup CD window appears, you are asked to select what you want to do. Select **Run the Setup Assistant now**.

2. Click the **Go button**.

You are asked to select the country where the router will operate.

3. Select your country. If you cannot find it (in our case, Romania was not on the list of options), select **Other**.

4. Click the **Begin** button.

   The Setup Assistant asks you to read the Quick Installation Guide found in the package of your router and confirm that all the steps outlined there have been completed.

5. Read the Quick Installation Guide, follow all the steps, and when you have finished, select the **I have completed all Quick Installation Guide steps** check box.

6. Click **Next**.

   The Setup Assistant takes a few seconds to connect to your router. It then asks you to name your home's wireless network.

BELKIN. | Setup CD

Version 1.1.2 [X]

Main Menu

Setup Assistant >

Security Assistant

Storage Manager

Network Status

Manual Setup

Language

User Manual

Help

Quit

Step 3 of 6: Naming your network

This name identifies your wireless network. Using a unique name helps people choose the right network when multiple networks are available in your neighborhood.

Network Name (SSID) | My Home Wireless

Examples: Jan's Network, XYZ Corp Visitors WiFi

☑ High Speed Enabled

Enabling High Speed Mode increases your network speed but may interfere with other nearby routers. We recommend that you try enabling this and turn it off later if you notice problems with other routers.

(Cancel)   (Back | Next)

7. In the **Network Name (SSID)** field, type the name that you want to apply to your home's wireless network.

8. Select the **High Speed Enabled** check box. This helps increase your wireless network speed.

9. Click **Next**.

The Setup Assistant begins a series of checks. When it is complete, you are asked to select the type of connection your ISP uses to connect your home to the Internet. Your choices are: Static IP, Dynamic IP, PPPoE, PPTP, or BigPond and Optus Cable.

BELKIN. | Setup CD

Version 1.1.2 ✕

Main Menu

Setup Assistant >
Security Assistant
Storage Manager
Network Status
Manual Setup
Language

User Manual
Help
Quit

Step 4 of 6: Internet account info - manual entry

Choose the connection type that your ISP uses. Your ISP provided this information when you signed up with them.

Connection Type:

○ Static IP
◉ Dynamic IP
○ PPPoE
○ PPTP
○ BigPond® and Optus Cable   Only available in Australia

If you are unsure of your connection type, please contact your provider.

Cancel   Back   Next

10. Select the appropriate type of connection, as provided by your ISP. In our case, we needed to select **Dynamic IP**.

11. Click **Next**.

    Depending on the choice you made, Setup Assistant might ask you to type certain connection details. For example, if you choose Static IP, you are asked to enter details such as the IP Address, Subnet Mask, Gateway, and DNS servers. For our exercise, we selected Dynamic IP, which means there's no need to type any details because the router will automatically receive them from the servers of our ISP.

12. Once you enter the connection details required, the Setup Assistant sends the data to the router. It then restarts the router so that the settings are applied and tries to connect to the Internet. In case you are using a modem to connect your router to the Internet, you are asked to unplug its power supply, wait for five seconds, and then plug it in again.

13. If you are using a modem to connect your router to the Internet, follow the instructions. If not, simply click **Next**.

The router tries again to connect to the Internet, then notifies you of the success of the operation.

14. Click **Next**.

The Setup Assistant asks you to connect the other computers to the router.

15. Connect all the other desktops to the router via Ethernet network cables, similar to the one found in the package of the router. Establish wireless connections for any laptops or notebooks.

16. When you have finished connecting all the other computers, click **Next**.

You are asked if all your wireless computers are able to connect.

BELKIN.   Setup CD   Version 1.1.2 ☒

Main Menu

Setup Assistant >

Security Assistant

Storage Manager

Network Status

Manual Setup

Language

User Manual

Help

Quit

Optional: Assistance connecting other computers

Often wireless connection problems are caused by interference from walls, electric appliances, or other nearby wireless networks.

Were all of your wireless computers able to connect?

⊙ Yes   ○ No   ○ Does not apply

Cancel   Back   │   Next

17. If you were able to connect the wireless computers, select **Yes**. If not, select one of the other answers that apply to your situation.

18. Click **Next**.

You are asked if all your wired computers are able to connect.

BELKIN.   Setup CD   Version 1.1.2 ☒

Main Menu

Setup Assistant >

Security Assistant

Storage Manager

Network Status

Manual Setup

Language

User Manual

Help

Quit

Optional: Assistance connecting other computers

Wired connection problems often result from incorrectly located plugs or bad cables.

Were all of your wired computers able to connect?

⊙ Yes   ○ No   ○ Does not apply

Cancel   Back   │   Next

19. If you were able to connect the wired computers, select **Yes**. If not, select another answer that applies to your situation.

20. Click **Next**.

You are informed that the network is now set up and computers can connect to it.

21. Click **Next**.

A window opens in which you can choose to start other configuration tools. Even though your network is now set up and fully functioning, there's one important thing missing: your wireless network is not secured and everybody can connect to it freely, including unauthorized users.

BELKIN. | Setup CD

Version 1.1.2 ☒

Main Menu >

Setup Assistant
Security Assistant
Storage Manager
Network Status
Manual Setup
Language

User Manual
Help
Quit

1. Setup Assistant

This tool automatically connects your router to the internet, helps you set up wireless security, and enables you to share USB storage devices via our router. Use this when setting up your router for the first time.

2. Security Assistant

Make your network private and secure. You may use this tool at any time.

3. Storage Manager

This software allows your computer to use storage attached to your router. Please install this application on every computer on your network.

Network Status

See the current status of your network and internet connection.

Manual Setup

Manually set details of your internet connection, network and security.

22. It's time to set up your network security. Click **Security Assistant**.

BELKIN. | Setup CD

Version 1.1.2 ☒

Main Menu

Setup Assistant
Security Assistant >
Storage Manager
Network Status
Manual Setup
Language

User Manual
Help
Quit

When to use the Security Assistant

We recomend setting up wireless security now.

Why use wireless security?

Without wireless security your neighbors can get on the internet via your account and potentially intercept your wireless data. Setting up security prevents others from using your bandwidth and keeps your data private.

Click "Next" to start the Security Assistant.

Cancel   Back   Next

23. Click **Next**.

The Security Assistant starts and informs you about the steps it will follow.

24. Click **Next**.

The Security Assistant checks for a connection to your router. Once found, it asks you to choose the type of security you want to use for your home's wireless network.

25. Choose WPA2—this is the most secure option—and then click **Next**.

You are asked to type the network key (or password) that will be used by other computers to connect to your home's wireless network.

26. Type a network key.

The network key must be a minimum of 8 characters. Also, it should be made up of a combination of letters, numbers, and special characters (such as $, #, +, and so on). This will make it harder for intruders to hack (decipher) your network key.

27. Click **Next**.

The Security Assistant sends the data to the router. When this is complete, it informs you about the network key being set.

BELKIN. | Setup CD

Version 1.1.2 ☒

Main Menu

Setup Assistant
Security Assistant >
Storage Manager
Network Status
Manual Setup
Language

User Manual
Help
Quit

Step 6 of 7: Transferring the key to your wireless computers

You will now need to transfer the key to your wireless computers or devices. This can be done easily with a thumb drive (also known as a flash drive). If you do not have one, print or write the information shown below and then manually enter it into each wireless computer. Instructions for connecting are included in the printouts.

Network Key

l0ngpaffw0rd

Transfer Key   Print

Cancel   Back   Next

28. You have the option to print the network key or transfer it to a USB memory stick. Click the appropriate button if either of these options is useful to you.

29. Click **Next**.

You are asked to verify if your wireless computers can connect to the network using the newly created network key.

BELKIN. | Setup CD

Version 1.1.2 ☒

Main Menu

Setup Assistant
Security Assistant >
Storage Manager
Network Status
Manual Setup
Language

User Manual
Help
Quit

Step 7 of 7: Verifying your computers can connect

Did you have trouble getting any of your computers to connect to your network now that it's secure?

⦿ **All computers were able to connect successfully.**

○ **I had problems with at least one computer.**

Cancel   Back   Next

30. If everything is working properly, select **All computers were able to connect successfully**.

31. Click **Next**.

You are informed that your wireless network is now private and secure.

32. Click **Finish**.

You are returned to the overall Setup CD window, where you can choose other tools you might want to launch.

Your home network is now set up and secured correctly. Both your wired and wireless computers are able to connect to it.

✖ CLEAN UP Close the Setup CD window.

Important If after the initial setup you want to configure any parameters for your Belkin N+ Wireless router, open your Internet browser and type **http://192.168.2.1**. When you want to change the settings of your router, you are asked for a password. Leave it blank and click Submit.

Installing and Configuring a D-Link DIR-615 Router

The second example router that we are using is the D-Link DIR-615. This model is generally recommended to those who want an entry-level device that satisfies most home networking situations at an affordable price.

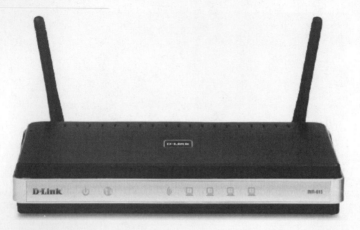

In this exercise, you will learn how to set up your router so that all computers on your home network can connect to it and access the Internet. The steps in this exercise apply to most D-Link routers.

SET UP Be sure that you know the details you need to use to connect your router to the Internet. Ask your ISP to provide them to you. Also, inform them that you are about to install a home router; the ISP might need to make some changes on their end in order for your router to connect to the Internet successfully. Once this is done, unpack your router carefully and identify the instruction manual and installation CD or DVD. Plug in the power adapter of your router and connect your computer to the router via the network cable provided in the package. Connect the router to the Internet using the cable from your Internet provider or from the modem your Internet provider has installed. Finally, insert the router's installation CD or DVD into your computer's CD/DVD-ROM drive and run the WIZARD.exe file.

1. Once the D-Link Setup Wizard appears, you are asked to select your language. Select the language that you prefer to use.

2. Click the **Start** button.

You are asked a series of questions about what you must do prior to continuing with the setup.

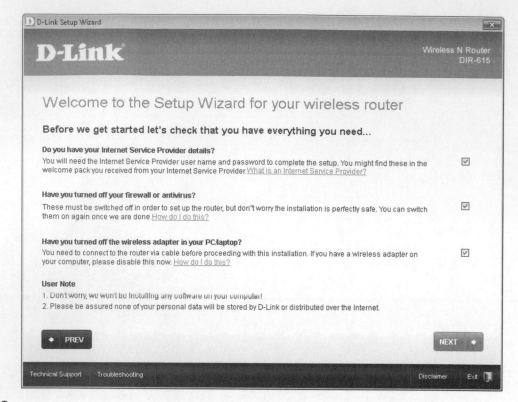

3. Follow the instructions recommended by the wizard and select the appropriate check boxes when done.

4. Click **Next**.

   You are asked what kind of installation you want to perform.

5. Select **First Installation**, and then click **Next**.

The wizard now asks you to set up the hardware.

6. Follow the instructions shown. When you have finished, click **Next**.

   You receive instructions about connecting your router to the computer.

7. Follow the instructions shown. When you have finished, click **Next**.

You are asked to connect the router to your set-top box or modem. Follow the instructions if your ISP provided such devices. If the connection is via a network cable, plug the cable into the gray Internet port on the back of your router.

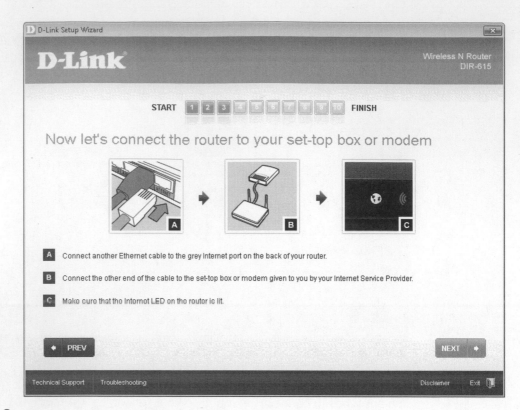

8. When you have finished, click **Next**.

You are asked to create a password for your router. This will be the password for the administrative user on the router. You can use this later to set up your router's parameters, if needed.

9. Type the same password in both fields, then click **Next**.

The Setup Wizard checks your Internet connection. When it is complete, you are asked to select the type of Internet connection you have.

10. Select the appropriate Internet connection from the list. For our Internet connection, we had to use a Static IP Address connection.

11. Type the requested connection details. For our connection, we entered the IP Address to be used by the router to connect to the Internet, the Subnet Mask, the Gateway, and the primary and secondary DNS servers. Depending on your type of connection, you might be required to enter other types of connection details.

12. When you have finished entering all the details, click **Next**.

    The Setup Wizard saves your settings and checks the Internet connection. If everything works well, you are asked to give a name for your home's wireless network.

13. Type the name of the network, then click **Next**.

You are asked to select the type of security to be applied to your wireless network.

14. Select **WPA2**, then click **Next**.

You are now asked to type a wireless network password (also known as an encryption key or security key). This password will be used by all computers that connect to the wireless network.

15. Type a network password.

The network password must be a minimum of 8 characters. Also, it should be made up of a combination of letters, numbers, and special characters (such as $, #, +, etc.). This will make it harder for intruders to hack (decipher) your network key.

16. When you have finished, click **Next**.

The Setup Wizard saves your wireless network settings. When it is complete, it informs you of the newly created wireless network name and password.

17. You can print these details by clicking the **Print Details** button. If you want the settings saved in a text file on your desktop, select the **Save these settings in a text file on my desktop** check box.

18. Click **Next**.

You are informed that your router is up and running.

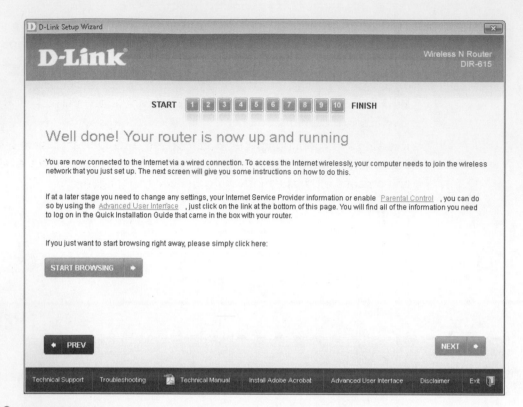

19. Click **Next**.

    The Setup Wizard has completed all of the steps. Finally, it informs you that you can join the newly created wireless network. Your home network is now set up and secured correctly. Both your wired and wireless computers should be able to connect to it.

CLEAN UP Close the D-Link Setup Wizard.

Important If after the initial setup you want to configure any parameters for your D-Link DIR-615 router, open your Internet browser and type **http://192.168.0.1**. This takes you to the logon window of the router. Type the user name **admin** and the password that you assigned in step 9. Once you log on, you can change all the settings of your router.

Key Points

- It's very important to install all hardware devices and their appropriate drivers properly.

- Device Stage is a Windows 7 feature that allows you to interact with devices in a very friendly manner.

- Installing and configuring your router is the most important task in setting up your home network. When setting up your router, talk to your Internet service provider and obtain the list of settings that you need to configure it.

Chapter at a Glance

Configure your user
account, **page 42**

Change your user
account picture with
anything you like,
page 51

Delete a user
account, **page 54**

Set Windows 7 to log you
in automatically, **page 57**

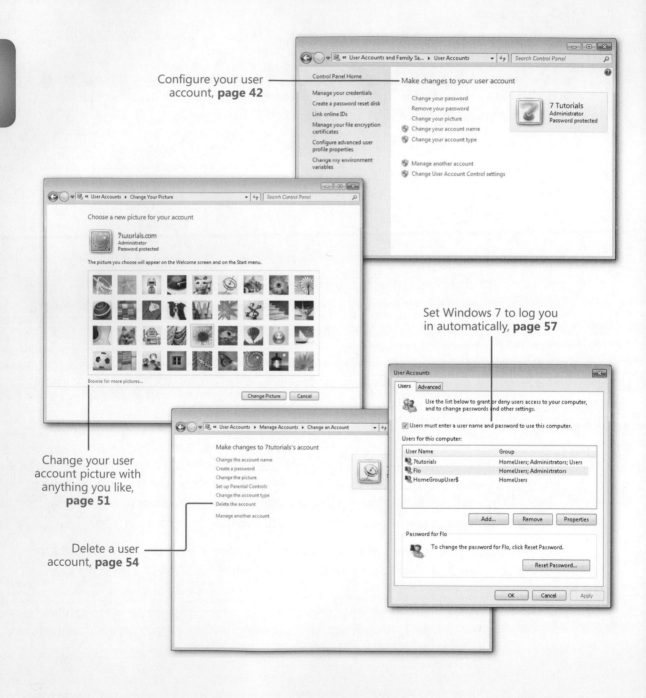

2 Setting User Accounts on All Computers

In this chapter, you will learn how to

- ✔ Access the User Accounts control panel.
- ✔ Create a new user account.
- ✔ Switch between user accounts.
- ✔ Turn the Guest user account on or off.
- ✔ Change, remove, or create the password for a user account.
- ✔ Change a user account picture, name, and type.
- ✔ Delete a user account.
- ✔ Log on to Windows 7 automatically.

Once you have the operating systems installed on all computers, the router and network connections configured, and all your external devices installed and working, it is time to set up the user accounts you need to use on all your home computers.

In a typical family, you might have a few computers that are used by only one person. For these computers, you need only the user account setup during the installation of the operating system. However, there will always be a few computers that are used by more than one person—it can be a computer used only by children, by parents, or the whole family. In such usage scenarios, it is best to create a user account for each person.

In this chapter, you will learn what user accounts are, understand how many you need to define on a computer, and how to manage user accounts and configure them the way you need.

> **Practice Files** You won't need any practice files to complete the exercises in this chapter.

What Is a User Account and How Many Do You Need?

User accounts allow multiple people to share the same computer, each having their own private Documents folder, e-mail inbox, settings, and so on. It also improves security and reduces file-sharing and network problems. Having your own account means that you can do all the customization you want to your Windows 7 environment, without affecting other user accounts. Other users will have their own visual customization, their own application settings, and so forth.

There are three types of user accounts: administrator, standard (or limited user), and Guest user account.

The administrator has full access to all user accounts. He can create and delete user accounts, create account passwords for other users, and change the name, password, picture, and account types for other accounts. Also, the administrator can install software, hardware, and configure every aspect of the operating system.

As a rule, there must be at least one administrator user account on a computer.

A user with standard account rights has access to programs that have already been installed on that computer and cannot install other software without the administrator password. He can change his account picture and create, change, or delete his password, but he cannot change his account name or type. Also, some programs (mostly old ones, created prior to Windows Vista and Windows 7) might not work properly on this type of account and might require a temporary or permanent change of the account type to administrator.

The Guest account is a special type of limited user account that has the following restrictions:

- Does not require a password
- Cannot install software or hardware
- Cannot change the Guest account type
- Cannot create a password for the account
- Cannot change the Guest account picture
- Cannot access the files in the Shared Documents folder

When you install Windows 7, you already have a default user account created. That user account always has administrator permissions. A new account should be created when there is another person who needs to work on the same computer.

For example, if you are a parent sharing the computer with your child, it is best to have two separate user accounts: one for you with administrator permissions, and one for your child with standard user permissions. By doing this, you make sure that the child can use the computer but cannot change important configuration aspects of it.

If you generally have temporary guests who need to use one of your computers to browse the Internet, check their e-mails, and perform other light computing activities, it is best to enable the Guest account and let them use that.

Accessing the User Accounts Control Panel

All the configuration options that are related to user accounts are set in the User Accounts control panel. There are several ways to access this panel.

In this exercise, you will learn how to access the User Accounts control panel.

SET UP Start your computer and log on.

1. Click the **Start** menu, then choose **Control Panel**.

   The Control Panel window opens.

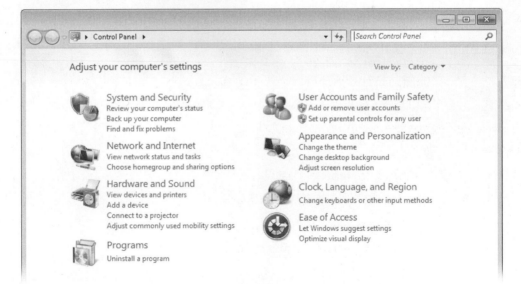

2. Click **User Accounts and Family Safety**.

   A window opens with several options that are related to user accounts and family safety.

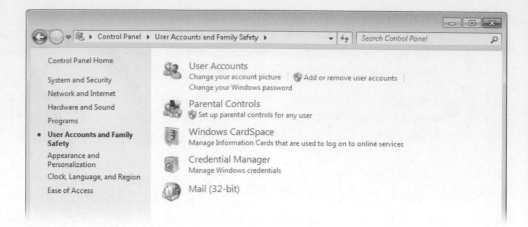

3. Click the **User Accounts** link.

The User Accounts window opens. Here you can configure your own account and, if you are an administrator, other user accounts as well.

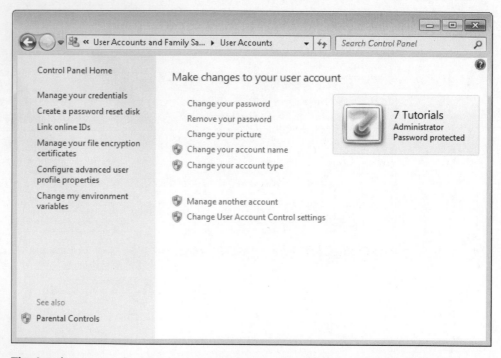

Tip Another way to find the User Accounts control panel is to go to the Start menu search box and enter **user account**, and then click the User Accounts search result.

 CLEAN UP Close the window.

Creating a New User Account

Creating a user account is a task that can be done by anyone with administrator permissions. In this exercise, you will learn how to create a new user account on your computer.

SET UP Log on as a user who has administrator permissions, then open the User Accounts window.

1. Click **Manage another account**.

The Manage Accounts window opens.

Choose the account you would like to change

7tutorials.com
Administrator
Password protected

Flo
Administrator
Password protected

Guest
Guest account is off

Create a new account
What is a user account?

Additional things you can do

Set up Parental Controls

Go to the main User Accounts page

2. Click **Create a new account**.

The Create New Account window opens.

Name the account and choose an account type

This name will appear on the Welcome screen and on the Start menu.

New account name

◉ Standard user

Standard account users can use most software and change system settings that do not affect other users or the security of the computer.

○ Administrator

Administrators have complete access to the computer and can make any desired changes. Based on notification settings, administrators may be asked to provide their password or confirmation before making changes that affect other users.

We recommend that you protect every account with a strong password.

Why is a standard account recommended?

Create Account   Cancel

3. Type the name of the new account.

4. Select the account type: **Standard user** or **Administrator**.

5. Click the **Create Account** button.

Windows 7 returns you to the Manage Accounts window.

A new folder with the new account name is created in the C:\Users folder, where all the personal files of the new user are kept. No user other than the administrator and the new user have access to this folder.

Tip By default, the new account doesn't have a password set. Therefore, it is best to create one as soon as you log on to it.

 CLEAN UP Close the Manage Accounts window.

Switching Between User Accounts

Switching between user accounts occurs when you leave the current user account turned on (with all running applications) and log on to a separate user account. You can switch back and forth between user accounts whenever you want.

In this exercise, you will learn how to switch between user accounts.

SET UP Open the Start menu.

1. Click the arrow symbol beside the **Shut down** button.

A menu with several options opens.

2. Click **Switch user**.

The Windows 7 logon window opens.

Tip An alternative is to press the Windows logo+L keys at the same time, then click Switch User.

3. Choose the user to which you want to switch.

4. Type the password of the selected user.

5. Press **ENTER**.

You are now logged on to the selected user account. The user account from which you switched still remains active with all applications running, and you can switch back to it at any time.

CLEAN UP When you are done working on the computer, make sure you save any open documents (or any of your work) in all user accounts to which you logged on.

Turning the Guest Account On or Off

The Guest account is, by default, disabled in Windows 7. You can easily turn it on whenever you have a guest who needs to use your computer, and then turn it off when it is no longer needed.

In this exercise, you will learn how to turn the Guest account on or off.

SET UP Log on as a user who has administrator permissions and open the User Accounts window.

1. Click **Manage another account**.

   The Manage Accounts window opens.

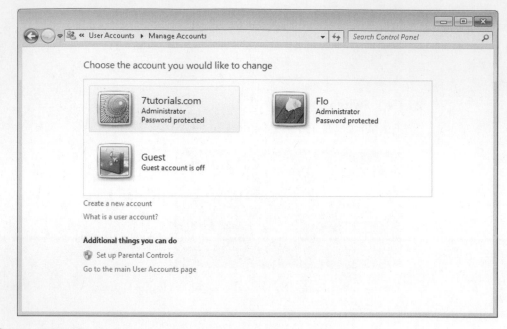

2. Click **Guest**.

   If the Guest account is turned off, you are now asked if you want to turn it on.

3. Click **Turn On**.

   The Guest account is enabled, and you are returned to the Manage Accounts window.

4. If you want to turn off the Guest account, follow steps 1 and 2.

The Change Guest Options window opens.

5. Click the **Turn off guest account** link.

The Guest account is disabled, and you are returned to the Manage Accounts window.

 CLEAN UP Close the Manage Accounts window.

Creating a Password for a User Account

Every user except Guest can create his own password if one has not already been set. Making the change doesn't require any administrator permissions, as long as you do not want to create a password for a user account other than your own.

In this exercise, you will learn how to create a password for your user account if one has not already been set.

SET UP Open the User Accounts window.

1. Click **Create a password for your account**.

The Create Your Password window opens.

Create a password for your account

7 Tutorials
Administrator

New password

Confirm new password

If your password contains capital letters, they must be typed the same way every time you log on.
How to create a strong password

Type a password hint

The password hint will be visible to everyone who uses this computer.
What is a password hint?

Create password   Cancel

2. Type the password that you want to use in the first two fields.

Security Tip To keep your computer safe, it is recommended that you use strong passwords. This means using passwords that contain a combination of letters, numbers, and special characters (like "@", "#", or "&"). Ideally, the password should be something that would be hard for you to forget but impossible for anyone else to figure out.

3. You can also type a password hint if you are likely to forget your password.

Tip The password hint will be visible to anyone trying to log on to your computer. Make it something simple enough to help you remember the password but hard enough so others cannot work out your actual password.

4. Click **Create password**.

You are returned to the User Accounts window.

 CLEAN UP Close the User Accounts window.

Changing the Password for a User Account

Every user except Guest can change her password. Making the change doesn't require any administrator permissions, as long as you do not want to change the password of a user account other than your own.

In this exercise, you will learn how to change the password of your user account.

SET UP Open the User Accounts window.

1. Click **Change your password**.

   The Change Your Password window opens.

   Change your password

   7tutorials.com
   Administrator
   Password protected

   •••••••

   •••••••••••

   •••••••••••

   If your password contains capital letters, they must be typed the same way every time you log on.
   How to create a strong password

   Type a password hint

   The password hint will be visible to everyone who uses this computer.
   What is a password hint?

   Change password   Cancel

2. Type your current password in the first (top) field.

3. Type your new password in the second and third fields.

   Security Tip To keep your computer safe, it is recommended that you use strong passwords. This means using passwords which contain a combination of letters, numbers, and special characters (like "@", "#", or "&"). Ideally, the password should be something that would be hard for you to forget but impossible for anyone else to figure out.

4. You can also type a password hint if you are likely to forget your password.

   Tip The password hint will be visible to anyone trying to log on to your computer. Make it something simple enough to help you remember the password but hard enough so others cannot work out your actual password.

5. Click **Change password**.

   You are returned to the User Accounts window.

 CLEAN UP Close the User Accounts window.

Removing the Password for a User Account

Every user except Guest can remove his password. Making the change doesn't require any administrator permissions, as long as you do not want to remove the password of a user account other than your own. The Guest user has no password, therefore there is nothing to remove for it.

In this exercise, you will learn how to remove the password of your user account.

➡ **SET UP** Open the User Accounts window.

1. Click **Remove your password**.

   The Remove Your Password window opens.

2. Type the current password.

3. Click **Remove Password**.

   You are returned to the User Accounts window.

✖ **CLEAN UP** Close the User Accounts window.

Changing a User Account Picture

Every user except Guest can change his account picture. Making the change doesn't require any administrator permissions, as long as you do not want to change the picture of a user account other than your own.

In this exercise, you will learn how to change the picture of your user account.

➡ **SET UP** Open the User Accounts window.

1. Click **Change your picture**.

   The Change Your Picture window opens.

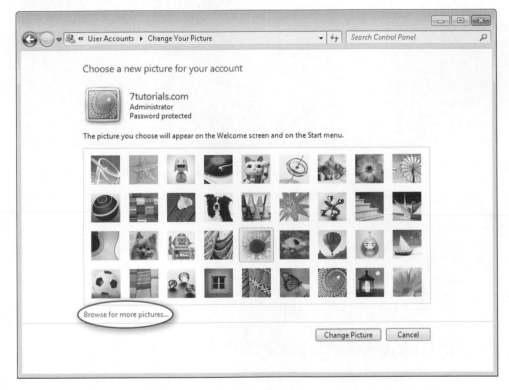

2. Select one of the available images for Windows 7 accounts, then click **Change Picture**.

3. If you don't see what you want in the available images and you want to select another picture, click **Browse for more pictures**.

The following Open window appears:

4. Browse to the folder where the image you want to use is located.

5. Select the image, and then click **Open**.

   The image for your user account is now changed and you are returned to the User Accounts window.

✖ **CLEAN UP** Close the User Accounts window.

Changing a User Account Name

Every user except Guest can change the name of his user account. However, making the change requires administrator permissions. If you are trying to change the name for a user account with standard permissions, you need to know the password of the administrator account.

In this exercise, you will learn how to change the name of your user account.

SET UP Open the User Accounts window.

1. Click **Change your account name**.

   The Change Your Name window opens.

Type a new account name

7tutorials.com
Administrator
Password protected

7tutorials

This name will appear on the Welcome screen and on the Start menu.

Change Name   Cancel

Tip If you are making this change as a standard user, you are first asked to enter the administrator password. Type the administrator password, and then click OK; this takes you to the Change Your Name window.

2. Type the new name you want to use for your user account.

3. Click **Change Name**.

   You are returned to the User Accounts window.

CLEAN UP Close the User Accounts window.

Changing a User Account Type

Every user except Guest can change his user account type. However, making the change requires administrator permissions. If you are trying to change the type for a user account with standard permissions, you need to know the password of the administrator account.

In this exercise, you will learn how to change the type of your user account.

SET UP Open the User Accounts window.

1. Click **Change your account type**.

The Change Your Account Type window opens.

Tip If you are making this change from a standard user, you are first asked to enter the administrator password. Type the administrator password, and then click OK. You are taken to the Change Your Account Type window.

2. Select between **Standard user** or **Administrator**.

3. Click **Change Account Type**.

You are returned to the User Accounts window.

✖ **CLEAN UP** Close the User Accounts window.

Deleting a User Account

Deleting user accounts is a task that can be done only by administrators. When an account is deleted, all the settings and files belonging to that user account will be deleted. This activity is done best by logging in to another user account and making the deletion from there. Also, make sure that the user account you are about to delete is not logged on when executing the deletion.

In this exercise, you will learn how to delete a user account.

SET UP Log on as a user who has administrator permissions, then open the User Accounts window.

1. Click **Manage another account**.

   The Manage Accounts window opens.

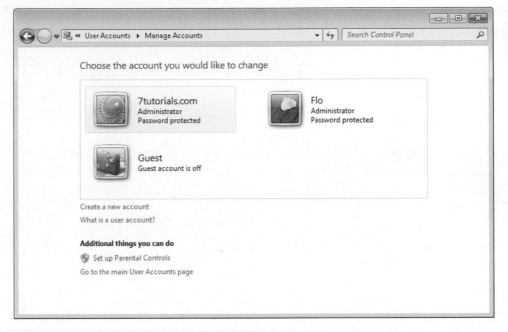

2. Click the user account you want to delete.

   This opens the User Accounts window, which presents the options available for the selected user.

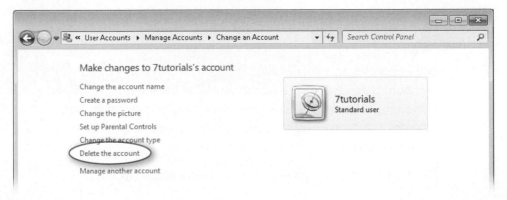

3. Click the **Delete the account** link.

The Delete Account window opens, and you are asked if you want to keep the files of that user account.

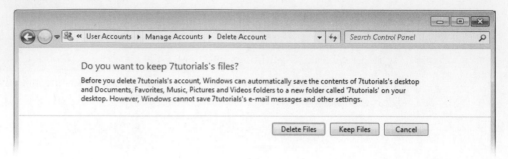

4. If you have already backed up the files of that user account, click **Delete Files**. If you have not yet done so and you want to keep the files, click **Keep Files**.

The Confirm Deletion window opens.

Note If you decide to keep the user's files, they will be saved in a folder on the desktop of the user account from which you are making the deletion. The folder name will be that of the deleted account.

Note If you choose Delete Files, you are asked to confirm your choice.

5. Click **Delete Account**.

The user account is now deleted, and you are returned to the Manage Accounts window.

CLEAN UP Close the Manage Accounts window.

Logging on to Windows 7 Automatically

You can set up Windows 7 so that it will log you on automatically, without requesting you to type your user account password every time. The next exercise will show you how.

 SET UP Open the Command Prompt.

1. Type **netplwiz.exe**, and then press **ENTER**.

The User Accounts window opens, and displays a list showing all users registered on your computer.

2. Select the user for which you no longer want to type the password when logging on.

3. Clear the check box beside **Users must enter a user name and password to use this computer**.

4. Click **OK**.

The Automatically Log On window opens.

Automatically Log On

You can set up your computer so that users do not have to type a user name and password to log on. To do this, specify a user that will be automatically logged on below:

User name: 7tutorials

Password: •••••••••••

Confirm Password: •••••••••••

OK   Cancel

5. Type the user's current password in the **Password** and **Confirm Password** fields.

6. Click **OK**.

The next time you start Windows 7, you will be automatically logged on with the user you just selected. This becomes the default logon user to Windows 7.

Important If you have multiple users defined on your computer, setting this up might be an inconvenience; Windows 7 will always log on automatically to the user you selected during this procedure. In order to log on to another user, you need to wait for Windows 7 to start up and log you in automatically, then log off and select the other user that you actually want to log on to. If you want to set things back to the way they were, follow the same procedure you just performed here, but this time select the Users Must Enter a User Name and Password to Use This Computer option.

 CLEAN UP Reboot your computer to test if it works.

Key Points

- If you have more than one person using a computer, it is best to create separate user accounts for each person.

- The Guest user account is useful when you have guests who need to temporarily use your computer.

- To create a user account, change user account names or types, or delete user accounts, you need administrator permissions.

- Any user can change her account password and picture except the Guest user account.

- The deletion of a user account is best done from another user account and only after you have backed up all the important files created by that user.

- You can set Windows 7 to automatically log you on, without having to type the password.

Chapter at a Glance

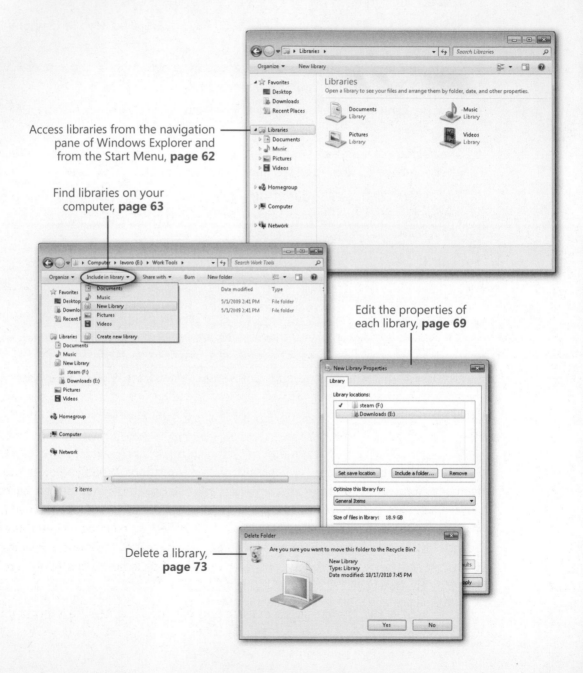

Access libraries from the navigation pane of Windows Explorer and from the Start Menu, **page 62**

Find libraries on your computer, **page 63**

Edit the properties of each library, **page 69**

Delete a library, **page 73**

3 Setting Up Your Libraries on All Windows 7 Computers

In this chapter, you will learn how to

✔ Access the libraries defined on your computer.

✔ Create a new library.

✔ Add folders to a library.

✔ Remove folders from a library.

✔ Edit the properties of a library.

✔ Delete a library.

Libraries are one of the coolest features introduced in Windows 7. Think of a library as a virtual collection of folders on your computer. Virtual, because it doesn't exist as an actual folder—it is only a reference to one or more folders on your computer and the files within them. For example, you can have documents stored in multiple locations: your Documents folder, on the Desktop, and some other locations. You can have a library called Documents that includes references to all these locations. When you open the Documents library, you will see all these folders and their contents as if they are subfolders of the Documents library. This feature helps you organize all your files together in one place, regardless of where they are stored. It also offers many benefits in terms of productivity when working with lots of files spread across several locations. For example, you can get access to all your documents with one single click, no matter the folders where they are stored.

By including folders in libraries, you are also telling Windows 7 where the important data is located. Therefore, Windows 7 will index the folders that are part of libraries, enabling fast searching and stacking, based on file properties.

Before starting to share files and folders between your computers, it is a good idea to set up your libraries on all of them. Each user account defined on your computer has its own set of libraries. So, you might want to do this exercise for all user accounts on each computer that has Windows 7 installed.

In this chapter, you will learn how to create a library, add folders to it, sort the contents of a library, edit its properties, and delete a library.

Practice Files You can complete the exercises in this chapter using your own files, folders, and libraries.

Accessing the Libraries Defined on Your Computer

By default, each computer that is running Windows 7 has the Documents, Music, Pictures, and Videos libraries defined. They initially contain only sample files, but they can be modified to contain whatever you need. You can find three of them—Documents, Pictures, and Music—on the upper-right side of the Start Menu.

You can find the entire list of libraries defined on your computer in Windows Explorer. Open the Computer shortcut or the shortcut for Windows Explorer and look on the left side of the window. There, you can find the Libraries section and all the libraries defined on your computer.

To open a library, just double-click it.

Creating a New Library

Libraries are specific to each user account on your Windows 7 computer. A user can have multiple libraries defined, and a folder can be a part of any number of libraries.

In this exercise, you will learn how to create a library in Windows 7.

 SET UP Open Windows Explorer.

 1. Click **Libraries** in the Navigation pane on the left side.

A list opens that shows the existing libraries.

2. Click the **New Library** button, located on the bar at the top of the **Libraries** window.

   This creates a library called New Library.

Tip An alternative way to create a library is to right-click anywhere in the empty space on the right side of the window and select New -> Library.

3. Type the name you want to use for your library.

4. Press **Enter**.

An empty library with the name you specified is created.

 CLEAN UP Repeat this procedure until you have created as many libraries as you need.

Adding Folders to a Library

Once you have created your library (or libraries), it's time to add the folders you want to have within it. There are many ways in which you can add folders to a library.

In this exercise, you will learn how to add folders to a library in Windows 7 using the simplest procedure available.

 SET UP Open Windows Explorer.

1. Browse to the folder you want to add to your library and select it.

2. Click the **Include in library** button, located toward the top of the Windows Explorer window.

A list opens that shows all existing libraries.

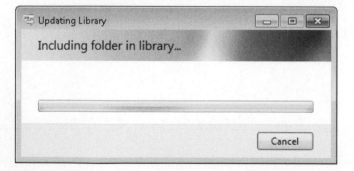

3. Select the library in which you want to include the folder.

The Updating Library window opens, which displays a progress bar to show you how the process of including the selected folder in the library is proceeding.

Note If the folder you added does not contain many items, chances are this window will disappear very quickly, or you might not even notice it. For larger folders, it takes a longer time until it disappears.

4. The folder you selected is now included in the library. To confirm that the procedure worked, click the library and you will see that the folder appears under it.

CLEAN UP Repeat this procedure until you have included all the folders that you want to have in the library.

Removing Folders from a Library

Removing a folder from a library is as easy as adding one, and of course, there is more than one way of doing this.

In this exercise, you will learn how to remove folders from a library in Windows 7 using the simplest procedure available.

SET UP Open Windows Explorer.

1. Browse to the library from which you want to remove the folder.

2. Click the library.

   The library expands to show the folders that are part of it.

Libraries	bin
▷ 📄 Documents	**Expand**
▷ 🎵 Music	Add to Winamp's Bookmark list
▲ 📑 New Library	Enqueue in Winamp
▷ 💾 steam (F:	Play in Winamp
▷ 🖼 Pictures	Open in new window
▷ 🎬 Videos	7-Zip ▶
▷ 🏠 Homegroup	Scan for Viruses
▷ 💻 Computer	Move to Quarantine
▷ 🖥 Network	Share with ▶
	Snagit ▶
	Shared Folder Synchronization ▶
	Restore previous versions
44 ite	Combine supported files in Acrobat...
	Back Up
	Send to ▶
	Copy
	Remove location from library
	Rename
	Open folder location
	New ▶
	Properties

3. Right-click the folder that you want to remove from the library.

4. Select **Remove location from library**.

   The folder is now removed from the library. However, the folder will continue to exist on your computer in its original location, and its contents will not be modified in any way by this procedure. The only difference is that Windows 7 will no longer index it automatically.

CLEAN UP Close Windows Explorer.

Editing the Properties of a Library

One very important configuration step you must make is to correctly set the properties of each library. This step should be done after you have added the folders you want to each library.

In this exercise, you will learn how to edit the properties of any library and make important settings, such as selecting the default save location for a library, the type of library, and others.

 SET UP Open Windows Explorer.

1. Select the library that you want to configure.
2. Right-click it to open the contextual menu.

3. Select **Properties**.

   The Properties window opens for the selected library.

4. If you have more than one folder in a library, it is a good idea to specify which one should be the default save location. This helps when you want to copy something to the library—it will be automatically copied to the default save location. To set a folder, select it and click **Set save location**.

5. It is a good idea to set the type of the library. Go to the **Optimize this library for** section.

6. Click the drop-down list.

   A list of available options opens. The options are: General Items, Documents, Music, Pictures, and Videos.

Optimize this library for:

General Items ▼

General Items
Documents
Music
Pictures
Videos

7. Select the option that is best suited to your library.

   Depending on your choice, the icon of the library will change, as well as the options made available by Windows 7 when working with the library.

8. If you want to include or remove folders, use the appropriate buttons: **Include a folder** or **Remove**.

9. If you want to have the library displayed in the Navigation pane of Windows Explorer, in the **Attributes** section, select the check box beside **Shown in navigation pane**.

   Note The Shared check box indicates whether or not the library is shared. You cannot make any changes to it.

10. If you are not happy with the settings you've made, you can click **Restore Defaults**. This restores the library to its initial settings, and you can change its properties from scratch.

11. When you're done setting the options as you want them, click **OK**.

   The library is now set according to your preference.

✖ **CLEAN UP** Repeat this procedure for all libraries.

Quick Sorting the Content of a Library

In order to help you more quickly find what you are searching for, Windows 7 provides a predefined set of sorting criteria, depending on the type of library you are working with (General Items, Documents, Music, Pictures, and Videos).

To access these quick sorting criteria, click the down arrow next to **Arrange by**.

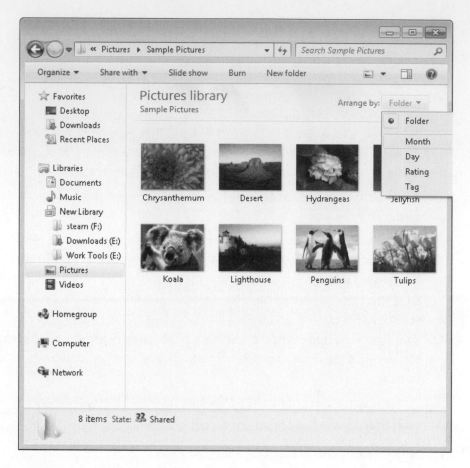

Depending on the type of library you are sorting, you have the following options:

- *Documents:* Folder, Author, Date modified, Tag, Type, Name
- *Pictures:* Folder, Month, Day, Rating, Tag
- *Music:* Folder, Album, Artist, Song, Genre, Rating
- *Videos:* Folder, Year, Type, Length, Name

Experiment with each option to better understand how they work.

Deleting a Library

As mentioned at the beginning of this chapter, a library is a virtual collection of files and folders. Deleting a library has no affect on its contents—only the virtual links between the library and the folders inside it are affected. Therefore, if you delete a library, the folders and files that were part of it will continue to exist on your computer, in the same location as they always did. The only difference is that you might not be able to access them so easily, and Windows 7 will no longer index them, which means you won't be able to take advantage of fast searching and stacking based on file properties.

In this exercise, you will learn how to delete a library.

 SET UP Open Windows Explorer.

1. Select the library you want to delete.
2. Right-click the library to open the contextual menu.

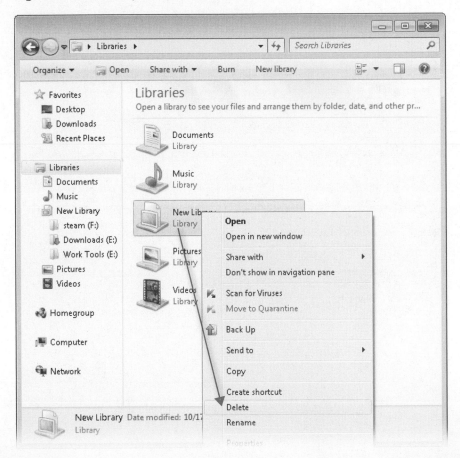

3. Select **Delete**.

Windows 7 asks you to confirm the deletion process.

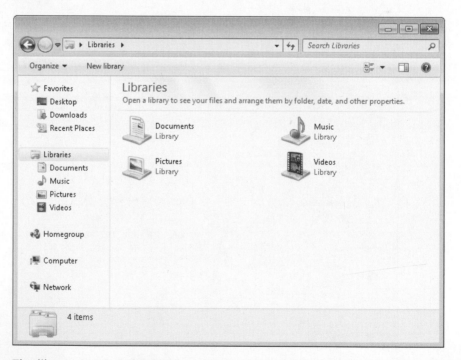

4. Click **Yes**.

This takes you to the **Libraries** window, in which you can see the remaining libraries.

The library you just deleted is no longer included in the list of available libraries.

 CLEAN UP Close Windows Explorer.

Key Points

- Libraries are virtual collections of folders.

- Libraries make it easy for you to organize and access your important files and folders.

- Windows 7 indexes the folders included in a library automatically, enabling fast searching and stacking, based on file properties.

- It is important to edit the properties of each library so that they function as you need them to.

- Deleting a library does not delete its content from the computer. Only the library's "virtual" content is deleted; the actual content remains intact in its original location.

Chapter at a Glance

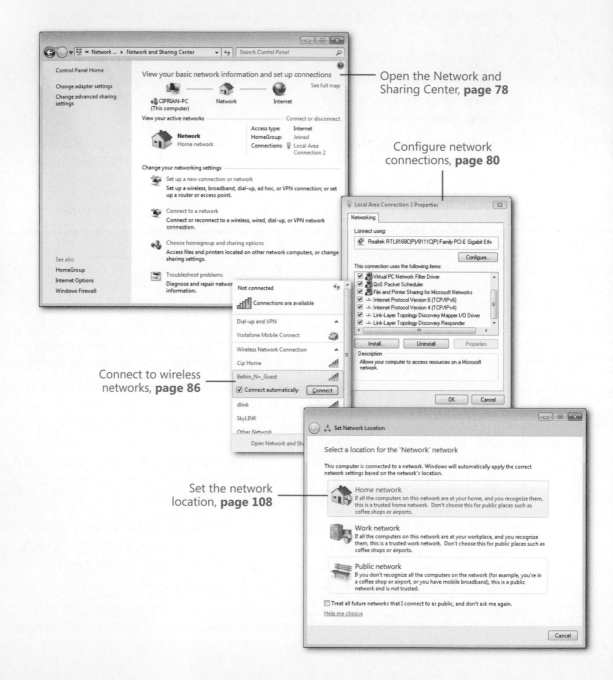

Open the Network and Sharing Center, **page 78**

Configure network connections, **page 80**

Connect to wireless networks, **page 86**

Set the network location, **page 108**

4 Creating the Network

In this chapter, you will learn how to

✔ Open the Network and Sharing Center.

✔ Configure network adapters.

✔ Enable or disable a network adapter.

✔ Connect to a wireless network.

✔ Connect to a hidden wireless network.

✔ Set up an ad hoc wireless network between computers.

✔ Create an ad hoc wireless network.

✔ Connect other computers to an ad hoc wireless network.

✔ Share files on an ad hoc wireless network.

The Network and Sharing Center was first introduced in Windows Vista and has been further fine-tuned in Windows 7, improving usability and access to certain features and configuration options. This tool is the main control panel for starting different network configuration tasks. In this chapter, you will learn first how to find and open the Network and Sharing Center. Next, you will learn how to access different configuration panels that are found in the Network and Sharing Center so that you can configure your network adapters, change your network location correctly (depending on the network to which you are connected), and set your workgroup so that computers with other operating systems installed can detect and connect to your computer.

On top of that, you will learn how to connect to different wireless networks, including those that are hidden and are not detected automatically by Windows 7. To completely cover the topic, you will also learn how to create your own ad hoc wireless network between two computers so that you can share files between them.

Tip Before completing the exercises in this chapter, make sure you have read Chapter 1, "Setting Up a Router and Devices" and followed the instructions for installing and configuring your hardware, drivers, and network router. If your router and other network devices are not installed and configured correctly, you will not get the desired results.

> **Practice Files** You won't need any practice files to complete the exercises in this chapter.

Opening the Networking and Sharing Center

You can launch the Network and Sharing Center in three ways.

One way is to click the network icon from the right side of the taskbar, then click Open Network and Sharing Center.

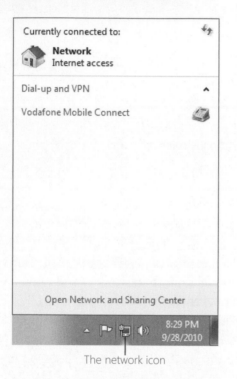

The network icon

A second (and the quickest) way is to launch the Run window by pressing the **Windows** key+**R**, typing **control.exe/name Microsoft.NetworkAndSharingCenter**, then clicking OK.

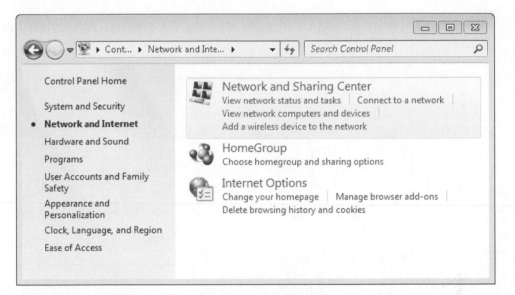

A third way is to choose Control Panel -> Network And Internet -> Network And Sharing Center.

The Network and Sharing Center window is split into two areas. On the left side, there is a column containing shortcuts toward tasks, such as managing your wireless networks, changing settings for all network adapters, and changing network sharing settings. On the bottom of the same column, there are shortcuts to the Homegroup settings panel, the Internet Options panel, and the Windows Firewall panel. On the right side, you have basic information about the current network connection and links to several wizards that allow you to change some of your network settings.

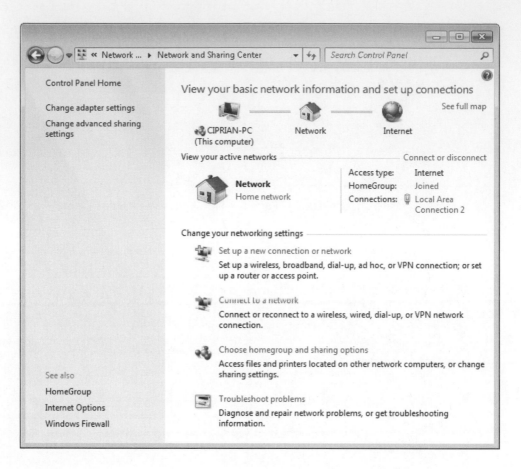

Configuring Network Adapters

In most cases, your home router is set to assign IP Addresses automatically to all computers on your network. This way, all you have to do is plug in the network cables to the router and your home computers, and the network connection works without any issues.

If you set the home router to assign IP Addresses in a static way to computers on your networks, or if you have some other special setup, you will need to configure the network adapters (network cards) on all or some of the computers in your network.

In this exercise, you will access the settings window of your network adapters and learn how to configure them.

SET UP Open the Network and Sharing Center.

1. In the left column, click the **Change adapter settings** link.

   The Network Connections window opens. Here, you see all network adapters and their status.

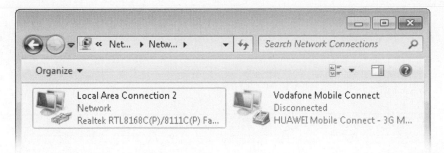

Important Each network adapter has three rows that describe them: the first shows the name of the adapter, the second shows the status of the adapter (disconnected, disabled, network, network cable unplugged), and the third shows the manufacturer and model name of the adapter.

Each adapter will have its own icon, colored in either gray or blue. Gray icons represent network adapters that are disconnected or disabled. Blue icons represent enabled and connected adapters.

If you have a network adapter that is enabled but not connected, you will see a red "X" near it. Also, in the second row of its description, it displays the text Network Cable Unplugged.

In such scenarios, you need to check the cable connection and ensure that the network cable is plugged in correctly to both the computer and the router.

2. Double-click the network adapter you want.

   A Status window opens (yours may look different).

   Note You can check the current settings of a network adapter and change them (if needed).

3. Click the **Details** button.

The Network Connection Details window opens.

4. When you're finished checking all the current settings, click **Close**.

Tip You can change any property of a network adapter. However, in most home networks, all you need to change is the IP Addresses and DNS settings. Therefore, we will stick mainly to these two settings, but we will mention the others briefly as well.

5. In the **Status** window, click the **Properties** button.

The Properties window of your local area connection opens (yours may look slightly different).

Tip Another way to go to the Properties window is to right-click the network adapter when you are in the Network Connections window (see step 1), and then click Properties.

6. To change the IP Address and DNS settings, double-click **Internet Protocol Version 4 (TCP/IPv4)**.

Note The Internet Protocol Version 4 (TCP/IPv4) Properties window will open. In it, you can either set the IP Addresses and DNS server to be set automatically (if your home router is configured to assign these settings automatically to all computers) or set them manually.

7. If you need to manually set IP addresses or DNS settings, select the appropriate boxes and type the needed information. DNS settings will be provided by your Internet provider while IP addresses should be according to how the home router is set to work with the home network.

8. If you want the IP addresses to be assigned automatically but you need to manually enter the DNS server addresses, you can leave the **Obtain an IP address automatically** option selected, then choose the **Use the following DNS server addresses** option.

9. If you click the **Advanced** button, you will be able to set more advanced parameters, such as NetBIOS settings (Network Basic Input/Output System), WINS addresses (Windows Internet Name Service), and other DNS-related details. For a typical home network, setting these parameters is not needed because the default values generally work, so we won't enter into detail about them.

10. Click **OK**.

✖ **CLEAN UP** If you are not comfortable with making your own home network settings, it is best to let the router set IP addresses and all other settings dynamically—leave the options for Obtain an IP Address Automatically and Use the Following DNS Server Addresses selected. This way, the home router will do all the work of setting the network for you while Windows 7 will automatically apply the right settings to your network devices and connections.

Enabling or Disabling a Network Adapter

Depending on your computing needs, you might want to enable or disable some of the network adapters that exist on your computer. For example, if you are a laptop user on the road and you connect to the Internet via a mobile modem, you might want to disable your wireless network adapter while in transit to save on battery so you can use your laptop for a longer period of time. When you get to a hotel room or other location where you can connect to the Internet again and you want to use the local wireless connection, you will need to re-enable the wireless network adapter.

To enable a network adapter, right-click its icon, then select Enable.

To disable a network adapter, right-click it, then select Disable.

Connecting to a Wireless Network

A growing number of people use laptops, notebooks, and netbooks instead of desktop computers. As a result of this trend—plus the growing number of devices like smartphones—more people use wireless networks on a regular basis. Windows 7 offers all you need to connect to wireless networks effortlessly.

In this exercise, you will learn how to detect wireless networks in Windows 7 and how to connect to them.

SET UP Before trying to connect to a wireless network, check if your wireless network adapter is detected by Windows 7, that it has the appropriate drivers installed, and that it is enabled.

1. On the right side of the taskbar, click the wireless network icon.

   A window with available network connections opens. The list is split by type of available network connections. At the top you have the available dial-up and virtual private network (VPN) connections, while at the bottom you have a list with the wireless networks that Windows 7 has detected. To refresh the list of available networks, click the Refresh icon, located at the upper-right side.

Not connected	⚡ —Refresh icon
📶 Connections are available	
Dial-up and VPN	⌃
Vodafone Mobile Connect	☎
Wireless Network Connection	⌃
Cip Home	📶
Belkin_N+_Guest	📶
dlink	📶
SkyLINK	📶
Other Network	📶
Open Network and Sharing Center	

   ⌃ ▸ 🎌 🔋 🔊 📶   9:28 PM
   28 Sep 2010

Troubleshooting If Windows 7 has not detected any connections and you know for a fact that there should be at least one wireless network available in your area, you should check whether your wireless network card has the appropriate drivers installed and that it is enabled.

2. Scroll down through the list of available networks.

Note If you hover your mouse cursor over a network icon for a second, you will see more details about it. Windows 7 will show the following: the network name, signal strength, the type of wireless security used (if any), and its Service Set identifier (SSID).

Not connected

Connections are available

Dial-up and VPN

Vodafone Mobile Connect

Wireless Network Connection

Cip Home

Belkin_N+_Guest

> Name: Cip Home
> Signal Strength: Excellent
> Security Type: WPA2-PSK
> Radio Type: 802.11n
> SSID: Cip Home

dlink

SkyLINK

Other Network

Open Network and Sharing Center

Important Be careful with wireless networks that have no security enabled—they can be used to steal personal data. If you connect to such networks, make sure your security solutions are turned on.

Not connected

Connections are available

Dial-up and VPN

Vodafone Mobile Connect

Wireless Network Connection

Cip Home

Belkin_N+_Guest

☑ Connect automatically   [Connect]

dlink

SkyLINK

Other Network

Open Network and Sharing Center

3. Once you decide which network to connect to, click it, and then click **Connect**.

Tip If you plan to use that network in the future, make sure you select the Connect Automatically check box before clicking Connect. This way, the next time you start your laptop in the same location, it will automatically connect to this wireless network without the need for manual intervention.

Important After a few seconds, you will be asked to enter the security key. Ask the administrator of the network for the wireless security key or, if you have connected to your own home network, take it from the control panel of your router.

Connect to a Network	✕

Type the network security key

Security key: securitykeygoeshere

☐ Hide characters

You can also connect by pushing the
button on the router.

OK   Cancel

4. Type the security key, then click **OK**.

Tip If you are in a public environment, it is best to select the Hide Characters check box so that other people can't see what you are typing.

CLEAN UP When you connect to the wireless network for the first time, make sure you assign it the correct network location. For instructions on how to do this, see the "Setting the Network Location" section on page 108.

If you are successful, the wireless icon on your taskbar changes to indicate your connection status and how powerful the wireless signal is.

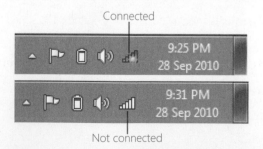

Connected

9:25 PM
28 Sep 2010

9:31 PM
28 Sep 2010

Not connected

Note If you typed an incorrect password, Windows 7 will prompt you to type it again and again until it matches the password of the network that you are connecting to. If everything is OK, Windows 7 will connect to the network you selected using the given security key.

Troubleshooting If you cannot connect to a wireless network from your Windows 7 computer, but all your other computers with older operating systems can, chances are you need to upgrade the firmware on your wireless router. Please consult the Internet page of your router's model to see if there are any upgrades available. If there are, download and install the latest version of firmware. Unfortunately, some older router models do not work very well with computers that use Windows 7 unless you perform a firmware upgrade.

Connecting to a Hidden Wireless Network

Hidden wireless networks are those networks that do not broadcast their Network ID (SSID). While not that many people use such networks, some feel a bit more secure by having their home wireless network hidden from unwanted guests. Therefore, if you've set your wireless network this way, you need to know how to connect to such networks.

Tip According to Microsoft TechNet's community and other reputable Web sites, hidden wireless networks are not undetectable. On the contrary, computers configured to connect to such networks are constantly disclosing the Network ID (SSID) of those networks, even when they are not in range. As a result, using such networks actually compromises the privacy of the clients connected to them.

In this exercise, you will learn how to connect to hidden wireless networks.

SET UP First and foremost, you need to know all the identification and connection details of the hidden wireless network to which you want to connect. Therefore, open your router's configuration page and go to the Wireless configuration menu. Write down the values for the Network ID (SSID) and Security fields.

Depending on what type of security your wireless network has, you will need to write down the value of another important field, as follows:

- For WEP security, note the value of the WEP Key field.

- For WPA-PSK, WPA2-PSK(AES) security, note the value of the Preshare Key field.

Note If your wireless network has no security enabled, then you only need to know the value of the Network ID (SSID) field.

1. Open the **Network and Sharing Center**, then click **Set Up a Connection or Network**.

   The Set Up A Connection Or Network window opens.

2. Select **Manually connect to a wireless network**, then click **Next**.

The Manually Connect To A Wireless Network wizard displays several fields in which you need to supply information.

3. In the **Network name** field, type the name of the wireless network you want to connect to; this is the equivalent of the Network ID (SSID) field from your router's wireless configuration menus.

4. In the **Security type** field (the type of security that's used by your wireless network), choose the appropriate option: WEP for WEP security, WPA-Personal for WPA-PSK security, or WPA2-Personal for WPA2-PSK (AES) security.

Note WPA2-Enterprise, WPA-Enterprise, and 802.1x are not covered in this book, as they are specific only to business networks not home networks. If you need to connect to a hidden business network, contact the organization's network administrator or the help desk team for guidance.

5. In the **Encryption type** field, if the wireless network is using WPA2-Personal (WPA2-PSK(AES)) security, select AES. Otherwise, leave the default value Windows 7 provides for you.

6. In the **Security Key** field (for WEP, WPA2 Personal, and WPA Personal), you will need to enter the security key used to connect to the wireless network.

This is the value of the WEP Key field (for WEP security) or the value of the Preshare Key field (for WPA-PSK, WPA2-PSK(AES) security).

Tip If you are in a public environment, it is best to select the Hide characters check box so that other people can't see what you are typing.

7. Don't forget to select the other two check boxes. **Start this connection automatically** will allow you to connect automatically to the wireless network each time you log on, and **Connect even if the network is not broadcasting** will allow you to connect to it even if the Network ID (SSID) is hidden, as is the case with hidden wireless networks.

8. Once you've entered all the necessary data, click **Next**.

When done, you will see a message indicating that you have successfully added the wireless network to your computer.

9. If you are unsure of any of the settings, you can click **Change connection settings** and review them all. A window opens where you can change all your settings.

CipHome2 Wireless Network Properties   [×]

| Connection | Security |

Name: CipHome2
SSID: CipHome2
Network type: Access point
Network availability: All users

☑ Connect automatically when this network is in range
☐ Connect to a more preferred network if available
☑ Connect even if the network is not broadcasting its name (SSID)

🛡 <u>Copy this network profile to a USB flash drive</u>

                                    [OK]   [Cancel]

Note The same window can be opened at any time by going to Control Panel -> Network and Internet -> Network and Sharing Center -> Manage Wireless Networks, and then double-clicking the wireless network.

10. Click **OK** to close the network properties window, then click **Close** to end the **Manually Connect to a Wireless Network** wizard. When done, Windows 7 automatically connects to the hidden wireless network.

✖ **CLEAN UP** When you connect to the hidden wireless network for the first time, make sure you assign it the correct network location. For instructions, check the "Setting the Network Location" section on page 108.

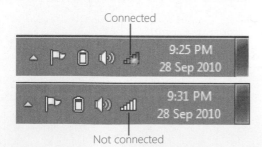

Connected

Not connected

The wireless icon on your taskbar shows your connection status and how powerful the wireless signal is.

Setting Up an Ad Hoc Wireless Network Between Computers

An ad hoc wireless network can be created between mobile computers, such as laptops or netbooks, and allow users to share files and folders between them quickly. This can be useful when you need to connect your laptop to another person's to quickly share files. With further configuration, you can also use this type of network connection to share the Internet connection on one of the computers.

The procedures are divided into three parts: creating the ad hoc wireless network, connecting other computers to it, and sharing files and folders on the newly created network.

Creating an Ad Hoc Wireless Network

Creating the ad hoc wireless network can be done on either of the two computers you are trying to connect.

In this exercise, you will learn how to create and configure an ad hoc wireless network.

 SET UP Before trying to create the ad hoc wireless network, check that your wireless network adapter is detected by Windows 7, that it has the appropriate drivers installed, and that it is enabled.

1. Open the **Network and Sharing Center**, and then click **Set Up a Connection or Network**.

   The Set Up A Connection Or Network window opens.

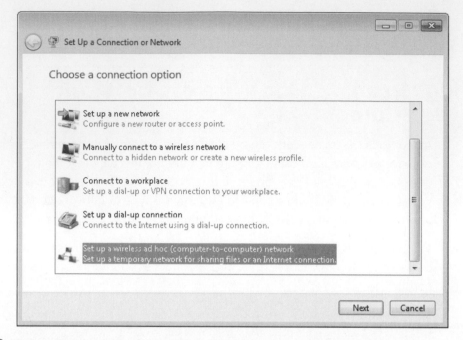

2. Select **Set up a wireless ad hoc (computer-to-computer) network**, then click **Next**.

   The Set Up An Ad Hoc Network window opens and describes the things you can do on a wireless ad hoc network.

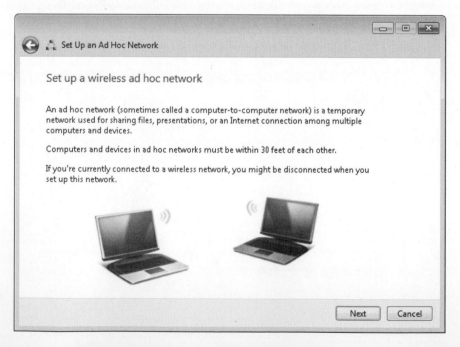

3. Read the contents of the window, then click **Next**.

The Set Up An Ad Hoc Network window opens.

4. Type the network name, then select the security type you want to use.

Tip For more security, I recommend you choose WPA2-Personal. It provides better encryption and is much harder to crack than WEP.

5. Type the password you want to use and, in case you want to use this network on other occasions, select the **Save this network** check box.

6. Click **Next**.

The wizard will create the network. This activity should take no more than a few seconds.

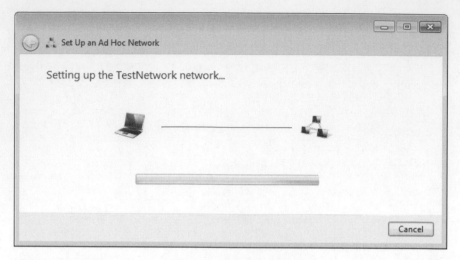

When finished, you will receive a notification that the network has been created and is ready to use.

7. Click **Close**.

Your laptop or netbook will now broadcast this newly created network and will wait for other computers to connect.

CLEAN UP Keep the laptop or netbook on which you created the network turned on and start configuring the client computer that will connect to it. Follow the instructions in Chapter 5, "Customizing Network Sharing Settings in Windows 7."

Connecting Other Computers to an Ad Hoc Wireless Network

Once the ad hoc network has been created on one of your computers, it is time to connect the second computer to it.

In this exercise, you will learn how to connect a computer to an existing ad hoc wireless network.

SET UP Before trying to connect to the ad hoc wireless network, check that your wireless network adapter is detected by Windows 7, that it has the appropriate drivers installed, and that it is enabled.

1. Click the **wireless** icon.

   You will see the list of all available wireless networks, including the ad hoc one you just created. Windows 7 will show the network's name plus the note that it is waiting for users.

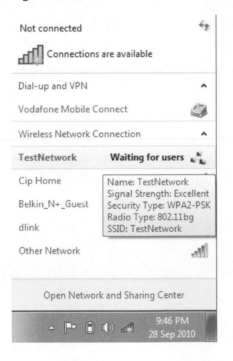

Tip If you don't see the ad hoc network, wait a few seconds and then click the refresh icon.

2. Select the test ad hoc network that you just created, then click **Connect**.

Connect to a Network	✕

Type the network security key

Security key: ☐ testpassword

☐ Hide characters

OK   Cancel

3. Type the password, then click **OK**.

Windows 7 will take a few seconds to connect to the network.

✖ CLEAN UP Before trying to share files or folders between computers, read the instructions in Chapter 5. There are some other settings you need to specify first.

Sharing Files on an Ad Hoc Wireless Network

After setting up an ad hoc computer-to-computer network and connecting the client computer, one would assume that features such as file sharing, networking discovery, and so on would be working and that you would be able to start sharing the content you need. Unfortunately, this is not the case.

After a client is connected, it will spend a few seconds identifying the network.

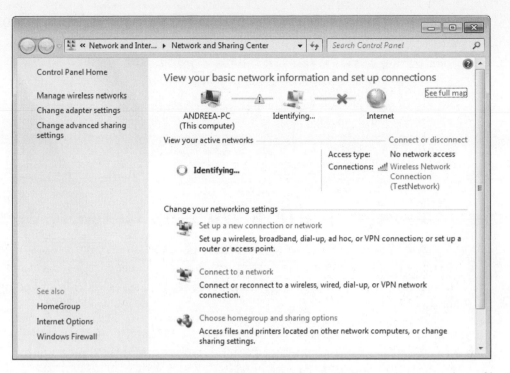

After the network is identified, Windows 7 will assign to it the public network profile. This means that you cannot share files and folders, as this option is disabled for public networks. Another problem is the fact that you cannot change the assigned network profile from public to work or home so that sharing of files and folders is enabled.

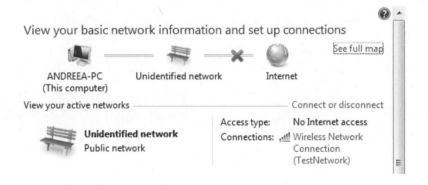

This means that you need to manually change the network and sharing settings for the public network profile so that the sharing of files and folders is enabled.

See Also To learn how to change the network and sharing settings for the public network profile, check the instructions detailed in Chapter 5.

Security Warning When you disconnect from the ad hoc network, make sure that you reset the network sharing settings for the public network profile. If you keep them unchanged, the next time you connect to a different public network, your computer might be at risk by allowing others to have access to your files and folders. So, be sure that you reset these settings to their default values when you are done.

Exporting and Importing Wireless Network Settings

One of the biggest annoyances when setting up wireless networks is remembering the security key and typing it correctly so that you can connect all laptops and netbooks to it. However, Windows 7 makes it easy to export your wireless settings from one machine to another.

The backup of the wireless networks settings can be easily done from Windows 7, saved to a USB stick, and then imported from the USB stick onto laptops and netbooks running Windows XP, Windows Vista, and Windows 7.

The procedures are divided in two parts: creating the backup of the settings on a USB memory stick, and importing the settings on other computers with Microsoft operating systems.

Exporting the Wireless Network Settings

All the settings of a wireless network that you have connected to are stored by Windows 7, and they can be reused when making another connection. These settings can be easily backed up on a USB memory stick.

In this exercise, you will learn how to back up the settings of any wireless network.

➡️ **SET UP** Make sure that you have connected to the wireless network from which you want to back up the settings at least once before starting this exercise. Also, open the Network and Sharing Center and make sure that you have a USB stick with you.

1. On the left side of the **Network and Sharing Center** window, click the **Manage Wireless Networks** link.

   In the Manage Wireless Networks window, you will see a list of all the wireless networks to which you have connected in the past.

2. Double-click the wireless network that you want to back up.

   A window presenting all the properties of the network appears.

3. To save the settings of the wireless network to a flash drive, click the **Copy this network profile to a USB flash drive** link.

The Copy Network Settings Wizard now opens.

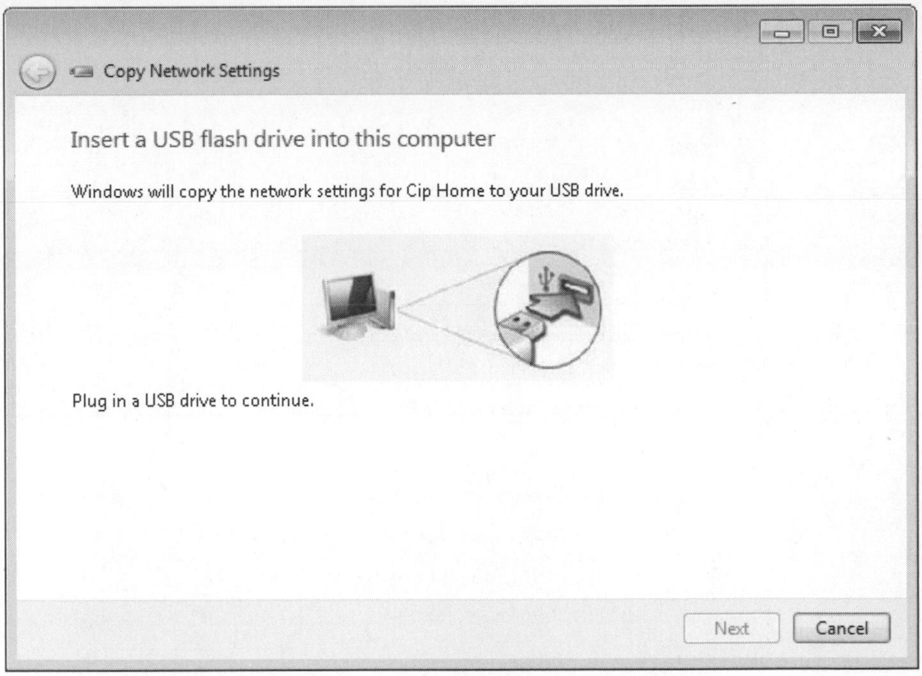

Copy Network Settings

Insert a USB flash drive into this computer

Windows will copy the network settings for Cip Home to your USB drive.

Plug in a USB drive to continue.

Next   Cancel

4. Insert the USB flash drive and wait until it is detected; you will know that it is ready for use when the **Next** button is no longer gray.

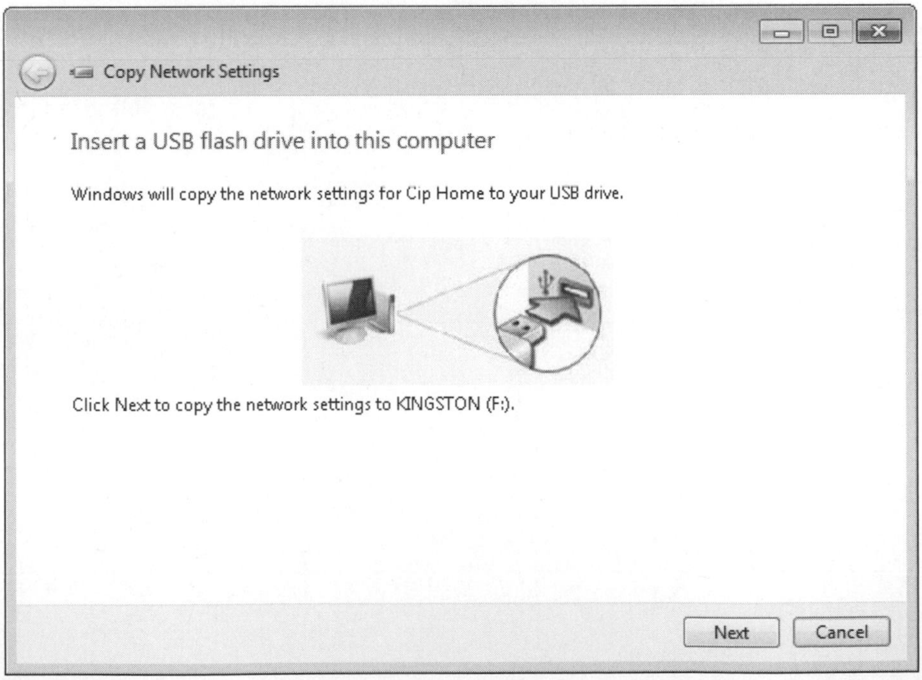

Copy Network Settings

Insert a USB flash drive into this computer

Windows will copy the network settings for Cip Home to your USB drive.

Click Next to copy the network settings to KINGSTON (F:).

Next   Cancel

5. Click **Next**. The copying process starts and, after a few seconds, you are notified of the success or failure of the operation.

6. Click **Close**. The backup operation is now done.

Look on your USB flash drive and you will see a setupSNK.exe file and a SMRTNTKY folder.

The Wireless Network window showing KINGSTON (F:) contents with SMRTNTKY file folder, AUTORUN setup information, and setupSNK application files, with 3 items total.

 CLEAN UP Make sure that you don't delete the files and folders created on the memory stick, and remove the stick safely before using it to import the wireless network settings on other computers.

Importing the Wireless Network Settings

By importing the settings of a wireless network onto other computers, you save time by not having to manually configure them. With just two clicks, you can get one computer correctly configured and ready to connect to the wireless network.

In this exercise, you will learn how to import the settings of a previously backed up wireless network.

SET UP Plug in the USB memory stick on which you backed up the wireless network settings and wait for your operating system to detect and install it correctly.

1. Run the **setupSNK.exe** file found on the memory stick.

   The Wireless Network Setup Wizard now opens and asks if you want to add your computer to the wireless network you have previously backed up.

2. Click **Yes**.

   The settings are now imported and you will be notified when done.

   Wireless Network Setup Wizard

   You have successfully added this computer to the "Cip Home" wireless network.

   OK

3. Click **OK**.

The settings of the wireless network have been installed on your computer and from this point forward, you will be able to connect to it when in range, without having to type its security key or adjusting any other settings.

 CLEAN UP Remove the USB memory stick from your computer. Do not delete its contents if you plan to use it in the future.

Setting the Network Location

A network location in Windows 7 is the profile that contains a collection of network and sharing settings that apply to the network to which you are connected. Based on the network location that is assigned to your active network connection, features such as file and printer sharing, network discovery, and others might be turned on or off.

These network locations are very useful to people who are very mobile and connect their computers to many networks. For example, you could use your work laptop to connect to your company network, take it home at the end of the day and connect to your home network, or connect to a network at your friend's place when you're visiting during the weekend. Each time you connect to a new network, Windows 7 will assign a network profile. With one choice, you get the entire set of network settings correctly changed. This way you won't compromise your security, and you have enabled only the network features that you actually need for each connection.

Network Locations: Home vs. Work vs. Public

Windows 7 allows you to choose among three types of network locations:

- **Home network**   Choose this location when you are connected to your home network or a network with people and devices you trust. By default, network discovery will be turned on and you will be able to see other computers and devices that are part of the network. Also, this will allow other computers from the network to access your computer. On home networks, you will also be allowed to create or join a Homegroup.

- **Work network**   This profile is good when connecting to your workplace network. It shares the same settings with Home network, with the exception that it won't allow you to create or join a Homegroup.

Share with other home computers running Windows 7

This computer can't connect to a homegroup.

⚠ To create or join a homegroup, your computer's network location must be set to Home.

What is a network location?

With a homegroup, you can share files and printers with other computers running Windows 7. You can also stream media to devices. The homegroup is protected with a password, and you'll always be able to choose what you share with the group.

Tell me more about homegroups

Change advanced sharing settings...

Start the HomeGroup troubleshooter

Create a homegroup   OK

- **Public network**   This profile is perfect when you are in a public place like an airport, pub, or coffee shop. When this profile is used, network discovery and sharing are turned off. Other computers from the same network will not be able to see yours. This setting is also useful when your computer is directly connected to the Internet (direct cable/modem connection, mobile Internet, and so on).

The default settings can be changed for all profiles. To learn how to do this, check the instructions detailed in Chapter 5.

NOTE There is also a fourth network location profile called Domain network. This profile cannot be set by a normal user. It is available for enterprise workplaces and can be set only by the network administrator. Under this profile, the network and sharing settings applied are the ones set by your company, and you cannot change them.

Changing the Network Location

When you connect to a network for the first time, Windows 7 automatically asks you about the type of location profile you want to assign to that network. Based on your choice, a specific set of network and sharing settings is applied.

In this exercise, you will learn how to change the network location applied to any network you are connected to.

SET UP Open the Network and Sharing Center.

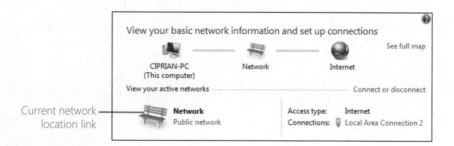

1. Click the link displaying the name of the current network location. This starts the **Set Network Location** Wizard.

Set Network Location

Select a location for the 'Network' network

This computer is connected to a network. Windows will automatically apply the correct network settings based on the network's location.

Home network
If all the computers on this network are at your home, and you recognize them, this is a trusted home network. Don't choose this for public places such as coffee shops or airports.

Work network
If all the computers on this network are at your workplace, and you recognize them, this is a trusted work network. Don't choose this for public places such as coffee shops or airports.

Public network
If you don't recognize all the computers on the network (for example, you're in a coffee shop or airport, or you have mobile broadband), this is a public network and is not trusted.

☐ Treat all future networks that I connect to as public, and don't ask me again.

Help me choose

Cancel

NOTE If you connect to a network for the first time, Windows 7 will show the Set Network Location Wizard automatically. You need to manually start it only if you want to change the current location assigned to the network.

2. Click the desired network location according to the recommendations detailed earlier in this chapter.

Windows 7 informs you of the change in network location.

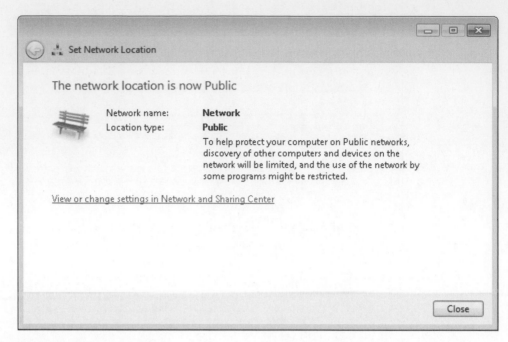

3. Click the **Close** button.

The network and sharing settings corresponding to the selected network location are now applied.

 CLEAN UP Close the Network and Sharing Center.

Setting the Workgroup

A workgroup is the name assigned to a group of computers connected in a network. Computers that are part of the same workgroup can easily detect each other and share files and folders among workgroup members. A computer can only be part of a single workgroup, and many computers can be part of the same workgroup.

Workgroups are used for small networks, and each computer has its own set of rules and settings. They work well for home or small-business networks. In order to access a computer within the workgroup, you need to have a user account defined on that computer. By default, Windows 7 assigns the workgroup "Workgroup" to a computer. If you have only Windows 7 computers in your home network, you won't need to make any changes. However, if you have multiple operating systems, then setting the same workgroup on all will help.

Changing the Workgroup

Change the workgroup so that it is set the same on all the computers that are part of your home network. This change will help ensure that all computers detect each other and work together properly when exchanging files and folders.

In this exercise, you will learn how to change the workgroup set for your computer.

SET UP Write down the workgroup set on all the computers from your home network and change it only for those that have different settings than the others. You need to make sure that it is set the same on all computers.

1. Choose **Control Panel -> System and Security -> System**.

   This opens the System window.

This section shows the
computer name and workgroup

Here, you will be able to see your computer name and the currently assigned workgroup.

2. To change the assigned workgroup, click **Change settings**.

   The System Properties window opens.

3. Click **Change**.

   The Computer Name/Domain Changes window opens.

4. In the **Workgroup** field, type the name of the workgroup you want your computer to join.

5. Click **OK**.

Windows 7 notifies you of the change with a welcome note.

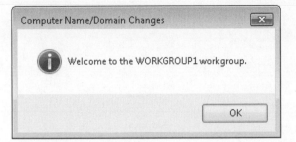

6. Click **OK**.

Windows 7 notifies you that you need to restart your computer in order for the change to be applied.

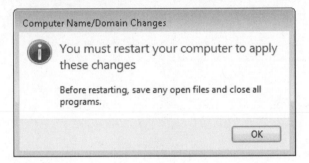

7. Click **OK**.

The System Properties window is shown again.

8. Click **Close**.

   Windows 7 asks if you want to restart your computer now or later.

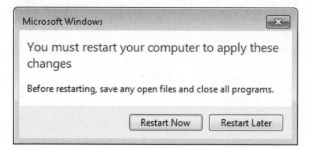

9. Close any open documents, then click **Restart Now**.

   After the restart, your computer joins the newly assigned workgroup.

   NOTE If you click Restart Later, the workgroup change will be applied the next time you reboot your computer.

   ✖ **CLEAN UP** Close the System window and (in case you chose to Restart Later) repeat the procedure on all computers for which you need to change the workgroup.

Key Points

- The Network and Sharing Center is the panel from which most network configuration settings can be accessed.

- You need to configure your network adapters correctly before being able to access the home network and the Internet.

- Most wireless networks require a security key in order to successfully connect to them.

- The network location is the profile that contains a collection of network and sharing settings that are applied to the network you are connected to.

- On a home network with many computers and diverse operating systems, it is important to set the same workgroup on all computers.

Chapter at a Glance

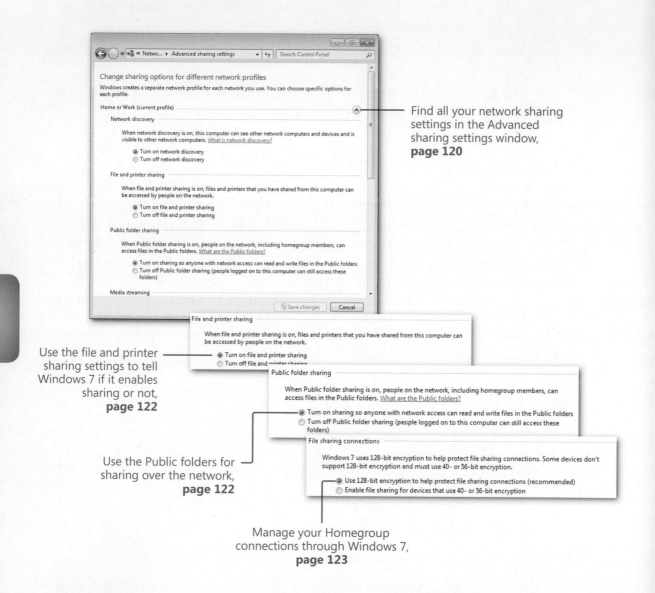

Find all your network sharing settings in the Advanced sharing settings window, **page 120**

Use the file and printer sharing settings to tell Windows 7 if it enables sharing or not, **page 122**

Use the Public folders for sharing over the network, **page 122**

Manage your Homegroup connections through Windows 7, **page 123**

5 Customizing Network Sharing Settings in Windows 7

In this chapter, you will learn how to

- ✔ Find the network sharing settings.
- ✔ Configure network sharing settings.

Compared to older versions of Microsoft operating systems, Windows 7 makes it much easier to configure network sharing settings. These settings are defined by a different network profile: one set of settings that apply to trusted network locations such as home and work, and another that applies to untrusted public networks.

See Also To learn more about network locations, see the "Network Locations: Home vs. Work vs. Public" section in Chapter 4, "Creating the Network."

In this chapter, you will learn where to find the network sharing settings, how to turn network discovery, file sharing, media streaming, and password protection on or off; how to set encryption for sharing connections; and how to configure Homegroup connections.

See Also To learn more about the Homegroup, see Chapter 6, "Creating the Homegroup and Joining Windows 7 Computers."

> **Practice Files** You do not need any practice files to complete the exercises in this chapter.

Finding the Network Sharing Settings

The great thing about Windows 7 is that it organizes all your network sharing settings in one panel. There's no need to go to several places to configure your setup.

In this exercise, you will learn how to find the network sharing settings.

SET UP Open the Network And Sharing Center.

See Also To learn more about the Network And Sharing Center, check the "Opening the Networking and Sharing Center" section in Chapter 4.

1. Click the **Change advanced sharing settings** link found on the top-left side of the **Network and Sharing Center** window.

   The Advanced Sharing Settings window opens, which contains all the sharing settings, displayed by network location type.

Minimize/Maximize list of settings

Change sharing options for different network profiles

Windows creates a separate network profile for each network you use. You can choose specific options for each profile.

Home or Work (current profile)

Network discovery

When network discovery is on, this computer can see other network computers and devices and is visible to other network computers. What is network discovery?

○ Turn on network discovery
○ Turn off network discovery

File and printer sharing

When file and printer sharing is on, files and printers that you have shared from this computer can be accessed by people on the network.

○ Turn on file and printer sharing
○ Turn off file and printer sharing

Public folder sharing

When Public folder sharing is on, people on the network, including homegroup members, can access files in the Public folders. What are the Public folders?

○ Turn on sharing so anyone with network access can read and write files in the Public folders
○ Turn off Public folder sharing (people logged on to this computer can still access these folders)

Media streaming

Save changes   Cancel

2. If you want to access the settings for only one of the network locations, use the arrows to the right of each profile.

   Clicking an arrow once minimizes the list of settings for that network location. To maximize the list, click it again.

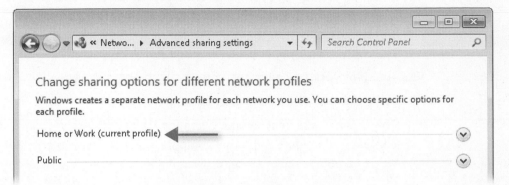

3. The profile currently assigned to your network connection is indicated by the **(current profile)** statement, just beside the name of one of the two profiles.

 CLEAN UP To learn how to configure the settings for each profile, see the next section in this chapter.

Configuring the Network Sharing Settings

Now that you have opened the panel with all the network sharing settings, it is time to customize them to fit your needs. In this exercise, you will learn how to do that.

SET UP Open the Advanced sharing settings window.

1. Click the network profile for which you want to customize the network sharing settings (the **Public** profile or the **Home or Work** profile).

   The entire list of settings for that profile opens.

2. Scroll down to the **Network Discovery** section.

   This shows the current setting. When turned on, this setting allows your computer to search for other devices on the network to which it is connected. Also, it allows other computers on the same network to find your computer.

Network discovery

When network discovery is on, this computer can see other network computers and devices and is visible to other network computers. What is network discovery?

◉ Turn on network discovery
◯ Turn off network discovery

Recommendation If you are connected to a home or work network, it is best to choose Turn On Network Discovery. For public networks, it is best to choose Turn off Network Discovery so that your computer won't be visible to other computers.

3. Turn **Network Discovery** on or off, depending on your needs.

4. Scroll down to **File and printer sharing**.

This shows the current setting. When turned on, this feature allows you to share content and printers with other computers on your network. With it turned off, you won't be able to share anything. Even if your computer is visible for other devices on the network, nobody will be able to access any shared files, folders, or printers.

File and printer sharing

When file and printer sharing is on, files and printers that you have shared from this computer can be accessed by people on the network.

◉ Turn on file and printer sharing
◯ Turn off file and printer sharing

Recommendation Choose Turn on file and printer sharing for home or work networks. Choose Turn off file and printer sharing for public networks.

5. Turn **File and printer sharing** on or off, depending on your needs.

6. Scroll down to **Public folder sharing**.

This shows the current setting. When turned on, the C:\Users\Public\ folder is shared with all the computers on the network. This folder contains the following subfolders: Public Desktop, Public Documents, Public Downloads, Public Music, Public Pictures, and Public Videos. Users from the other computers can read the contents of the Public folder and write files inside it and its subfolders. When turned off, this folder is not shared with your network.

Public folder sharing

When Public folder sharing is on, people on the network, including homegroup members, can access files in the Public folders. What are the Public folders?

◉ Turn on sharing so anyone with network access can read and write files in the Public folders
◯ Turn off Public folder sharing (people logged on to this computer can still access these folders)

Recommendation Turn off Public Folder Sharing unless using this folder for sharing is something you find very useful. Depending on your personal preference, you might choose to share files and folders directly with others, without the need to copy them to the Public folder.

7. Turn **Public folder sharing** on or off, depending on your needs.

8. Scroll down to **Media Streaming**.

This shows the current setting. This feature allows you to stream multimedia files (pictures, video, and music) using Windows Media Player 12. When turned on, you will be able to stream your media with the home network and the Internet. When turned off, no media streaming is possible using Windows Media Player 12.

Media streaming

When media streaming is on, people and devices on the network can access pictures, music, and videos on this computer. This computer can also find media on the network.

Media streaming is on.
Choose media streaming options...

Recommendation Turn Media Streaming on only if you plan to use this feature.

9. Turn **Media Streaming** on or off, depending on your needs.

See Also **To learn more about Media Streaming and how to set it up, see Chapter 9, "Streaming Media Over the Network and the Internet."**

10. Scroll down to **File sharing connections**.

This shows the type of encryption used for file sharing connections. By default, this is set to 128-bit encryption. You can also set it to 40-bit or 56-bit encryption.

File sharing connections

Windows 7 uses 128-bit encryption to help protect file sharing connections. Some devices don't support 128-bit encryption and must use 40- or 56-bit encryption.

◉ Use 128-bit encryption to help protect file sharing connections (recommended)
◯ Enable file sharing for devices that use 40- or 56-bit encryption

Recommendation Leave this set to 128-bit encryption, unless you have problems with some older devices or computers that cannot properly access your shared files and folders.

11. Set the type of encryption you need to use, depending on your home network.

12. Scroll down to **Password protected sharing**.

This shows the current setting. Password protected sharing allows people to access your shared files and folders only if they have a user account and password set on your computer. If they don't know such details, they cannot connect to your shared items.

Password protected sharing

When password protected sharing is on, only people who have a user account and password on this computer can access shared files, printers attached to this computer, and the Public folders. To give other people access, you must turn off password protected sharing.

○ Turn on password protected sharing
◉ Turn off password protected sharing

Recommendation Choose Turn off password protected sharing for home or work networks. Choose turn on password protected sharing for public networks.

13. Turn **Password protected sharing** on or off, depending on your needs.

14. Scroll down to **Homegroup connections**.

This shows the current setting. Once your computer has joined the Homegroup, Windows 7 will automatically manage your connections. That's why the option for Allow Windows to manage Homegroup connections is selected. If you choose the Use user accounts and passwords to connect to other computers option, you will need to manually type a user name and password when you connect to other computers instead of letting Windows 7 do the job for you.

HomeGroup connections

Typically, Windows manages the connections to other homegroup computers. But if you have the same user accounts and passwords on all of your computers, you can have HomeGroup use your account instead. Help me decide

◉ Allow Windows to manage homegroup connections (recommended)
○ Use user accounts and passwords to connect to other computers

Recommendation Use only Allow Windows to manage Homegroup connections.

Note This setting is available only for Home or Work network profiles. It is not for Public profiles.

15. Set **Homegroup connections** according to your needs.

16. When you have finished with all settings, click **Save changes**.

All your network sharing settings are applied to the customized network profile. Each time you connect to a network using this profile, all these settings will be automatically applied.

 CLEAN UP Close the Advanced Sharing Settings and Network and Sharing Center windows.

Key Points

- All network sharing settings can be found in one panel.
- The network sharing settings are separated and customized by network profile.
- The network sharing settings are applied automatically to the network you are connected to, depending on the profile you assign to it.
- Homegroup connection settings can be customized only for home or work networks.

Chapter at a Glance

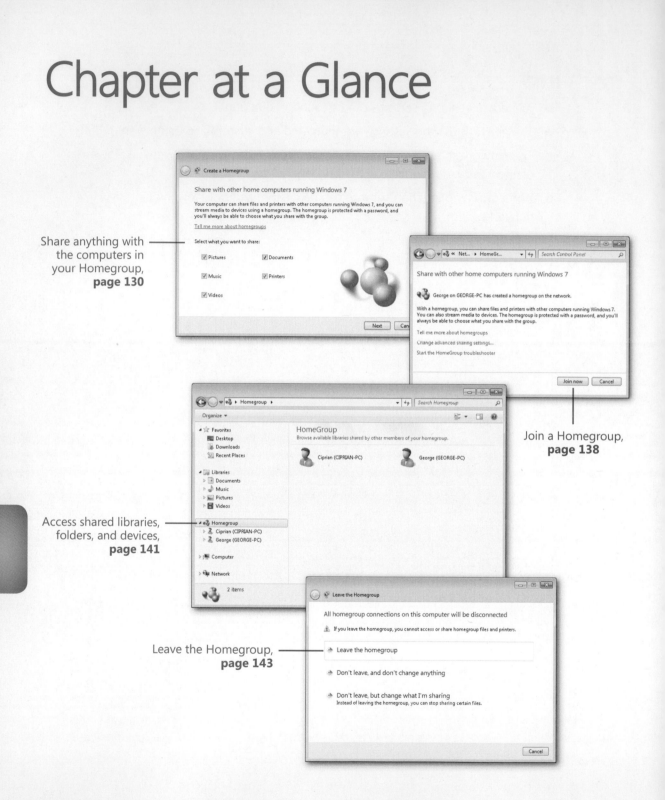

Share anything with the computers in your Homegroup, **page 130**

Join a Homegroup, **page 138**

Access shared libraries, folders, and devices, **page 141**

Leave the Homegroup, **page 143**

6 Creating the Homegroup and Joining Windows 7 Computers

In this chapter, you will learn how to

- ✔ Create a Homegroup.
- ✔ Find or change the existing Homegroup password.
- ✔ Join a computer to a Homegroup.
- ✔ Access files, folders, and devices shared on the Homegroup.
- ✔ Leave a Homegroup.
- ✔ Solve some of the known issues encountered with the Homegroup feature.

Homegroup is a new feature introduced in Windows 7 that aims to simplify the process of sharing content and devices on your home network. In older versions of Windows, sharing content was a tedious and sometimes painful process, especially for home users. By using the Homegroup, you can now access all shared files and devices in your home network with very few clicks and without the need to type any user names and passwords.

This feature is designed to be available for computers connected to a home network. Each time you connect your computer to a new network, Windows 7 asks you to set the network location. If you select Home Network, it means you are in a trusted network of computers, and Windows 7 allows you to use the Homegroup feature. If you select Work Network or Public Network, this feature will not be available.

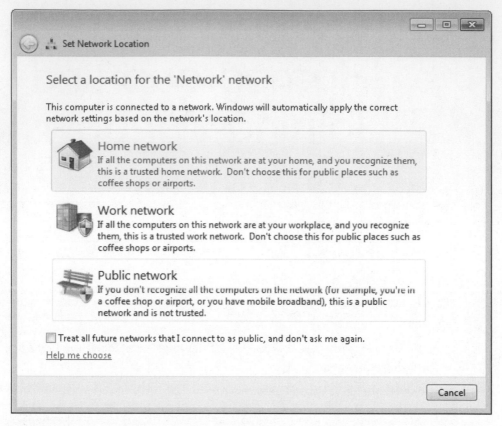

See Also To learn more about Network locations, read the "Setting the Network Location" section found in Chapter 4, "Creating the Network."

Even though this feature is very useful and easy to use, unfortunately it has a very important limitation: it is available only for computers running Windows 7. Only computers with Windows 7 can join a Homegroup and take advantage of it.

See Also If you own computers with Windows XP and Windows Vista installed, see Chapter 10, "Sharing Between Windows XP, Windows Vista, and Windows 7 Computers," for instructions on how to share files, folders, and devices with your Windows 7 computers.

See Also If you own computers with Mac OS X and Ubuntu Linux installed, see Chapter 11, "Sharing Between Mac OS X and Windows 7 Computers," and Chapter 12, "Sharing Between Ubuntu Linux and Windows 7 Computers," respectively, for instructions on how to share files, folders, and devices with your Windows 7 computers.

In this chapter, you learn how to create a Homegroup, add other home computers to it, access content and devices shared by them via the Homegroup feature, and manage the password used to connect all computers to the Homegroup. Last but not least, you will learn how to set a computer to leave the Homegroup and how to solve one of the most common problems encountered with this feature.

> **Practice Files** You won't need any practice files to complete the exercises in this chapter.

Creating the Homegroup

After you have created the network and customized the network sharing settings, it is time to create the Homegroup for your home computers to join and exchange libraries, files, folders, and devices.

In this exercise, you will learn how to create a Homegroup for your home network computers.

 SET UP Open the Network and Sharing Center and make sure the network location is set to Home Network.

 1. Click the **Homegroup** link located at the lower-left side of the **Network and Sharing Center** window.

The Homegroup Creation Wizard opens.

Share with other home computers running Windows 7

There is currently no homegroup on the network.

With a homegroup, you can share files and printers with other computers running Windows 7. You can also stream media to devices. The homegroup is protected with a password, and you'll always be able to choose what you share with the group.

Tell me more about homegroups

Change advanced sharing settings...

Start the HomeGroup troubleshooter

[Create a homegroup] [Cancel]

Note If, when you click the Homegroup link, you do not see a window similar to the one shown here, but something with the settings of an existing Homegroup, it means the computer is already part of a Homegroup. In this scenario, you either keep the computer as part of that Homegroup or leave it and create a new one. To learn how to leave a Homegroup, read the "Leaving a Homegroup" section on page 143.

2. Click **Create a Homegroup**.

   This opens the Create A Homegroup window, where you can select the items you want to share with the other computers that will join the Homegroup. A limited list of libraries is available for sharing: Pictures, Documents, Music, and Videos. You can also share your printers.

See Also To learn more about libraries in Windows 7, read Chapter 3, "Setting Up Your Libraries on all Windows 7 Computers."

3. Select the items you want to share, then click **Next**.

   After a few seconds, Windows 7 will show an automatically generated password for the Homegroup. This password will be used by other computers to join the Homegroup.

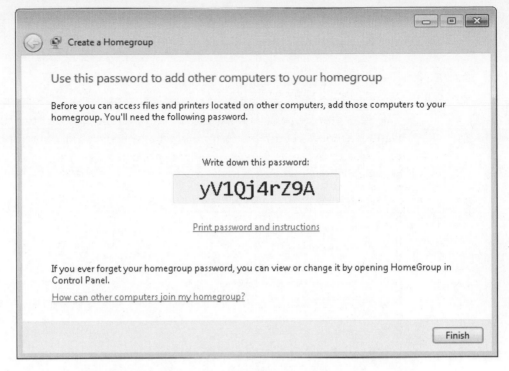

4. Write down the password, then click **Finish**.

The Homegroup is now created and other computers from your home network can join it. At the end of the wizard, you return to the Homegroup window, where you see the list of available settings.

Change homegroup settings

This computer belongs to a homegroup.

Share libraries and printers

☑ Pictures   ☑ Music   ☑ Videos

☑ Documents   ☑ Printers

How do I share additional libraries?   How do I exclude files and folders?

Share media with devices

☑ Stream my pictures, music, and videos to all devices on my home network

Choose media streaming options...

Note: Shared media is not secure. Anyone connected to your network can receive your shared media.

Other homegroup actions

View or print the homegroup password

Change the password...

Leave the homegroup...

Change advanced sharing settings...

Start the HomeGroup troubleshooter

Save changes   Cancel

5. If you want to customize the Homegroup settings, select the appropriate options, then click **Save changes**.

✖ **CLEAN UP** Close the Homegroup window.

Finding Your Homegroup Password

If you want to add another computer to the Homegroup and you forgot the password, you can easily access it on the computers that have already joined or created the Home-group in the first place.

In this exercise, you will learn how to find the password defined for your Homegroup.

SET UP Start a computer that is part of the Homegroup, then open the Network and Sharing Center.

1. Click the **Homegroup** link.

   The Homegroup window opens, displaying all the available configuration options.

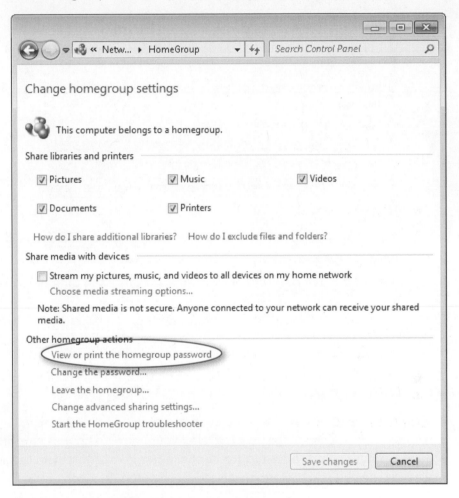

2. Click **View or print the Homegroup password**.

   A window opens in which the password is shown in a big yellow box.

View and print your homegroup password

Password for the homegroup on
your network:

shoshoshome

Use this password to connect other computers running Windows 7 to the homegroup.

On each computer:

1. Click Start, and then click Control Panel.
2. Under Network and Internet, click Choose homegroup and sharing options.
3. Click Join now, and then follow the HomeGroup wizard to enter the password.

Note: Computers that are turned off or sleeping will not appear in the homegroup.

Print this page   Cancel

3. Write down the password or click the **Print this page** button to print it out.

4. When done, close the window.

✖ **CLEAN UP** Close the Homegroup window.

Changing the Password of a Homegroup

Changing the password of a Homegroup can be done from any computer that joined it. However, if you change the password after your home computers have joined the Homegroup, you will need to retype it on all computers in order for them to join again. If you change the password before joining other computers, you don't need to rejoin them.

In this exercise, you will learn how to change the password of an existing Homegroup.

 SET UP Open the Network and Sharing Center.

1. Click on the **Homegroup** link.

   The Homegroup window opens.

2. Click **Change the password**.

   A dialog box appears in which Windows 7 notifies you that changing the Home-group password will disconnect everyone who has joined it thus far.

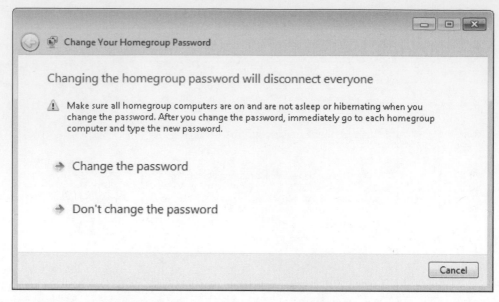

3. Click **Change the password**.

   Windows 7 now generates a new random password for your Homegroup.

4. If you prefer another new password, you can type your own custom password or click the **Refresh** button to have Windows 7 generate another one for you.

If you type your own password, ensure that it is at least eight characters long. Otherwise, Windows 7 won't accept it as a valid password.

5. When done, click **Next**.

Windows 7 notifies you that the password has been changed.

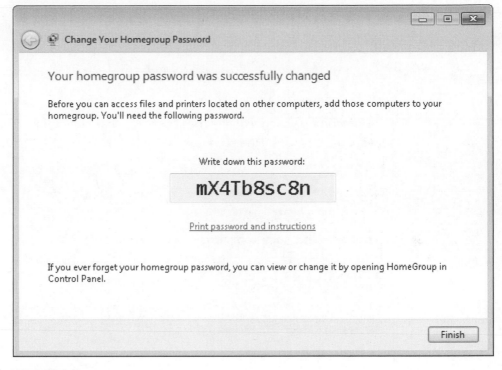

6. Click **Finish**.

The password for the Homegroup is now changed and can be used by other computers to join the Homegroup, too.

✖ **CLEAN UP** Don't forget to rejoin all computers that have been disconnected from the Homegroup due to the password change.

Joining a Homegroup

Once the Homegroup is created, it is time to join other computers so that you can exchange files, folders, and devices. Any computer on the network can be part of a Homegroup, but they can only be in one Homegroup at a time.

In this exercise, you will learn how to add a computer running Windows 7 to a previously created Homegroup.

 SET UP Open the Network and Sharing Center.

1. Click the **Homegroup** link.

   The Homegroup window opens and shows you that one of the computers on your network has created a Homegroup.

   > Share with other home computers running Windows 7
   >
   > George on GEORGE-PC has created a homegroup on the network.
   >
   > With a homegroup, you can share files and printers with other computers running Windows 7. You can also stream media to devices. The homegroup is protected with a password, and you'll always be able to choose what you share with the group.
   >
   > Tell me more about homegroups
   >
   > Change advanced sharing settings...
   >
   > Start the HomeGroup troubleshooter
   >
   > [Join now]   [Cancel]

2. Click **Join now**.

   This opens the Join A Homegroup window, in which you can select the items you want to share with the other computers on the Homegroup. A limited list of libraries is available for sharing: Pictures, Documents, Music, and Videos. You can also share your printers.

See Also To learn more about libraries in Windows 7, read Chapter 3, "Setting Up Your Libraries on All Windows 7 Computers."

3. Select the items you want to share, then click **Next**.

A window opens in which you are asked to type the Homegroup password.

4. Type the password, then click **Next**.

Windows 7 notifies you that you have joined the Homegroup.

> ⬅ 🖳 Join a Homegroup
>
> You have joined the homegroup
>
> You can begin accessing files and printers shared by other people in the homegroup.
>
> How can I access files and printers on other computers?
>
> Finish

5. Click **Finish**.

The computer is now part of the Homegroup and is able to share libraries, files, folders, and devices with the other computers. It can also access the things shared by them.

❌ **CLEAN UP** Repeat this procedure for all the computers on your home network that are running Windows 7.

Accessing Homegroup Computers

Once the Homegroup is created and all computers are joined, accessing their shared libraries and devices is a simple task—all it takes is a few clicks. You no longer need to type any user names and passwords in order to access what is shared in the Homegroup.

In this exercise, you will learn how to access the libraries, files, folders, and devices shared by other computers in the Homegroup.

➡ **SET UP** Turn on the computers you want to access.

1. Open the **Computer** window.

   Tip You can select the Computer shortcut from the Desktop or the Start menu, or by pressing Windows+E on your keyboard simultaneously.

The Computer window looks similar to the one shown here.

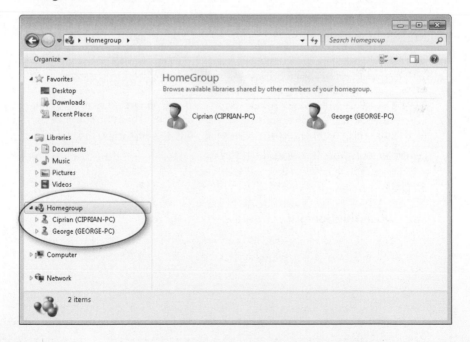

2. Click **Homegroup**.

You now see the list of computers that are part of the Homegroup and that are also running at the moment.

3. Double-click the name of the computer you want to access.

You now see the complete list of libraries, folders, and devices shared by that computer.

4. Double-click the library, folder, or device that you want to access.

You now have access to the items that are shared by that computer and can work with them according to the defined sharing settings.

Tip By default, libraries and folders are shared with the other Homegroup computers as read-only. Therefore, you will be able to access them or copy them to your computer, but you won't be able to delete them or change them in any way.

See Also For more information on permission levels and how to share folders and libraries, read Chapter 7, "Sharing Libraries and Folders."

✖ **CLEAN UP** When you are done accessing other Homegroup computers, close the Computer window.

Leaving a Homegroup

Leaving a Homegroup is as easy as joining one. If you leave a Homegroup, you stop sharing files, folders, and devices with other members of the group, and you won't be able to access what is shared as part of that Homegroup. After leaving a Homegroup, you can create another one, or at any time, rejoin the Homegroup you left.

In this exercise, you will learn how to leave a Homegroup.

SET UP Open the Network and Sharing Center.

1. Click the **Homegroup** link found on the lower-left side of the **Network and Sharing Center** window.

   The Homegroup window opens.

2. Click the **Leave the Homegroup** link.

Windows 7 informs you that all the Homegroup connections on your computer will be disconnected.

3. Click **Leave the Homegroup**.

Windows 7 informs you that you have successfully left the Homegroup.

4. Click **Finish**.

Your computer is no longer part of the Homegroup.

Tip If you repeat this procedure on all computers that are part of the Homegroup, the Homegroup will no longer exist. This is the only way to "delete" a Homegroup.

✖ **CLEAN UP** Close the Network and Sharing Center.

Known Issues and Solutions

If you are trying to connect to the Homegroup but you receive an error message indicating that "The password is incorrect," even though you have typed it correctly, it means you might have encountered a bug. According to Microsoft, this can happen because the computer's date and time does not match the date and time of the system that owns the Homegroup. In this case, the only solution is to adjust the date and time settings on the computer that is joining the Homegroup to match that of the computer that owns the Homegroup, and then try to join again. The computer that owns the Homegroup is the one on which it was first created.

Key Points

- The Homegroup is a Windows 7-specific feature that allows easy sharing of files, folders, libraries, and devices, without requiring you to type user names and passwords each time you want to access something that is shared over the network.

- The Homegroup is available only for home networks and not for public or work networks.

- In order to join a Homegroup, you need to know and type the Homegroup password defined by the computer that created it.

- A computer can join only one Homegroup at a time. In order to join another Homegroup, the computer needs first to leave the current one, then join the other.

Chapter at a Glance

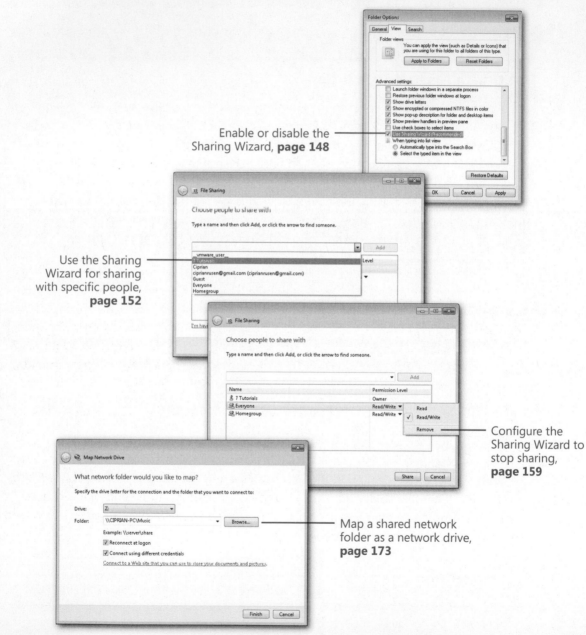

Enable or disable the
Sharing Wizard, **page 148**

Use the Sharing
Wizard for sharing
with specific people,
page 152

Configure the
Sharing Wizard to
stop sharing,
page 159

Map a shared network
folder as a network drive,
page 173

7 Sharing Libraries and Folders

In this chapter, you will learn how to

- ✔ Enable or disable the Sharing Wizard.
- ✔ Use the Sharing Wizard to share with the Homegroup.
- ✔ Use the Sharing Wizard to share with specific people.
- ✔ Use the Sharing Wizard to stop sharing.
- ✔ Use Advanced Sharing to share your folders or partitions.
- ✔ Use Advanced Sharing to stop sharing your folders or partitions.
- ✔ Map a shared network folder as a network drive.
- ✔ Map an FTP server as a network drive.
- ✔ Delete a mapped network drive.

While developing Windows 7, Microsoft directed a lot of effort toward improving the networking experience. Windows Vista was a first step in the right direction. Windows 7 raises things to a new level and makes it easier than ever to share files, folders, libraries, and devices with the other computers on your network.

With the help of file sharing wizards and the Homegroup feature, it takes only a few clicks to share and access the things you want to.

In this chapter, you will learn how to share libraries and folders over your home network by using the sharing wizard and the advanced sharing options and menus. You will also learn what the Public folder is and how to use it for sharing. At the end of this chapter, you will learn how to map a shared folder on your home network as a network drive and how to map an FTP site as a network drive.

> **Practice Files** You can use any of your libraries, folders, and files to complete the exercises in this chapter. Until you get the hang of it, it is best not to use any important files. Also, back up the files and folders you are about to use, just to make sure you don't lose them by mistake.

Enabling or Disabling the Sharing Wizard

The Sharing Wizard in Windows 7 is designed so that you can easily share anything you want with the other computers on your home network. But even though it simplifies the sharing experience, some people might prefer the old Windows XP/Windows 2000 way of sharing things. In this circumstance, it is best to disable the Sharing Wizard. The procedure is pretty simple and involves nothing more than editing a configuration setting in Windows Explorer.

In this exercise, you will learn how to enable or disable the Sharing Wizard, depending on your preference.

> **Practice Files** No practice files are required for this exercise.

SET UP Open Windows Explorer or the Computer shortcut.

1. Click the **Organize** button on the upper-left side of Windows Explorer window.

   The Organize menu appears.

2. Click **Folder and search options**.

The Folder Options window opens.

![Folder Options dialog box showing the View tab selected, with Folder views and Advanced settings sections. The Advanced settings list shows options including Launch folder windows in a separate process, Restore previous folder windows at logon, Show drive letters, Show encrypted or compressed NTFS files in color, Show pop-up description for folder and desktop items, Show preview handlers in preview pane, Use check boxes to select items, Use Sharing Wizard (Recommended) highlighted, When typing into list view, Automatically type into the Search Box, Select the typed item in the view. Buttons include Apply to Folders, Reset Folders, Restore Defaults, OK, Cancel, and Apply.]

3. Click the **View** tab.

4. Scroll down the Advanced settings list and find the **Use Sharing Wizard (Recommended)** check box.

5. If you want to enable the Sharing Wizard, select the check box. If you want to disable it, clear the check box.

6. Click **OK**.

This takes you back to the Windows Explorer window, and the setting you made is now applied.

 CLEAN UP Close Windows Explorer.

Using the Sharing Wizard to Share with the Homegroup

If you have set up a Homegroup and you want to share something with other computers that have joined it, the Sharing Wizard makes the procedure extremely simple.

In this exercise, you will learn how to use the Sharing Wizard to share anything you want with your Homegroup.

> **Practice Files** You can use any of your libraries or folders to complete this exercise. Until you get the hang of it, it is best not to use any important libraries or folders. Also, back up the folders and libraries you are about to use, just to make sure you don't lose any data by mistake.

SET UP Open Windows Explorer or the Computer shortcut.

1.   Navigate to the library or folder you want to share and right-click it.

The contextual menu appears.

2. Click **Share with** to open the list of sharing options, which includes the following:

- **Nobody**   This option prevents the selected item from being shared. It can be useful when you share a library or collection of folders and files, but you don't want to share a specific item. For example, you might share your entire pictures library, but you want some pictures to remain private while leaving the rest accessible to others on your network. By using this option, you can quickly filter out those items from your collection that you don't want to share.

- **Homegroup (Read)**   This option shares the selected item with the Homegroup and gives read-only permissions to all computers in the Homegroup. The item will be shared only when you are connected to the Homegroup, and other computers will only be able to view/read the shared item but not modify it, delete it, or change it in any way.

- **Homegroup (Read/Write)**   This shares the item with others in your Homegroup and gives full permissions to modify it, delete it, or change it. The item will not be shared when you disconnect from the Homegroup or connect to another network.

- **Specific people**   This option allows you to share the selected item with whomever you want, including computers that are not a part of the Homegroup and specific user accounts. This option will be described in more detail in the next section of this chapter.

3. Select the option that works for you. Depending on the size of the shared library or the folder and its contents, you might see a **File Sharing** progress window.

Note If the shared library or folder is small or contains very few files, you might not see this progress window, and the items will be shared instantly with the Homegroup.

Important Depending on what you have shared, you might see an additional window, asking you to confirm that you want to start sharing. Make the appropriate confirmation and you are done.

4. Wait for the **File Sharing** progress window to disappear.

The selected library or folder is now shared.

 CLEAN UP Repeat the procedure for all the items you want to share. When you have finished, close Windows Explorer.

Using the Sharing Wizard to Share with Specific People

If you have computers that are not running Windows 7, you can use the Sharing Wizard to share libraries and folders with them. However, the procedure is slightly longer than when sharing items with the Homegroup.

In this exercise, you will learn how to use the Sharing Wizard to share libraries and folders with people using operating systems other than Windows 7.

➜ **SET UP** Open Windows Explorer or the Computer shortcut.

1. Navigate to the library or folder that you want to share and right-click it.

The contextual menu appears.

2. Click **Share with**, then choose **Specific people**.

   The File Sharing Wizard opens, which shows the user accounts with which the selected item is already shared.

3. Click the drop-down menu.

A list opens that shows the user accounts with which you can share.

Note The drop-down menu shows all the user accounts defined on your computer, the Homegroup you have joined, and a user account called Everyone. The Homegroup user represents all the computers from your Homegroup, while Everyone is a generic user account—this is any user on the list.

4. Select the user account with which you want to share.

5. Click **Add**.

This adds the selected user account to the list below the drop-down menu.

6. Repeat steps 3 to 5 until you add all the user accounts with which you want to share.

7. By default, all the added user accounts are granted **Read** permissions to the shared item. If you want to change that, click the **Permission Level** assigned.

A list appears showing the available permission levels you can assign.

8. Select the desired permission level for each of the user accounts with which you want to share the item.

9. When done adding user accounts and setting permission levels, click **Share**.

   If you are trying to assign permissions to a library that contains many folders, you might receive a request for confirmation.

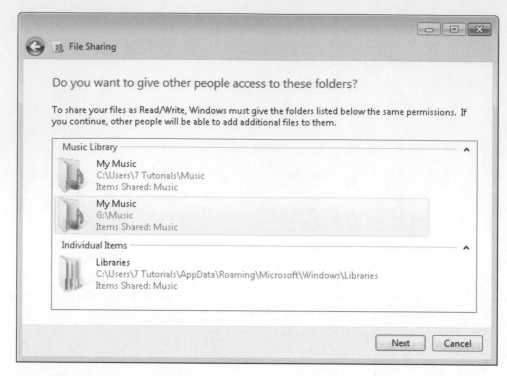

Note This window might not appear if you shared a library containing only one folder.

10. Click **Next**.

If you are not asked to confirm the access permissions to the shared item, skip to the next step.

After a few seconds, you are informed that the selected item (library or folder) has been shared.

Tip If problems occur when trying to share the selected library or folder, you will see a message at the bottom similar to the following: "1 error(s) occurred when sharing this library (or folder)." If you click the error message, you can view details about the root cause of the problem so that you can fix it and try again.

11. Click **Done**.

The selected library or folder is now shared with the user accounts you specified.

✗ CLEAN UP Repeat the procedure for all the items that you want to share. When you have finished, close Windows Explorer.

Using the Sharing Wizard to Stop Sharing

At some point in your home networking experience, you might want to stop sharing a folder or library. To discontinue sharing an item, you have the following options:

- Stop sharing it with everybody on the home network.
- Stop sharing it with the Homegroup.
- Stop sharing it with a specific user account.

In this exercise, you will learn how to use the Sharing Wizard to discontinue sharing an item.

 SET UP Open Windows Explorer or the Computer shortcut.

1. Navigate to the library or folder that you want to stop sharing and right-click it. The contextual menu appears.

2. Click **Share with**, and then choose **Specific people**.

The File Sharing Wizard opens, showing the user accounts with which the selected item is currently shared.

3. If you want to stop sharing with a specific user account only, click on the **Permission Level** column of that user and select **Remove**. If you select the **Homegroup** user account, you will stop sharing with all the computers on your Homegroup. If you select the **Everyone** user account, you will stop sharing with the users who don't have an account on your computer.

> **Tip** If you want to completely discontinue sharing the item so that only you have access to it, select Remove for all the user accounts in the list, except your user account.

4. Once you are done selecting the user account with which you want to stop sharing, click **Share**.

After a few seconds, you are notified that the selected item (library or folder) is now shared. Don't be fooled by the message. It simply means that the item is shared with the new list of user accounts. If you removed all the user accounts except yours, this means the item is actually no longer shared.

The selected library or folder is no longer shared with the user accounts you
selected.

Your library is now shared.

You can e-mail someone links to these shared items, or copy and paste the links into another program.

Music Library

My Music
\\CIPRIAN-PC\Users\7 Tutorials\Music

⚠ 1 error(s) occurred when sharing this library.
Show me all the network shares on this computer.

Done

Tip If problems occur during the procedure, you will see a message at the bottom of the
screen similar to the following: "1 error(s) occurred when sharing this library (or folder)."
If you click the error message, you can view details about the root cause of the problem
so that you can fix it and try again.

5. Click **Done**.

The selected library or folder is no longer shared with the user accounts you
selected.

 CLEAN UP Repeat the procedure for all the items that you want to stop sharing.
When you have finished, close Windows Explorer.

Using Advanced Sharing to Share Your Folders or Partitions

If you want to have more control over how you share a folder and who can access
it, you might prefer to use Advanced Sharing instead of the Sharing Wizard. With
Advanced Sharing, you can set options in more detail. The downside is that you cannot
use Advanced Sharing to share libraries. For an unknown technical reason, you can use
Advanced Sharing to share only folders or partitions, but not libraries.

In this exercise, you will learn how to share a folder or partition using Advanced Sharing.

➡ **SET UP** Disable the Sharing Wizard and then open Windows Explorer or the
Computer shortcut.

1. Navigate to the folder or partition that you want to share and right-click it. The contextual menu appears.

2. Click **Share with**, then choose **Advanced sharing**.

The Properties window of the selected folder or partition opens.

Tip An alternative is to right-click the folder, select Properties, then go to the Sharing tab.

3. Click **Advanced Sharing**.

The Advanced Sharing window opens.

4. Select the **Share this folder** check box.

5. By default, the share name is the name of the folder that you want to share. You can change it in the **Share name** field. This won't modify the name of the folder on your computer, but only changes the name used to share it over the network.

6. Click **Permissions**.

The Permissions window opens, in which you can set who has access to the shared folder and the level of access.

7. By default, the item is shared with **Everyone**. This means anyone can access the item, even though the person doesn't have a user account defined on your computer. To add a user account, click **Add**.

The Select Users Or Groups window opens.

Note If you do not want to add another user account, simply skip to step 12.

8. Click **Advanced**.

   This opens a new Select Users Or Groups window with more advanced options for selection.

9. Click **Find Now**.

   After a few seconds, a list of all the user accounts and user groups defined on your computer appears.

10. Select the user account or the user group with which you want to share, then click **OK**.

    This takes you back to the first Select Users Or Groups window, where you can see the user account or group you just selected being added.

Select Users or Groups

Select this object type:

Users, Groups, or Built-in security principals   [Object Types...]

From this location:

CIPRIAN-PC   [Locations...]

Enter the object names to select ([examples]):

CIPRIAN-PC\Administrators   [Check Names]

[Advanced...]   [OK]   [Cancel]

Tip To select more than one user account or user group, press and hold the **CTRL** key on your keyboard and select each account or group with the mouse.

Important If you want to share with the Homegroup, select the HomeUsers user group from the list.

11. Click **OK**.

You are returned to the Permissions window.

Permissions for downloads

Share Permissions

Group or user names:

Administrators (Ciprian-PC\Administrators)

Ciprian (CIPRIAN-PC\Ciprian)

Everyone

[Add...]   [Remove]

Permissions for Administrators	Allow	Deny
Full Control	☑	☐
Change	☑	☐
Read	☑	☐

Learn about access control and permissions

[OK]   [Cancel]   [Apply]

12. You can now see all the user account and user groups that you have selected. If you want to remove one of them, select it and click **Remove**. Otherwise, go to the next step.

13. Select the type of permissions for each of the user accounts or user groups. Choose the access level you want to assign to each user or group by selecting the appropriate check box:

- **Full Control**   This setting is self-explanatory. With this level assigned, users or groups who have access to this shared folder can do anything they desire: view, modify, delete, and so on.

- **Change**   With this level assigned, users or groups can change contents of the shared folder but cannot delete any of its content.

- **Read**   With this level assigned, users or groups can only view the existing content without being able to make any changes to it.

14. When you have finished, click **OK**.

You are returned to the Advanced Sharing window.

15. Use the **Limit the number of simultaneous users** field to set the maximum amount of users that can connect to a shared folder. (For home networks, this setting is optional.)

16. You can also set options related to **caching** and how the shared folder is available to users who are offline. To do this, click **Caching**, enter the settings the way you want them, then click **OK**. Again, this is not an important setting, especially for home networks, so you may choose to ignore this step.

17. Click **OK**.

You are returned to the Properties window.

18. Click **Close**.

The selected folder or partition is now shared with the user accounts or groups that you have specified, using the permission levels that you have set for each.

 CLEAN UP Repeat the procedure for all the items you want to share. When you have finished, close Windows Explorer.

Using Advanced Sharing to Stop Sharing Your Folders or Partitions

If you want to stop sharing a folder or partition, the procedure is actually easier when using Advanced Sharing instead of the Sharing Wizard. In this exercise, you will learn how.

 SET UP Open Windows Explorer or the Computer shortcut.

 1. Navigate to the folder or partition that you want to stop sharing and right-click it.

The contextual menu appears.

2. Click **Share with**, then choose **Advanced sharing**.

The Properties window of the selected folder or partition opens.

Tip An alternative is to right-click the folder, select Properties, then go to the Sharing tab.

3. Click **Advanced Sharing**.

The Advanced Sharing window opens.

4. Clear the **Share this folder** check box.

The Advanced Sharing window grays out completely.

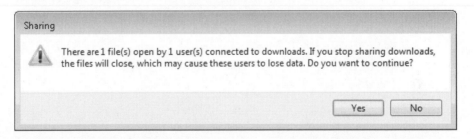

5. Click **OK**.

You might be notified that a number of files are open by a certain number of users connected to the shared folder or partition.

6. Announce to the users connected to your shared item that you are about to discontinue sharing it so that they can save and close any work that is at that location. When you have finished notifying any affected users, click **Yes**.

You are returned to the Properties window of the selected folder or partition.

7. Click **Close**.

The selected folder or partition is no longer shared.

✖ CLEAN UP Repeat the procedure for all the items you want to share. When you have finished, close Windows Explorer.

Note If you want to stop sharing a folder or partition only with a certain user account or user group, follow the procedure detailed in the "Using Advanced Sharing to Share Your Folders or Partitions" section on page 162 and pay special attention to step 12.

Using the Public Folder for Sharing

In the "Configuring the Network Sharing Settings" section in Chapter 5, "Customizing Network Sharing Settings in Windows 7," there is mention of enabling the Public folder for sharing. When turned on, the C:\Users\Public\ folder is shared with all the computers on the network. This folder contains the following subfolders: Public Documents, Public Downloads, Public Music, Public Pictures, and Public Videos. These folders contain some sample files of music, pictures, and videos. The Public folder also contains a series of hidden folders such as: Favorites, Libraries, and Public Desktop. By default, these folders are empty.

Users from the other computers can read its contents and write files inside this folder and its subfolders. When turned off, this folder is not shared with your network.

Using the Public folder is a matter of choice and personal style, and in certain scenarios, it can be useful. For example, if multiple people are using the same computer—each person with his own user account—you can use the Public folder to share files between all these user accounts. Everything you place inside this folder will be accessible to other user accounts.

The Public folder can also be used for sharing files with other computers on your network. If you choose to share this folder, other computers can access its contents.

Recommendation Use Public folder sharing if

- **You want to share files from a single location for ease of management.**
- **You want to keep everything you share separate from your personal data.**
- **It is okay to apply the same permissions for all users of your home network.**

Note By default, the Public folder is not shared unless you are connected to a Homegroup. To stop sharing this folder, you need to follow the instructions found in the "Configuring the Network Sharing Settings" section in Chapter 5, "Customizing Network Sharing Settings in Windows 7".

Mapping a Shared Network Folder as a Network Drive

Drive mapping is the procedure by which you can associate a local drive letter (for example, A to Z, just like your disk drives) with an area on another network computer (for example, a shared folder) or Internet location (for example, an FTP site). Using drive mappings can be very useful, especially when working with different operating systems on the same network. For example, if you use both Windows 7 and Windows XP in your home network, you cannot take full advantage of the Homegroup feature. Using drive mappings can be a pretty good alternative because you can easily access the shared folders from the other computer.

In this exercise, you will learn how to map a shared folder from another computer as a network drive on your Windows 7 computer.

➡ **SET UP** Open Windows Explorer or the Computer shortcut.

1. At the top of the window, in the toolbar, click the **Map network drive** button. If you cannot see it, maximize the window and it will appear.

   The Map Network Drive Wizard opens.

Tip An alternative to start the Map Network Drive Wizard is to right-click on the Computer shortcut, then select Map Network Drive.

2. Click the **Drive** drop-down list.

A list opens showing the available letters that you can assign to the network drive.

3. Select the drive letter you want to assign.

4. In the **Folder** field, click **Browse**.

The Browse For Folder window opens, in which you can select the shared folder that you want to map.

5. Wait until all the computers on your network are displayed, then browse to the computer where the shared folder is found.

6. If the computer you want to access is set to allow access to a user account only after a password is provided, a Windows Security window pops up.

You are asked to type a user account and password that has access to that computer. If you don't see this window, skip to step 11.

7. In the first field, type the name of the computer to which you want to connect. Type a \ (the backslash character) and a user account defined on that computer.

    For example, if you want to connect to a computer called Ciprian-PC, which has Ciprian as a user account defined on it, type **Ciprian-PC\Ciprian**.

8. In the second field, type the password for that user account.

9. Select the **Remember my credentials** check box so that you are not asked to type the user account and password each time you want to access it.

10. Click **OK**.

    You are returned to the Browse For Folder window.

11. Select the folder that you want to map and click **OK**.

    You are returned to the Map Network Drive Wizard.

12. Select the **Reconnect at logon** check box.

    This allows your computer to automatically connect to the shared folder and make it accessible as a network drive each time you log on.

13. If your user account doesn't have access to the shared folder, select the **Connect using different credentials** check box.

14. Click **Finish**.

A Windows Security window appears, in which you are asked to type a user name and password in order to access the shared folder. In this window, by default, the last user account you used to access shared folders on the remote network computer will be selected.

15. If the user specified is correct, simply type the password and select the **Remember my credentials** check box.

Important Pay attention to the computer name specified before the user name. If it is your computer name and not that of the remote computer that is sharing the folder, then the drive mapping won't work. In such a scenario, select Use Another Account and follow steps 6 to 10 in this exercise to type the correct user name and password.

16. Click **OK**.

After a while, the shared folder is mapped and opened in a Windows Explorer window.

Now, each time you log on, the shared network folder will be mapped on your computer as a local drive.

 CLEAN UP Close the Computer and Windows Explorer windows.

Mapping an FTP Server as a Network Drive

Depending on your needs, it can be a good idea to map an FTP server as a network drive so that you can easily access it whenever you need it. This is very useful if you want to connect to a Web site that you own so you can manage the files and folders that reside on the hosting provider's servers, or if you want to connect to an FTP server at work to share files and documents with your coworkers. The procedure for mapping an FTP server is different; however, there's nothing complicated about it.

In this exercise, you will learn how to map an FTP server as a network drive in Windows 7.

SET UP Open Windows Explorer or the Computer shortcut.

1. At the top of the window, in the toolbar, click the **Map network drive** button. If you cannot see it, maximize the window and it will appear.

The Map Network Drive Wizard opens.

↩ 🔍 Map Network Drive

What network folder would you like to map?

Specify the drive letter for the connection and the folder that you want to connect to:

Drive: `Z:` ▾

Folder: `_____` ▾ Browse...

Example: \\server\share

☑ Reconnect at logon

☐ Connect using different credentials

Connect to a Web site that you can use to store your documents and pictures.

Finish   Cancel

Tip An alternative to start the Map Network Drive Wizard is to right-click the Computer shortcut and select Map Network Drive.

2. Click the **Connect to a Web site that you can use to store your documents and pictures** link located in the lower part of the window.

The Add Network Location Wizard opens.

↩ Add Network Location

Welcome to the Add Network Location Wizard

This wizard helps you sign up for a service that offers online storage space. You can use this space to store, organize, and share your documents and pictures using only a web browser and Internet connection.

You can also use this wizard to create a shortcut to a website, an FTP site, or other network location.

Next   Cancel

---

3. Click **Next**.

You are asked where you want to create the network location.

4. Click **Choose a custom network location**.

The Next button is no longer grayed out.

5. Click **Next**.

You are asked to specify the location of the FTP server to which you want to connect.

6. Type **ftp://** followed by the IP address or the web address of the FTP site.

7. Click **Next**.

   You are asked to specify the user name and password required to connect to the FTP server.

8. If your FTP server allows anonymous connections, simply click **Next** and skip to step 11. If the FTP server requests authentication in order to connect to it, clear the **Log on anonymously** check box.

9. Type the user name required to connect to the FTP server.

10. Click **Next**.

   You are asked to type the name of the location.

11. Type the name you want to use for this mapping. Choose a name that suggests where the mapping points to.

12. Click **Next**.

You are informed that you have successfully created a new network location using the name you entered in step 11.

Add Network Location

Completing the Add Network Location Wizard

You have successfully created this network location:

my FTP site

A shortcut for this location will appear in Computer.

☑ Open this network location when I click Finish.

Finish   Cancel

13. Click **Finish**.

If the FTP server doesn't allow for anonymous access, you are asked to type a user name and password. If it does allow anonymous access, you can skip to the end of this exercise.

Log On As

Could not login to the FTP server with the user name and password specified.

FTP server: 205.186.130.

User name: test

Password: ●●●●●●●●

After you log on, you can add this server to your Favorites and return to it easily.

⚠ FTP does not encrypt or encode passwords or data before sending them to the server. To protect the security of your passwords and data, use WebDAV instead.

☐ Log on anonymously   ☑ Save password

Log On   Cancel

14. Type the user name in the appropriate field.

15. Type the password.

16. Select the **Save password** check box.

17. Click **Log On**.

After a while, the FTP server opens and you can view its content.

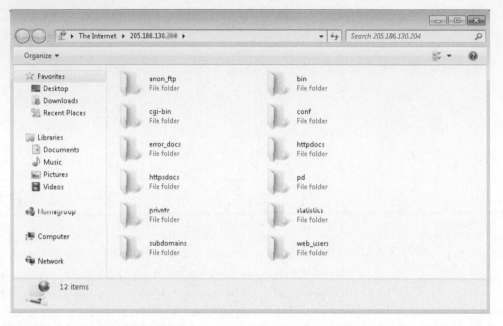

The FTP server is now mapped and you can access it whenever you need to work with it.

 CLEAN UP Close the FTP location window, the Map Network Drive Wizard, and the Computer window.

Deleting a Mapped Network Drive

Deleting a mapped network drive is a very simple procedure. In this exercise, you will learn how to do it.

 SET UP Open the Computer shortcut.

 1. In the **Computer** section, scroll down to the **Network Location** section.

You will find the drive mapping(s) you have made so far (shared network folders or FTP servers).

2. If you want to delete an FTP server mapping, right-click it (if you want to delete a shared network folder mapping, skip to step 5).

3. From the contextual menu, select **Delete**.

You are asked to confirm the deletion.

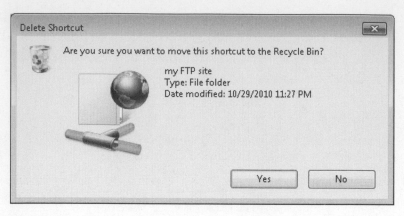

4. Click **Yes**.

The FTP server mapping is no longer available.

5. If you want to delete a shared network folder mapping, right-click it.

The contextual menu opens.

6. Select **Disconnect**.

The drive mapping is no longer available.

You have now deleted the selected drive mappings.

 CLEAN UP Close the Computer window.

Key Points

- The Sharing Wizard makes it easy for you to share libraries and folders with your home network.

- In order to use only Advanced Sharing in Windows 7, you need to disable the Sharing Wizard.

- You cannot use the Advanced Sharing Wizard to share libraries. You can use it to share only folders and partitions.

- You can map shared network folders as well as FTP servers for easier access.

Chapter at a Glance

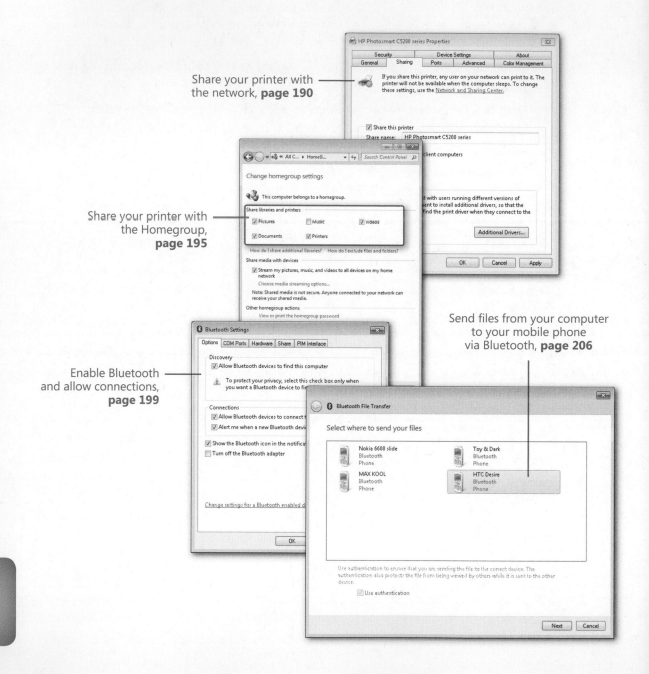

Share your printer with the network, **page 190**

Share your printer with the Homegroup, **page 195**

Enable Bluetooth and allow connections, **page 199**

Send files from your computer to your mobile phone via Bluetooth, **page 206**

8 Sharing and Working with Devices

In this chapter, you will learn how to

✔ Share a printer with computers on your home network.

✔ Enable Bluetooth on your computer and allow connections.

✔ Pair your computer with your mobile phone.

✔ Exchange files between your computer and your mobile phone.

✔ Remove the pairing between your computer and your mobile phone.

In the previous chapter, you learned how to share libraries, folders, and files with the computers on your home network. Fortunately, the list of things you can share on your network does not end here. You can also share some of the devices connected to your computer, the most common being the printer. Other devices include scanners, removable disk drives (such as USB memory sticks), or external hard disk drives.

Another positive is that you can connect yet more devices to the computers on your network and transfer files between them. One great example is your mobile phone. With the use of Bluetooth technology, you can connect your laptop or notebook with your mobile phone and exchange files among them (photos, short videos, music, and so on).

In this chapter, you will learn how to share a printer with the network or Homegroup and how to stop sharing it when you no longer need to use it as a network printer. Then, you will learn how to share a removable disk drive and how to transfer files between your mobile phones and your Windows 7 computers using Bluetooth.

> **Practice Files** You can use any of your printers, phones, and files to complete the exercises in this chapter. Until you get the hang of it, it is best not to use any important files. Also, back up the files you are about to use, just to make sure you don't lose them by mistake.

Sharing a Printer with Computers on Your Home Network

In Chapter 1, we talked a lot about Device Stage and how this feature allows you to interact with all the external devices attached to your computer. This feature comes in handy, especially when working with printers. Your printer is accessible in the Devices And Printers panel. From here, you can perform all the configuration tasks, including sharing it with the other computers on your home network.

In this exercise, you will learn how to share a printer with your network in Windows 7. The exercise and illustrations were created using an HP Photosmart C5280 printer, but the same steps apply to any model of printer.

 **SET UP** Connect the printer to your computer, start it, and install the latest drivers for it.

1. Open the **Start Menu** and click **Devices and Printers**.

    The Devices And Printers panel opens, in which you can access all the external devices connected to your computer, including your printer.

2. Select your printer and right-click it.

The contextual menu for the printer opens.

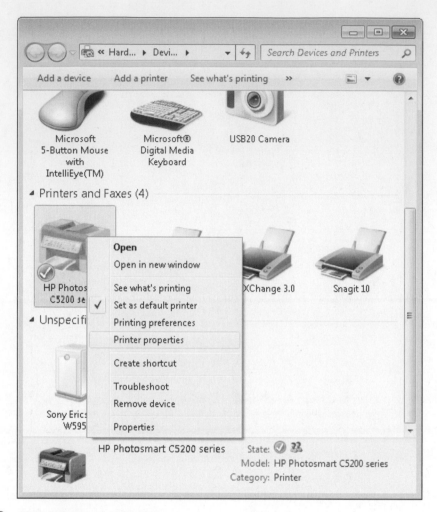

3. Click **Printer properties**.

   The Properties window for the selected printer opens.

4. Click the **Sharing** tab.

   Here, you can see whether the printer is already shared.

HP Photosmart C5200 series Properties

Security		Device Settings		About
General	Sharing	Ports	Advanced	Color Management

If you share this printer, any user on your network can print to it. The printer will not be available when the computer sleeps. To change these settings, use the Network and Sharing Center.

Change Sharing Options

☐ Share this printer

Share name: HP Photosmart C5200 series

☑ Render print jobs on client computers

Drivers
If this printer is shared with users running different versions of Windows, you may want to install additional drivers, so that the users do not have to find the print driver when they connect to the shared printer.

Additional Drivers...

OK   Cancel   Apply

5. Click the **Change Sharing Options** button.

The sharing fields can now be edited.

6. Select the **Share this printer** check box.

HP Photosmart C5200 series Properties

| Security | | Device Settings | | About |
| General | Sharing | Ports | Advanced | Color Management |

If you share this printer, any user on your network can print to it. The printer will not be available when the computer sleeps. To change these settings, use the Network and Sharing Center.

☑ Share this printer

Share name: HP Photosmart C5200 series

☑ Render print jobs on client computers

Drivers
If this printer is shared with users running different versions of Windows, you may want to install additional drivers, so that the users do not have to find the print driver when they connect to the shared printer.

Additional Drivers...

OK   Cancel   Apply

7. By default, the **Share name** of the printer is its model name. If you want to change it, type a new share name.

8. If you want a negligible performance increase on your computer, check **Render print jobs on client computers**.

   When this option is enabled, printing jobs are no longer rendered on the computer to which the printer is attached but on the computers ordering the printing jobs. This prevents any performance impact on the host computer when the client computers start printing large files. However, modern computers are very powerful and the performance impact of this setting is negligible. It is up to you whether you want this setting enabled.

9. Click **OK**.

   The printer is now shared with the computers on your network and they can install it and use it.

 CLEAN UP Close Devices And Printers.

Sharing a Printer with Your Homegroup

Sharing a printer with the Homegroup is extremely easy. Simply open the Home-group settings window and, in the Share Libraries And Printers section, check Print-ers, and then click Save Changes.

See Also For more information about the Homegroup and how to find its settings window, see Chapter 6, "Creating the Homegroup and Joining Windows 7 Computers."

The printer will automatically show up in the Devices And Printers panel of all the computers that are part of the Homegroup and they will be able to use it.

Stop Sharing the Printer

If you want to discontinue sharing the printer with the network, follow steps 1 to 5, detailed in the "Sharing a Printer with Computers on Your Home Network" section on page 190. Clear the Share This Printer check box, then click OK.

The printer is no longer shared with the other computers on the network. This procedure stops sharing the printer with computers that are not a part of the Homegroup and that are running operating systems other than Windows 7. To stop sharing a printer with the Homegroup, open the Homegroup settings window, and in the Share Libraries And Printers section, clear the Printers check box, then click Save Changes.

Change homegroup settings

This computer belongs to a homegroup.

Share libraries and printers

☐ Pictures   ☐ Music   ☐ Videos

☐ Documents   ☐ Printers

How do I share additional libraries?   How do I exclude files and folders?

Share media with devices

☑ Stream my pictures, music, and videos to all devices on my home network

Choose media streaming options...

Note: Shared media is not secure. Anyone connected to your network can receive your shared media.

Other homegroup actions

View or print the homegroup password

Change the password...

Leave the homegroup...

Change advanced sharing settings...

Start the HomeGroup troubleshooter

[Save changes]   [Cancel]

See Also For more information about the Homegroup and how to find its settings window, see Chapter 6.

The printer will no longer show up in the Devices And Printers panel of all the computers that are a part of the Homegroup.

Sharing a Removable Disk Drive

Removable disk drives (such as USB memory sticks or external hard disk drives connected through USB) are another type of device that you can share on your network. Sharing such devices is relatively easy—simply follow the instructions found in the "Using

Advanced Sharing to Share Your Folders or Partitions" section in Chapter 7, "Sharing Libraries and Folders."

Unfortunately, sharing disk drives of any type cannot be done using the simple Sharing Wizard found in Windows 7. You can only share them by using Advanced Sharing.

Transferring Files Between Mobile Phones and Your Windows 7 Computer via Bluetooth

Bluetooth is a popular wireless technology used to exchange data between devices over short distances. One very common use for it is transferring files between two mobile phones or between a mobile phone and a laptop or netbook computer. An important downside of Bluetooth support for Windows 7 is the fact that some manufacturers do not provide full support for Windows 7 in their drivers. Therefore, you might experience problems connecting your mobile phone to your Windows 7 computer. This is especially true for older or less expensive mobile phones. Newer, more popular and expensive models generally benefit from good support and drivers that enable successful connections to Windows 7 computers.

Before trying to connect your computer to your mobile phone, it is highly recommended that you install the latest drivers for the Bluetooth device on your computer and the latest drivers for your phone. These usually come packaged in the PC suites created by the manufacturer of your phone (for example: Nokia Ovi Suite, Sony Ericsson PC Suite, Motorola Phone Tools, or Samsung PC Studio). Another aspect worth keeping in mind is that desktop computers generally are not equipped with Bluetooth devices, so you cannot use them to establish such connections. If you want to establish Bluetooth connections on your desktop computer, you need to purchase and install a separate adapter.

Also, not all mobile computers such as laptops or notebooks have Bluetooth devices. Therefore, it is best for you to check the configuration of your specific model and confirm whether it has Bluetooth support. If it does have a Bluetooth device, then read the next sections.

If your computer does not have a Bluetooth device, then your only solution is to connect your mobile phone via a computer cable. This is usually provided by the manufacturer of your phone in the original packaging.

See Also For instructions on how to connect your mobile phone to your computer via the computer cable, check the manual for your specific model.

Assuming that you have a Bluetooth device on your computer and the latest drivers are installed, you need to follow a series of steps—in the correct order—before you begin transferring anything via Bluetooth. These steps are covered comprehensively in the next sections, so read them carefully; otherwise, you might run into some problems.

Enabling Bluetooth on Your Computer and Allowing Connections

The first task is to enable Bluetooth, both on your computer and on your mobile phone. The procedure is not very complicated, but it does require attention—especially during the setup process—so pay attention to the steps described in this chapter.

In this exercise, you will learn how to enable Bluetooth on your Windows 7 laptop or netbook. You will also learn how to set it to allow connections from other devices such as your mobile phone.

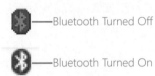

—Bluetooth Turned Off

—Bluetooth Turned On

SET UP Install all the drivers provided by the manufacturer of your laptop, including those for Bluetooth. Then, make sure the Bluetooth device is turned on. To turn it on, locate the button on the side of your computer or above its keyboard. Typically, you can determine whether Bluetooth is enabled by an illuminated Bluetooth LED icon on the surface of your laptop or netbook. In addition, the Bluetooth icon from the taskbar turns from red (or completely missing) to white.

See Also For complete instructions on how to turn on the Bluetooth device on your laptop or netbook, read the instruction manual provided by the manufacturer.

1. Go to the notification area of the Windows 7 taskbar and open the list of icons.

2. Right-click the **Bluetooth** icon.

   The contextual menu, which contains a list of Bluetooth-related configuration options, opens.

3. Click **Open Settings**.

The Bluetooth Settings window opens.

Tip An alternative to steps 1 to 3 is to search for the word "bluetooth" in the search box of the Start Menu, then click the Change Bluetooth Settings search result.

4. In the Options tab, select the **Allow Bluetooth devices to find this computer** check box.

    This allows your computer to be discovered by other Bluetooth devices.

5. Select **Allow Bluetooth devices to connect to this computer**.

    If this setting is not enabled, other devices will not be able to connect to your computer.

6. Select **Alert me when a new Bluetooth devices wants to connect**.

    With this setting enabled, you are notified when new—and possibly unauthorized—devices want to connect to your computer, which allows you to act, if needed.

7. Select **Show the Bluetooth icon in the notification area**.

    This allows you to easily access the Bluetooth capabilities on your computer and use them as required.

8. Click **OK**.

    The Bluetooth on your computer is now enabled, correctly configured, and ready to establish connections to and interact with other devices.

✖ CLEAN UP No cleanup is required.

Turning On Bluetooth on Your Mobile Phone

Now that your computer is correctly configured, it's time to turn on Bluetooth on your mobile phone. How to do this depends on the type of phone you have. We will try to help by sharing a few examples.

On smartphones running the Android operating system (version 2.1 or 2.2), go to Settings -> Wireless & Networks, and then simply select the Bluetooth check box.

On Sony Ericsson phones, go to Settings -> Connectivity -> Bluetooth, and then choose Turn On.

For Nokia phones (which are more popular in Europe), the setup is very similar to Sony Ericsson: go to Settings -> Connectivity -> Bluetooth. Here you simply need to change the value of the Bluetooth field to On.

See Also If you can't find the Bluetooth settings on your phone, consult the instruction manual for guidance on how to turn it on.

Pairing Your Computer with Your Mobile Phone, Starting from Your Phone

Before being able to transfer files, you need to pair the devices together. This procedure can be started from your mobile phone or from your computer. The end result is the same, so you can choose which one works best for you.

In this exercise, you will learn how to pair your computer with your mobile phone, starting from your phone.

 SET UP Go to the Bluetooth configuration menu on your phone.

1. Set your phone to scan for Bluetooth devices.

   This option is found in the same Bluetooth menus. On Nokia phones, go to Paired Devices -> Add New Device. On Android phones, go to Bluetooth Settings -> Scan For Devices. On Sony Ericsson phones, go to Bluetooth -> My Devices -> New Device. A scan process starts, and after a few seconds, the phone shows the results.

See Also To learn how to do this, refer to the manual provided by the manufacturer of your phone.

2. From the list of identified devices, select the computer to which you want to connect.

3. You are asked to type a personal identification number (PIN) code that will be used to establish the pair. Type the four-digit code you want to use. This can be any number you want.

4. Press **OK**.

   On your computer, you are notified that a Bluetooth device is trying to connect.

5. Click the notification.

   The Add A Device Wizard opens, in which you are asked to type the pairing code.

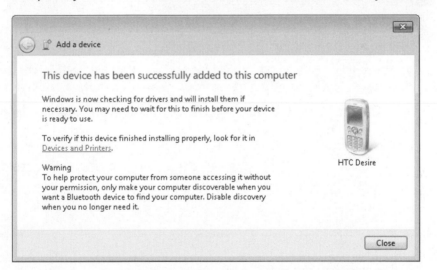

6. Type the same PIN code you entered on your phone.

7. Click **Next**.

   Windows 7 now starts installing the drivers for your phone. When the installation is complete, you are notified that the device has been successfully added.

Important If Windows 7 is not able to install the appropriate drivers, this procedure fails. In such scenarios, download and install the Windows 7 drivers for your phone prior to establishing the Bluetooth pairing. They are usually packed in the PC suites created by the manufacturer of your phone (for example, Nokia Ovi Suite, Sony Ericsson PC Suite, Motorola Phone Tools, or Samsung PC Studio). Installing these suites first will help solve the driver problems.

8. Click **Close**.

Your computer and mobile phone are now paired and can begin exchanging files.

✖ **CLEAN UP** Keep both devices turned on and do not change any of their settings.

Pairing Your Computer with Your Mobile Phone, Starting from Your Computer

As mentioned in the previous section, the pairing procedure can be started from any device.

In this exercise, you will learn how to pair your computer with your mobile phone, starting from your computer.

➡ **SET UP** Go to the Bluetooth configuration menu on your phone and set your phone so that it can be discovered. Depending on your phone, this means turning on settings named Discoverable or setting your phone's visibility to "Shown to all." When you have finished, open the Devices and Printers panel on your computer.

See Also To learn how to make your phone discoverable via Bluetooth, refer to the manual provided by the manufacturer of your phone.

1. On your computer, click the **Add a device** button in the **Devices and Printers** panel.

This starts the Add A Device Wizard, which automatically scans for new devices, including Bluetooth devices.

2. Once your mobile phone is detected, select it and click **Next**.

The wizard displays a code that you need to type on your mobile phone.

3. On your mobile phone, you are notified that the computer wants to connect via Bluetooth. Press **OK**, then type the code shown on your computer (from step 2). Once the code is entered, the pairing is created and Windows 7 automatically searches for drivers for your mobile phone, then installs them. When done, you are informed that the device has been successfully added to the computer.

4. Click **Close**.

Your computer and mobile phone are now paired and can begin exchanging files.

 CLEAN UP Close the Devices And Printers window.

Exchanging Files Between Your Computer and Your Mobile Phone

Your Bluetooth devices are finally ready to exchange files. You can now send files from your computer to the mobile phone and vice versa.

In this exercise, you will learn how to initiate file transfers from your computer to your mobile phone, via Bluetooth.

 SET UP Go to the notification area of your taskbar and identify the Bluetooth icon.

1. Right-click the **Bluetooth** icon.

The contextual menu appears, containing a list of Bluetooth-related configuration options.

Add a Device
Allow a Device to Connect
Show Bluetooth Devices

Send a File
Receive a File

Join a Personal Area Network

Open Settings

Remove Icon

Customize...

2. Click **Send a File**.

The Bluetooth File Transfer Wizard opens and shows you the list of Bluetooth devices with which your computer is paired.

3. Select the phone to which you want to send the file, then click **Next**.

   You are asked to select the file that you want to send.

4. Click **Browse**, then select the file you want to transfer.

Tip To select more than one file, press and hold the **Ctrl** key on your keyboard while using your mouse to select the files you want to transfer. When you have finished, click OK.

5. Click **Next**.

   The file transfer process starts.

6. Depending on your phone and how it is configured, the file transfer starts immediately and without user input, or it stops until you confirm on your phone that you want to allow the transfer. For example, on our Nokia phones, the transfer started immediately, while on our Android-based smartphones, we needed to confirm the transfer before it started.

Once the file transfer finishes, you are notified of its success.

7. Click **Finish**.

The file is now transferred to your phone.

CLEAN UP If you have finished transferring files, it is better to turn off Bluetooth on your mobile phone. This will save your battery. If you need to use it again, don't forget to turn it on first.

Exchanging Files Between Your Mobile Phone and Your Computer

As mentioned earlier in this chapter, the transfer of files can also be initiated from your mobile phone. If you've made some interesting pictures with your phone, a small video clip or anything else, you can transfer it to your computer.

In this exercise, you will learn how to initiate file transfers from your mobile phone to your computer, via Bluetooth.

 SET UP The first steps need to be done on your computer. Do not do anything on the phone yet. Go to the notification area of your taskbar and identify the Bluetooth icon.

 1. Right-click the **Bluetooth** icon.

The contextual menu opens, containing a list of Bluetooth-related configuration options.

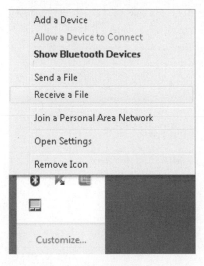

2. Click **Receive a File**.

The Bluetooth File Transfer Wizard opens and informs you that it is waiting for a connection. After this step (and only after this step), you can go to your phone and initiate the transfer.

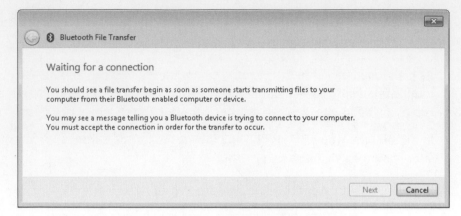

3. On your mobile phone, select the files you want to transfer.

4. Choose the options required to send the files via Bluetooth.

5. The phone asks you to select the Bluetooth device you want to send them to. Select your computer, then confirm your choice.

   The file transfer automatically begins; you can see both your mobile phone and computer showing the progress of the operation.

6. Wait for the file transfer to end.

   When it has finished, you are shown a summary of the transfer. The Bluetooth File Transfer Wizard lists the files that were received and asks for a location to save them to. The default location is your Documents folder for your user account.

Bluetooth File Transfer

Save the received file

Save the file to the location below, or click Browse to choose a different location.

File name:

File Name	Size
02.jpg	1.51 MB
01.jpg	1.35 MB

Location: C:\Users\MAX\Documents   Browse...

Finish   Cancel

7. To select a different location to save the received files, click **Browse**, then select the new location.

8. When you have finished, click **Finish**.

The data is now transferred to your computer.

CLEAN UP If you finished transferring files, it is better to turn off Bluetooth on your mobile phone. This will save your battery. If you need to use it again, don't forget to turn it on first.

Removing the Pairing Between Your Mobile Phone and Your Computer

If you have changed your phone, it is broken, or you simply you don't need to use it anymore to transfer files via Bluetooth with your computer, you can remove the pairing you've created so that it no longer appears in the Devices and Printers panel.

In this exercise, you will learn how to remove the pairing between your computer and your mobile phone from your Windows 7 computer.

 SET UP Open the Devices and Printers panel on your computer.

1. Right-click the phone that you want to remove.

The contextual menu opens, which contains options for the selected phone.

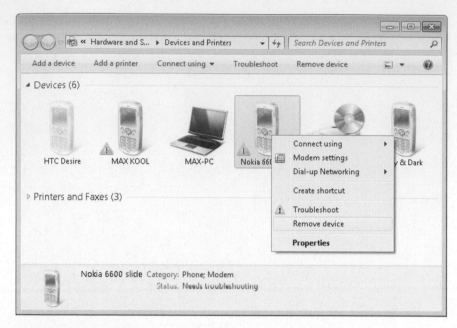

2. Click **Remove device**.

   You are asked to confirm the deletion process.

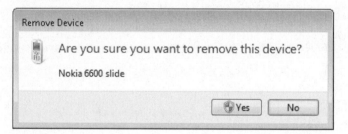

3. Click **Yes**.

   The removal process begins and the Remove Device progress window appears.

4. After a while, the progress window disappears and you are returned to the **Devices and Printers** window. The removal process for the pairing with the selected mobile phone is done.

✖ **CLEAN UP** Close the Devices and Printers window.

Key Points

- You can share your printer both with your Homegroup computers and the computers that are not a part of it but are part of the home network.
- Homegroup greatly simplifies the process of sharing your printer.
- Sharing a removable disk drive can be done only by using Advanced Sharing.
- Before using Bluetooth to transfer files between your mobile phone and your computer, you need to install all the appropriate drivers and enable Bluetooth on both devices.
- Pairing your devices can be initiated by either your computer or your mobile phone.
- Sending files via Bluetooth can be initiated by any of the paired devices.

Chapter at a Glance

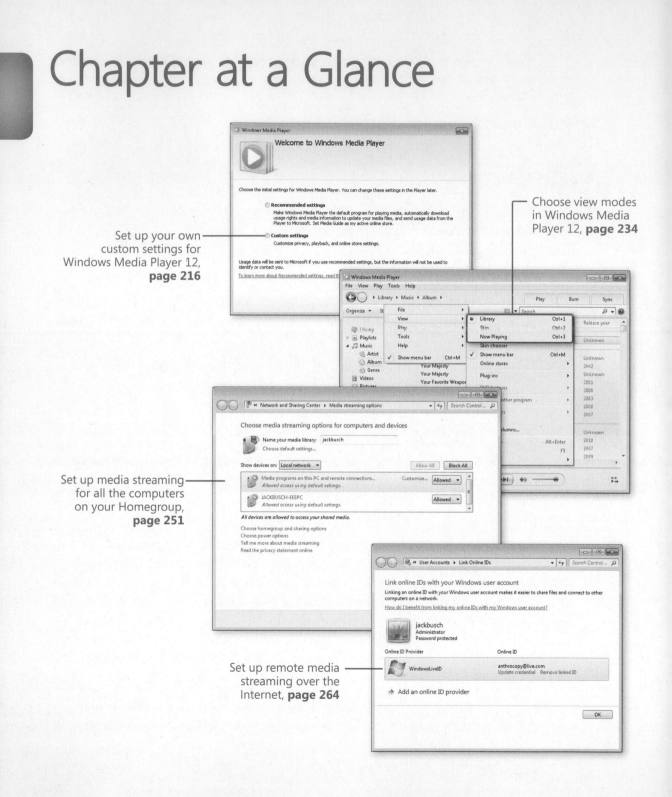

Set up your own custom settings for Windows Media Player 12, **page 216**

Choose view modes in Windows Media Player 12, **page 234**

Set up media streaming for all the computers on your Homegroup, **page 251**

Set up remote media streaming over the Internet, **page 264**

9 Streaming Media Over the Network and the Internet

In this chapter, you will learn how to

✔ Set up Windows Media Player 12.

✔ Add files to your media library.

✔ Search in Windows Media Player 12.

✔ Create quick playlists in Windows Media Player 12.

✔ Create advanced playlists in Windows Media Player 12.

✔ Stream your media library over the network.

✔ Stream your media library over the Internet.

Windows Media Player in its different incarnations has always been the default media player for Microsoft Windows operating systems. With this application, users are able to listen to music, play movies or DVDs, and view pictures and other types of media, such as recorded TV shows, for example.

Windows 7 ships with the new Windows Media Player 12, which looks and feels very similar to Windows Media Player 11, but has a few new tweaks and additions. The interface has been somewhat pared down and the tabbed navigation of Windows Media Player 11 has been replaced with a separate **Now Playing** view and a collapsible, tabbed list pane on the right side for playlists, burning, and syncing. Perhaps most significant is the functionality with the new Windows 7 taskbar, which lets you control playback with the Windows Media Player 12 minimized. Another great feature of the new version is the fact that you can use it to stream media over your home network and the Internet.

In this chapter, you will learn how to use Windows Media Player 12, add files to your media libraries, create playlists, and use the search, sort, and view functionalities. You will also learn some useful keyboard shortcuts that you can use to improve your productivity when working with Windows Media Player 12. Last but not least, you will learn how to stream your media between the computers on your home network and over the Internet.

> **Practice Files** You can use any of your media files to complete the exercises in this chapter.

Setting Up Windows Media Player 12

When you first run Windows Media Player 12, you'll be asked to set some configuration settings about how this application is going to be enabled on your computer and how it is going to function.

In this exercise, you will learn how to set up Windows Media Player 12 when you start it for the first time, using your own custom settings instead of the recommended defaults.

SET UP Open Windows Media Player 12.

1. The Windows Media Player 12 setup window opens, displaying the initial settings.

   You can choose between **Recommended settings** and **Custom settings**. **Recommended settings** means that all the default settings will be applied without you having any control over the setup. **Custom settings** means you can define all the important settings about how Windows Media Player 12 will work on your computer.

2. Choose Custom settings.

3. Click **Next**.

The Select Privacy Options window opens.

Note If you choose Recommended Settings, the Next button will be replaced by Finish. If you click Finish, the entire setup is done, and no further input is required from you.

4. Select the privacy options from the **Enhanced Playback Experience** section. These options are handy for retrieving album artwork and other artist information, and if you have purchased music, you can choose to download the usage rights automatically when you play the file. It is highly recommended to select these options.

5. The **Enhanced Content Provider Services** section is about providing information to the content providers that you will interact with in Windows Media Player 12. If you do not want to send them any information, clear the **Send unique Player ID to content providers** check box.

Tip You can also click the Cookies button and customize settings that affect cookies and what information is transmitted over the Web to the content providers with whom you will be working. However, it is best to leave those settings to their default because they will be applied to other Web sites as well, and it will also impact your browsing experience in Internet Explorer.

6. The **Windows Media Player Customer Experience Improvement Program** section lets you choose whether to provide information to Microsoft about how you are using this tool. The information is sent anonymously, and the purpose of it is to understand how people use the application. If you want to opt out of this program, clear the check box.

7. In the **History** section, you decide if you want Windows Media Player 12 to store your history for Music, Pictures, Video, or Playlists. Check the items for which you want to store your history.

8. If you are curious about the **Privacy Statement**, click the tab and you can read the entire statement from Microsoft.

9. When you have finished configuring all the settings, click **Next**.

    This opens a new window in which you are asked to choose which file types will be opened by default with Windows Media Player 12.

10. It is highly recommended to select the **Choose the file types that Windows Media Player will play** option, unless you plan on using Windows Media Player 12 for every movie, audio, video, and picture file.

11. Click **Next**.

    This opens a window in which you can set the associations for Windows Media Player 12.

12. Select the type of media files you want Windows Media Player 12 to play.

> **Tip** If you want Windows Media Player 12 to play all files, choose the Select All check box. Otherwise, spend a bit of time selecting the types of files you want played with this application.

13. When done, click **Save**.

Windows Media Player 12 now asks you to set up the online store.

14. Unless you want to start buying music right away, select **Don't set up a store now**. (You will be able to set up the store later.)

Note If you select Media Guide, you will be asked to select between a list of available stores. From there forward, the steps vary depending on the store. Make sure you follow the instructions, and you will be set up in no time. Also, be aware that setting up a store means that you will likely be requested to provide details such as your bank card number, and so on.

15. Click **Finish**.

Windows Media Player 12 now starts and is set up according to your needs.

CLEAN UP If you don't plan to use Windows Media Player 12 for now, close it; otherwise, keep it turned on.

Adding Files to Your Windows Media Player 12 Library

Now that you have done the initial setup of Windows Media Player 12, it is time to set up your media library and start using this application to play your media files. Windows Media Player 12 takes you directly to the Library view. This is your main command center and, for now, will only contain the songs that come standard with your Windows 7 installation.

In this exercise, you will learn how to add your media files to the Windows Media Player 12 library.

 **SET UP** Open Windows Media Player 12.

1. To set up your library, click **Organize -> Manage Libraries**.

   Another menu opens that shows the following options: Music, Videos, Pictures, and Recorded TV.

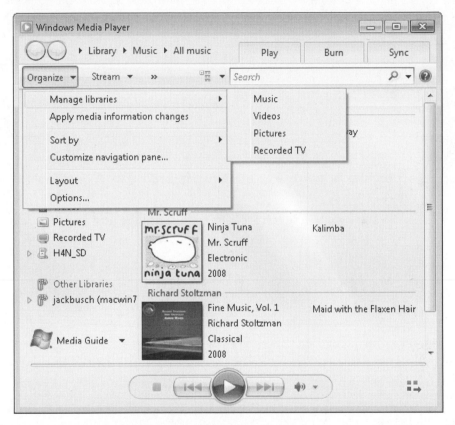

2. To add a certain type of media, select the appropriate option. For this specific exercise, choose **Music**.

   A window opens that shows your Music libraries.

See Also **To learn more about libraries, see Chapter 3, "Setting Up Your Libraries on All Windows 7 Computers."**

3. To add new libraries and folders to the list, click **Add** and then select the items that you want to include. Add all the libraries and folders that make up your music collection.

4. When you have finished, click **OK**.

You are returned to the Library view of Windows Media Player 12.

5. Next, click **Organize -> Apply media information changes**.

At this point, you may want to go grab a sandwich, depending on how extensive your music collection is. When you come back, you'll see your library, replete with all of your tunes.

Apply Changes   ⊠

Retrieving media information and updating files...

Progress

Percent complete: 5

Status: In progress

Cancel

Your music library is now added to Windows Media Player 12, and you can start playing it at any time.

Tip If you want to also add your videos, pictures, and recorded TV shows to the media library, repeat the same steps but select the corresponding option at step 2, depending on what you're adding.

✖ **CLEAN UP** Close Windows Media Player 12 when you are done using it.

The Navigation Pane, Back/Forward Buttons, and Breadcrumbs

Now that you have set up your library, it is time to learn how to navigate your way through Windows Media Player 12. When you click on a media type (for example, Music, Pictures, Video) in the Navigation Pane on the left side of the Windows Media Player 12 window, it will expand to show the subcategorizations. If you click Artist, it will list your music files by artist. As you move deeper into your library, you'll also notice the Breadcrumbs along the top of the screen. In the screenshot that follows, they read Library -> Music -> Artist.

Back and Foward
Breadcrumbs
Navigation Pane

You can click any of these terms to return to that level of your library.

Note The Breadcrumbs change dynamically, depending on your selections.

Alternatively, you can use the Back and Forward arrows to return to previous screens, exactly the way you would while using a Web browser.

Searching in Windows Media Player 12

If you have an extensive library of music, videos, or pictures, it won't be very easy to quickly find what you want to play or view. The best way to find something fast is to use the search functionality.

In this exercise, you will learn how to use the search functionality in Windows Media Player 12.

SET UP Open Windows Media Player 12.

1. For this exercise, let's search through the music library for a specific artist. Click **Music** and select the **Artist** view.

   This shows the entire list of artists found in your music library.

   — Artist View   — Search box

Album artist	Count	Length	Rating
W			
Wir sind Helden	91	5:47:48	☆☆☆☆☆

2. In the Search box located on the upper-right side of the Windows Media Player 12 window, type the name of the artist that you want to play.

3. Windows Media Player 12 instantly narrows your choices as you type. If your particular view does not contain any matches, Windows Media Player 12 will point you toward other matches in your library.

4. Click the links below **Matches in your library for**. Clicking **Artist** will show the list of artists matching your search, **Albums** will return the list of albums, and **Songs** will return the list of songs found.

CLEAN UP Close Windows Media Player 12 when you are done using it.

Working with View Options and Sorting

There are three different View options for Windows Media Player 12: Icon, Tile, and Details. You can choose one by clicking the arrow next to the View Options button or scroll through them by clicking the button itself.

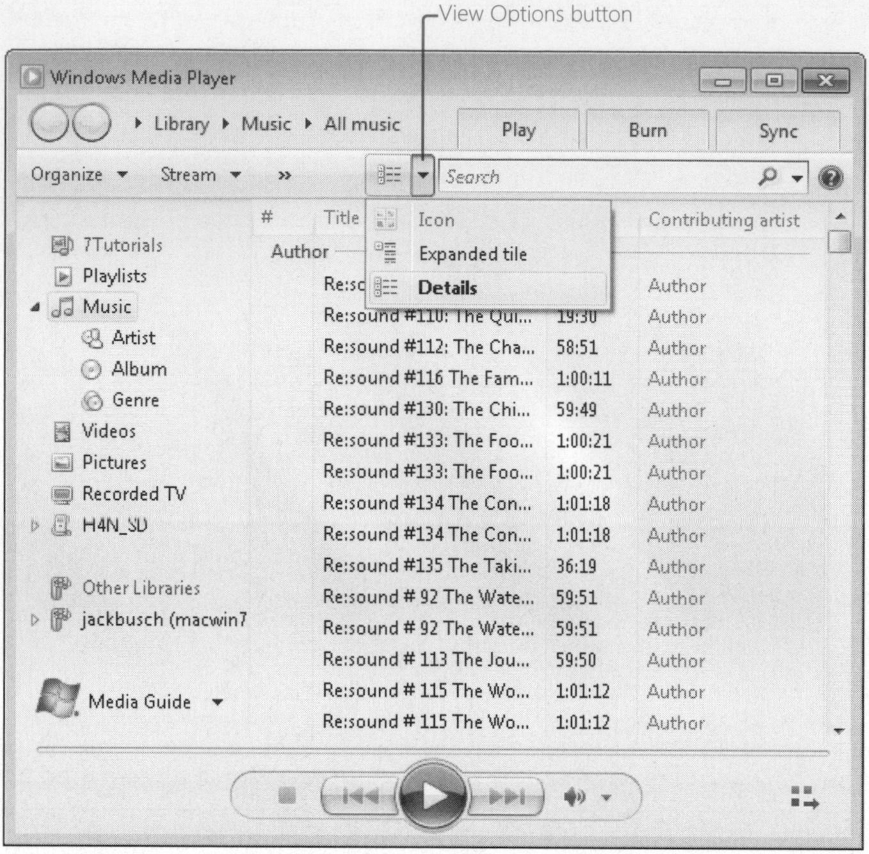

These views behave very similarly to the views in Windows Explorer. Let's see each view in action:

- **Icon view** This view is pretty self-explanatory. The only details shown are the file name and the album covers (if you have them downloaded). How much information is displayed below the album cover depends on which level of the library you're viewing. For example, in the screenshot following, we are at the Album level, so it shows the artist name below the album name (if available). When viewing the Artist level, only the album name is displayed.

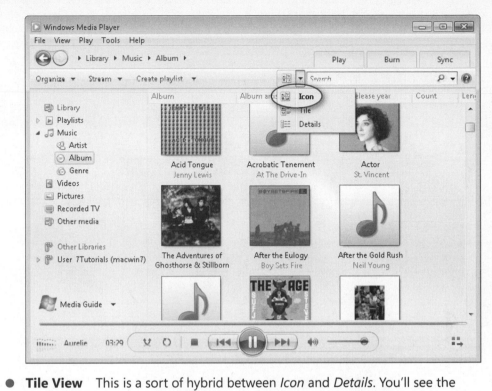

- **Tile View**   This is a sort of hybrid between *Icon* and *Details*. You'll see the album artwork in addition to a bit more information displayed to the right. In the Album level, you see the artist name, album name, genre, and year. In the Artist view, you also see the number of songs and length. If the album has been rated, this information will also be displayed.

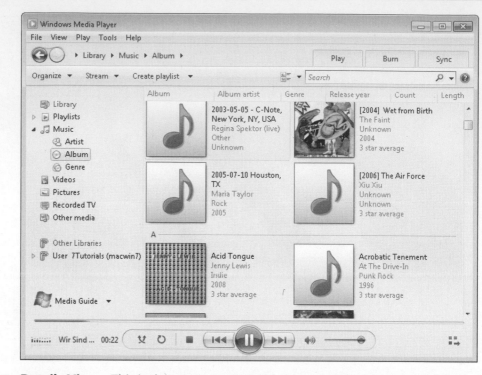

- **Details View**   This is the most customizable view and the most powerful for sorting and searching. It allows you to see the category columns and quickly sort your songs according to these columns. Click the column once to sort the items in ascending order. Click it again to sort it in descending order.

You'll notice that some View options aren't available at certain levels in the Library. For example, you cannot use Tile or Details view at the top (Library) level, nor can you use Icon when viewing from the Music level.

With all three View options, you can change the way the items are sorted by clicking the appropriate category column. For example, click Album once to sort the items in ascending order based on album name. Click Album again to sort the items in descending order by album name.

Switching Between View Modes

When you open it, Windows Media Player 12 operates by default in the Player Library view mode. From the left side you can access your media libraries, and based on your selections, the middle section of the window changes to show you the content.

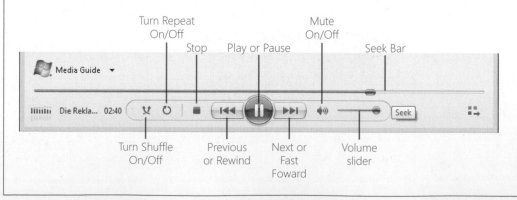

No matter where you are in the Player Library view mode, you will be able to see the Playback controls. The function of each of these buttons is annotated in the following screenshot.

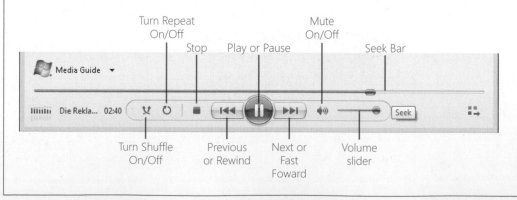

While this view works for most purposes, there are also two additional view modes available: Skin mode and Now Playing mode. Let's see the differences between them:

- **Now Playing**   This is a compact mode designed to sit unobtrusively on your desktop. By default, Now Playing mode shows the album artwork, but you can also have it display visualizations (as shown in the screenshot that follows). If you have lyrics downloaded, they will also appear here. The play controls, as always, are embedded at the bottom and you can switch back to the Player Library view mode by clicking the icon in the upper-right corner.

- **Skin**   This mode displays the player in the customized skin you've chosen. The appearance and layout will vary depending on the selected skin. The following screenshot shows the Revert skin.

You can switch to any of the modes by right-clicking a blank area anywhere in Windows Media Player 12, selecting View, and then the desired view mode.

Tip You can also use keyboard shortcuts to access these views: **Ctrl**+**1** for the Player Library view, **Ctrl**+**2** for the Skin view and **Ctrl**+**3** for the Now Playing view.

Using Keyboard Shortcuts

You can also quickly perform actions on Windows Media Player 12 by using keyboard shortcuts that are listed in the following table:

Action	Keyboard Shortcut
Video size 50%	Alt+1
Video size 100%	Alt+2
Video size 200%	Alt+3
Toggle display for full screen video	Alt+Enter
Retrace your steps back through your most recent views in the Player	Alt+Left Arrow
Retrace your steps forward through your most recent views in the Player	Alt+Right Arrow
Switch to Player Library	Ctrl+1

Action	Keyboard Shortcut
Switch to skin mode	Ctrl+2
Switch to Now Playing mode	Ctrl+3
Add to play list	Ctrl+7
Add to burn list	Ctrl+8
Add to sync list	Ctrl+9
Select all in list pane	Ctrl+A
Previous (item or chapter)	Ctrl+B
In the Player Library, put the cursor in the search box	Ctrl+E
Next (item or chapter)	Ctrl+F
Turn shuffle on or off	Ctrl+H
Eject CD or DVD (this doesn't work on computers equipped with two or more CD or DVD disc drives)	Ctrl+J
In the Player Library, show or hide the menu bar	Ctrl+M
Create a new playlist	Ctrl+N
Open a file	Ctrl+O
Play or pause playing	Ctrl+P
Stop playing	Ctrl+S
Turn repeat on or off	Ctrl+T
Specify a URL or path to a file	Ctrl+U
Close or stop playing a file	Ctrl+W
Previous playlist	Ctrl+Left Arrow
Next playlist	Ctrl+Right Arrow
Restart video	Ctrl+Shift+B
Turn captions and subtitles on or off	Ctrl+Shift+C
Fast forward through video or music	Ctrl+Shift+F
Use a fast play speed	Ctrl+Shift+G
Play at normal speed	Ctrl+Shift+N
Use a slow play speed	Ctrl+Shift+S
Display Windows Media Player Help	F1
Edit media information on a selected item in the Player Library	F2
Switch the view of items in the details pane	F4
Increase the size of album art	F6
Decrease the size of album art	Shift+F6
Mute the volume	F7
Decrease the volume	F8

Action	Keyboard Shortcut
Increase the volume	F9
Show menu bar in Player Library	F10
Show shortcut menu	Shift+F10

Note Some keyboard shortcuts only work in Player Library or Now Playing Mode.

Creating Quick Playlists in Windows Media Player 12

If you are the type of person who listens mostly to the same music on a frequent basis, it is a good idea to create simple playlists so you can easily find and play the artist, albums, or tracks that you are most interested in.

In this exercise, you will learn how to create simple playlists in Windows Media Player 12.

Practice Files You can use any of your music, video, or picture files to complete the exercises in this chapter.

→ **SET UP** Open Windows Media Player 12 and use the Player Library view mode.

1. All the playlists can be found by clicking the **Playlists** button, located on the left side of the Windows Media Player 12 window.

   This shows the currently defined playlists. If you have no playlist defined, a message displays, indicating that there are no playlists in this library.

2. To create your first playlist, click the **Create playlist** button.

   This creates an empty playlist.

3. Type the name of the playlist, and then press **Enter**.

4. Now click **Music** and browse your music library.

5. Select the artist, albums, or tracks that you want to add to the playlist.

6. Drag the selection on top of the playlist that you just created until you see a plus sign followed by **Add to** and the name of the playlist you want to add it to.

7. Drop the selection.

If you click the playlist you just created, you will see that it now contains the selection you just added.

CLEAN UP Listen to the playlist you just created to check if it is the way you want it. When you have finished listening, close Windows Media Player 12.

Creating Advanced Playlists in Windows Media Player 12

You can also create more advanced playlists, which can meet lots of custom criteria, such as type of media, artist, genre, track, year, size, length, and so on. You can be very creative with the type of playlists you can define.

In this exercise, you will learn how to create advanced playlists in Windows Media Player 12 using custom criteria.

> **Practice Files** You can use any of your music, video, or picture files to complete the exercises in this section.

SET UP Open Windows Media Player 12 and use the Player Library view mode.

1. Click the down arrow adjacent to the right side of **Create playlist**.

   This shows some additional options.

2. Click **Create auto playlist**.

The New Auto Playlist window opens.

3. In the Auto Playlist name field, type the name of the playlist you want to create.

4. You now have several fields in which you can define your criteria of selection. Click the plus sign beneath **Music in my library**.

A long list of fields opens that contains anything from album artist to file types and other characteristics, which can define your music.

5. Select the first criterion. For this exercise, we selected **Album artist**.

Set the condition that the criterion must meet.

Note By default, a condition is set, depending on the field you choose. For example, if you select Album artist, the default condition is "Contains." If you do not agree with this condition, click it and select another one.

6. Click **[click to set]**.

A list opens that contains all the available options.

7. Select the value that you want. For this exercise, we selected **Enya** as the value we want to have for **Album artist**.

8. Add all the conditions that you want your playlist to meet in the **Music in my library** section.

9. In the **And also include** section, you can add conditions about what else to include except the music in your library. Click the plus sign to see your options.

10. For example, if you want to also add videos of your favorite band in the playlist, but not the actual music files, you can select **Video in my library**. If you do not want to add other types of files, do not select anything in this section.

11. In the **And apply the following restrictions to the auto playlist** section, you can add limits related to the number of items included in the playlist, total duration, or total size of it. Click the plus sign to see your options.

New Auto Playlist

Select the criteria that you want to change in the auto playlist.
The auto playlist is updated automatically each time you open it.

Auto Playlist name: Playlist Name

Create an auto playlist that includes the following:

♪ Music in my library

▼ Album artist <u>Contains</u> <u>Enya</u>

✚ [Click here to add criteria]

And also include:

🎬 Video in my library

✚ [Click here to add criteria]

And also include:

✚ [Click here to add criteria]

And apply the following restrictions to the auto playlist:

✚ ▼

Limit Number Of Items
Limit Total Duration To
Limit Total Size To

| Remove | | OK | Cancel | Help |

12. Select the option you desire. For this exercise we selected **Limit Total Duration To**. Set the limit as you prefer.

New Auto Playlist

Select the criteria that you want to change in the auto playlist.
The auto playlist is updated automatically each time you open it.

Auto Playlist name: Playlist Name

Create an auto playlist that includes the following:

♪ Music in my library

▼ Album artist <u>Contains</u> <u>Enya</u>

✚ [Click here to add criteria]

And also include:

🎬 Video in my library

✚ [Click here to add criteria]

And also include:

✚ [Click here to add criteria]

And apply the following restrictions to the auto playlist:

▼ Limit total duration to [click to set] <u>Hours</u>

✚ [Click here to add criteria]

| Remove | | OK | Cancel | Help |

13. Click **[click to set]**.

14. Type the value of the limit that you want to set.

Note By default, a unit of measure is set depending on the field you choose. For example, if you select Limit Total Duration To, the default measure is hours. If you prefer a different unit of measure, click it and select another one.

15. Repeat steps 4 to 14 until you have set all the conditions you want the playlist to meet.

16. When you have finished, click **OK**.

When you access the newly created playlist, you see within it all the music (plus videos or pictures, if you set this in the list of conditions) that meets the criteria you defined. For this exercise, we set our playlist to load all songs and videos from Enya.

CLEAN UP Listen to the playlist you just created to check if it is the way you wanted. When done listening, close Windows Media Player 12.

Streaming Your Windows Media Player 12 Library Over the Network

One of the greatest features in Windows Media Player 12 is the fact that it allows you to stream your music library across all computers from your Homegroup. You can access remote media libraries, and you can also control what is played on other devices on the Homegroup remotely.

See Also To learn more about the Homegroup, see Chapter 6, "Creating the Homegroup and Joining Windows 7 Computers."

In order to take advantage of this feature to its fullest, you need to set a series of configurations. Let's look at them one by one.

Important In order for streaming to work between two or more computers, they all need to be running Windows 7, with the network location set as Home and the Homegroup set up and joined by all computers.

Setting Up Media Streaming with the Homegroup

The first step in streaming your media library over the network is to set up media streaming with the Homegroup on the computers that you want to use for this activity.

In this exercise, you will learn how to set up media streaming with the Homegroup.

SET UP Open Windows Media Player 12 and use the Player Library view mode

1. Click **Stream**.

   A list opens that displays options related to media streaming.

2. Click **Turn on media streaming with HomeGroup**.

Windows 7 now briefs you on the security implications of enabling media streaming. Essentially, enabling media streaming will modify your firewall settings to allow access from networked computers. For this reason, we don't recommend enabling media streaming unless you are on a secure network that you trust (for instance, avoid enabling network media streaming if you are on a public wireless network, such as at a café, library, airport, and so on).

3. Click **Turn on media streaming**.

The Media Streaming Options window opens.

4. In the **Name your media library** field, type the name you want to use for your media library.

This is how your media library is identified when other computers on the network connect to it.

5. In the **Show devices on** drop-down list, choose **Local network**.

This reveals all the computers that have successfully connected to the Homegroup.

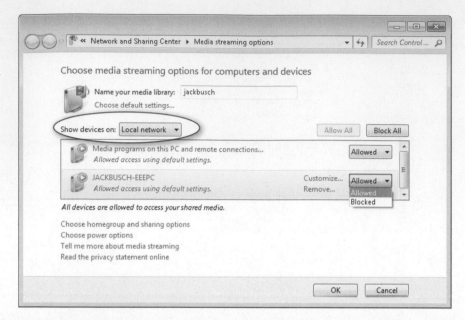

6. Now it is time to set which devices on your network you want to be able to access your media library. For each of the computers shown, you can allow or block access. Select **Allowed** for the computers that you want to allow access to your media library and **Blocked** for those computers that you do not.

7. For the computers for which you selected **Allowed**, you can further customize access by clicking **Customize**.

   The Customize Media Streaming Settings window opens.

Customize media streaming settings

Choose what is streamed to 'JACKBUSCH-EEEPC'

☐ Use default settings
☐ Make all of the media in my library available to this device

Choose star ratings:
◉ All ratings
◯ Only:

Rated 1 star or higher   ▾

☑ Include unrated files

Choose parental ratings:
◉ All ratings
◯ Only:

☑ Music: Unrated
☑ Pictures: Unrated
☑ Recorded TV: Unrated
☑ Video: Unrated

How do I customize sharing?

OK   Cancel

8. You can filter what is streamed to the selected computer based on star or parental ratings (in case you don't want your children to access certain types of media). Make the selections that best fit your needs.

9. When you have finished, click **OK**.

   You are returned to the Media Streaming Options window.

10. Click **OK**.

Your media library is now connected to the Homegroup.

 CLEAN UP Repeat this procedure for all computers you want to use for streaming media across the Homegroup.

Displaying Remote Media Libraries in the Navigation Pane

Once you have set up media streaming with the Homegroup on all computers, you can access remote media libraries directly from Windows Media Player 12. All you need to do is open the application and look at the bottom portion of the Navigation Pane. In the Other Libraries section, you should see a list with all the computers that are turned on and sharing their media library with the Homegroup. Accessing their media libraries is as simple as clicking on these computers and browsing with the mouse.

![Windows Media Player window showing the navigation pane with Other Libraries, Ciprian (ciprian-pc), George (george-pc) expanded to show Music, Videos, Pictures, Recorded TV, and User 7tutorials (george-pc)]

However, chances are you won't be able to see the media libraries of other computers because of how your Windows Media Player 12 is set up.

In this exercise, you will learn how to customize the navigation pane so that it shows the media libraries shared by other computers on the Homegroup or the Internet.

SET UP Open Windows Media Player 12.

1. Make sure that you are in the **Player Library** view mode. If you are not, Press **Ctrl+1** to switch to this view.

2. Click **Organize**.

3. Select **Customize navigation pane**.

The Customize Navigation Pane window opens.

4. Choose **Other Libraries** from the drop-down menu.

5. Select the **Show Other Libraries** check box.

6. Select the boxes next to the remote media libraries that you want to see in your Navigation Pane.

7. When you have finished, click **OK**.

The selected media libraries are now displayed in the Other Libraries section of the Navigation Pane.

 CLEAN UP Repeat this procedure for any other computers that you want configured in this manner.

Allowing Remote Control and Enabling the "Play To" Functionality

Another option that is handy for sharing media libraries is remote control. With this option enabled, you can play songs from your computer to others on the Homegroup. For example, if you have a living room computer hooked up to your entertainment system, you can play songs from your netbook via the network using Remote Control and the Play To functionality.

In this exercise, you will learn how to allow remote control of a computer and enable the Play To functionality.

SET UP Open Windows Media Player 12 and use the Player Library view mode.

 1. Click **Stream**.

2. To enable remote control of your computer, select the **Allow remote control of my Player** check box.

3. To enable the Play To functionality on your computer, select the **Automatically allow devices to play my media** check box.

Other computers can now control your Windows Media Player 12 remotely and also play music directly to your computer.

CLEAN UP Repeat this procedure for any other computers for which you want to use these features.

Playing Media Remotely to Another Computer

Now that you have set things up, it is time for the fun part: playing media remotely from your computer to another on your Homegroup.

In this exercise, you will learn how to use the Play To functionality.

SET UP Open Windows Media Player 12 on your computer as well as on the computer on which you want to play media remotely. Use the Player Library view mode.

1. In the **Playlists** section, you see all playlists currently defined in Windows Media Player 12.

2. Select the playlist that you want to play remotely.

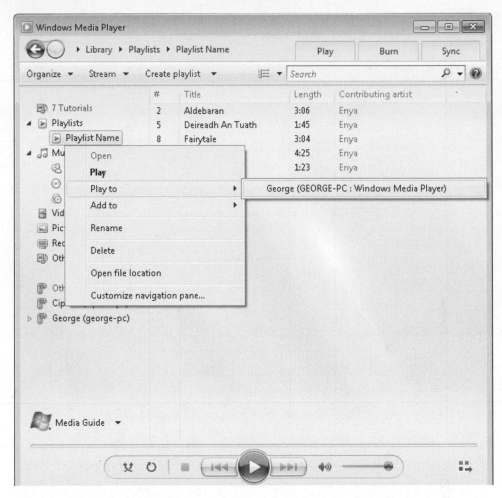

3. Right-click the playlist then select **Play to**.

4. From the list of options, select the computer on which you want to play that playlist.

The Play To window opens. Here, you are given control over the remote computer.

5. You can **Play** or **Pause** songs, **Skip** to the next song on the **Play To** list, and even adjust the volume.

On the remote computer, the songs begin to play.

Tip You can override remote control and manage songs locally, if you want.

CLEAN UP When you have finished playing media remotely, close Windows Media Player 12.

Streaming Your Windows Media Player 12 Library Over the Internet

Windows Media Player 12 has another cool feature that allows you to play your entire media library from any Windows 7 computer over the Internet. And that means everything: songs, videos, photos, even purchased media. This is useful for when you want to enjoy your Windows Media Player 12 library at the office, on your laptop, or simply from another computer in your home.

In order to take advantage of this feature to its fullest, you need to set a series of configurations. Let's look at them one by one.

Important In order for remote streaming via the Internet to work between two or more computers, they all need to be running Windows 7, and media streaming must be enabled in Windows Media Player 12.

Creating and Linking an Online ID for Remote Media Streaming

The first step in setting up remote media streaming over the Internet is to set up an Online ID by downloading the appropriate software from Microsoft. This online ID provider software, called Windows Live ID Sign-in, simply lets you link one of your online accounts (such as the one you use for email and instant messaging) to your Windows 7 user accounts. At the time of this writing, you can only link your Windows Live account, but there are plans to roll out other online ID providers (such as Google, OpenID, and Facebook). The Online ID you set up needs to then be linked with the user account on your Windows 7 computer. Once this link is set up, you can start using remote media streaming.

In this exercise, you will learn how to install the Online ID software from Microsoft, set it up, and link it to a user account from a Windows 7 computer.

 SET UP Go to the Windows 7 online ID providers Web site at *http://windows .microsoft.com/en-US/Windows7/OnlineIDProviders*.

 1. On the Windows 7 online ID providers page, you can see two download buttons: one for 32-bit editions of Windows 7 and the other for 64-bit editions.

2. Download the version suited to the type of operating system you have installed on your computer.

3. Run the downloaded file (wllogin_32.msi for 32-bit editions of Windows 7, wllogin_64.msi for 64-bit).

   You might receive a security warning, asking for your confirmation to run the file.

4. Click **Run**.

The Windows Live ID Sign-In Assistant Setup starts.

5. Click **Install**.

You are asked if you want to provide help to improve Windows Live programs.

6. If you want to help Microsoft, select the **Help improve Windows Live** check box. Otherwise, leave it unchecked.

7. Click **Next**.

The installation process now starts.

Important If you have any Windows Live Software already installed, such as Windows Live Essentials, the installation process ends and Windows displays the notification, "Newer version already installed." Click OK.

8. After a while, you are notified that the installation has completed.

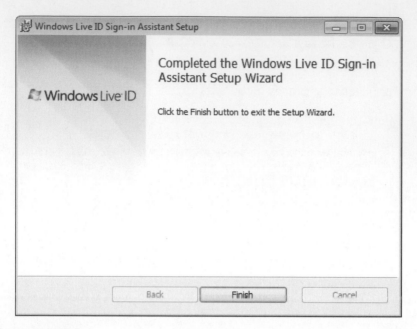

9. Click **Finish**.

   You are done installing the Windows Live ID Sign-iI Software. Now it is time to set it up.

10. Go to **Control Panel -> User Accounts and Family Safety -> User Accounts**.

11. In the **User Accounts** window, click **Link online IDs**.

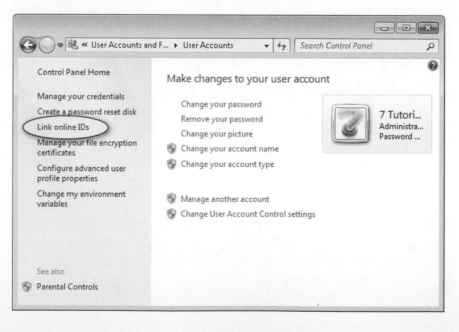

The Link Online IDs window opens. You can see here the current user plus the WindowsLiveID provider that you just installed.

12. Click the **Link online ID** link.

The **Windows Live ID** window opens, in which you can log on with your ID (if you have one) or create one (if you don't).

13. If you have a Windows Live ID, type the e-mail and password, then click **Sign In**.

14. For this exercise, we will assume that you don't have a Windows Live ID. If this is the case, click **Sign up**.

   The Create Your Windows Live ID page opens in your Internet browser.

15. Type all the required details and follow the instructions on the Web page.

16. Once your account is created, you are automatically signed in and returned to the **Link Online IDs** window. There, you can see that your user account is now linked with your Online ID.

17. Click **OK** and you are done.

Now you can set up Windows Media Player 12 to work with remote media streaming over the Internet.

CLEAN UP Repeat this procedure on any computers for which you want remote media streaming functionality.

Allowing Internet Access to Home Media

The second important step is to allow Internet access to home media on the computer where you keep your media files. Obviously, your host machine should be connected to the Internet, and you should already have some folders added to your Music, Pictures, or Videos libraries.

In this exercise, you will learn how to allow Internet access to your home media in Windows Media Player 12.

SET UP Open Windows Media Player 12 and use the Player Library view mode.

1. Click **Stream**.

2. Click **Allow Internet access to home media**.

The Internet Home Media Access window opens.

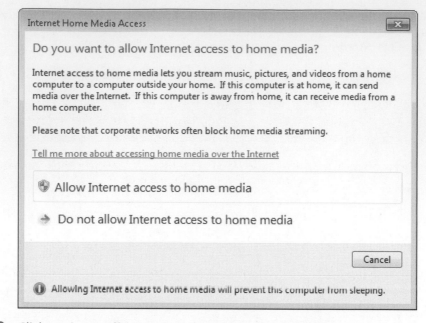

3. Click again on **Allow Internet access to home media**.

   This also opens a User Account Control (UAC) prompt.

4. Click **Continue**.

   You are informed that Internet access to home media is now enabled.

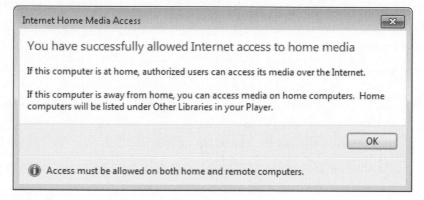

5. Click **OK**.

You are now done and other computers can begin accessing your media library via the Internet.

CLEAN UP Repeat this procedure on any computers for which you want remote media streaming functionality.

Playing Media Remotely over the Internet

Now that you have set up Internet access of your media, you can start playing it whenever you want to. In order for remote media playing to work, your remote host computer needs to be turned on and Windows Media Player 12 must be launched.

In this exercise, you will learn how to play remote media over the Internet in Windows Media Player 12.

→ **SET UP** Open Windows Media Player 12 and use the Player Library view mode.

 1. In the **Navigation Pane**, go to the **Other Libraries** section.

Here you should see all the computers and libraries that are available for media streaming, both from your network and the Internet.

The libraries that are available for remote streaming over the Internet have a slightly different icon and use the format: *User + Name of the User on that PC + name of the PC*. In our example, it is **User 7 Tutorials (ciprian-pc)**.

2. Click the remote computer you want to access.

3. Browse its media library and play the items that you are interested in listening to or viewing.

 CLEAN UP Close Windows Media Player 12 when you are done using it.

Troubleshooting If you are using a router for your home network and Windows Media Player 12 doesn't display the remote computers and their libraries, it means you need to map ports 44442 to 10245 and 443 to 10245 on your router. To learn more about how to troubleshoot this problem, see Chapter 15, "Troubleshooting Network and Internet Problems."

Key Points

- It is better to use your own custom settings when setting up Windows Media Player 12 instead of the recommended settings.

- Your media library can include music, video, pictures, and recorded TV shows.

- Windows Media Player 12 allows you to create advanced playlists that meet very specific criteria.

- With the help of the Homegroup feature, you can use Windows Media Player 12 to stream media over your home network.

- With the help of Online IDs, you can stream your media remotely over the Internet.

Chapter at a Glance

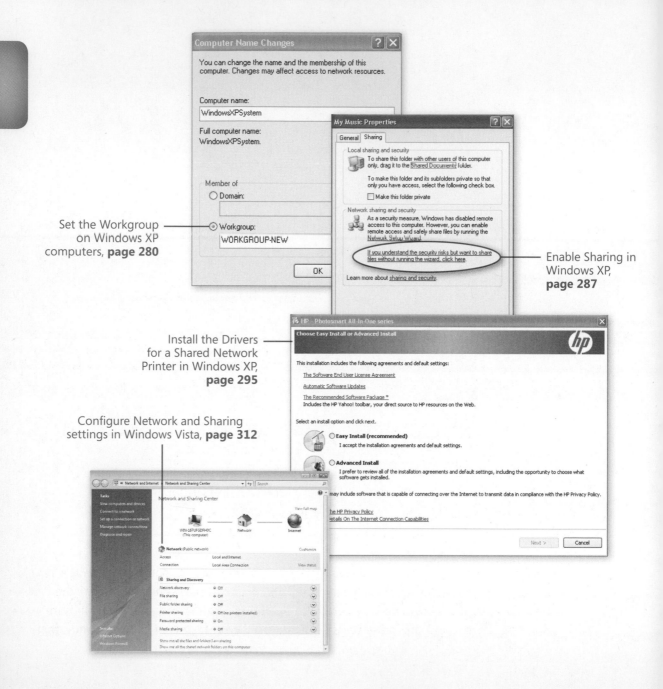

Set the Workgroup on Windows XP computers, **page 280**

Enable Sharing in Windows XP, **page 287**

Install the Drivers for a Shared Network Printer in Windows XP, **page 295**

Configure Network and Sharing settings in Windows Vista, **page 312**

10

Sharing Between Windows XP, Windows Vista, and Windows 7 Computers

---

In this chapter, you will learn how to

✔ Set the workgroup on your Windows XP computer.

✔ Enable the Computer Browser and Print Spooler services in Windows XP.

✔ Enable sharing in Windows XP.

✔ Access shared network folders from Windows XP.

✔ Access Windows XP shared folders from Windows 7.

✔ Install drivers for a shared network printer in Windows XP.

✔ Install a shared network printer in Windows XP.

✔ Set the workgroup on your Windows Vista computer.

✔ Configure network and sharing settings in Windows Vista.

✔ Share folders in Windows Vista.

✔ Install drivers for a shared network printer in Windows Vista.

✔ Install a shared network printer in Windows Vista.

Sharing folders and printers between Windows 7, Windows Vista, and Windows XP is not as easy as it should be, particularly as they all are Microsoft operating systems. Before being able to share anything between these operating systems, you need to make sure that the network and sharing settings are configured correctly on all computers and that they all joined the same workgroup.

In this chapter, you will first learn how to set up Windows XP and Windows Vista so that you can share folders with other Windows computers. You will then learn how to access these shared folders and also how to access a Windows 7 shared printer from both Windows XP and Windows Vista so that you can print the files you need.

> **Practice Files** You can use any of your folders on your Windows XP or Windows Vista computer to complete the exercises in this chapter. Until you get the hang of it, it is best not to use any important folders. Also, back up the files and folders you are about to use, just to make sure you don't lose them by mistake.

Setting the Workgroup on Your Windows XP Computer

In order to share files and folders between computers that are running different operating systems—and without too much hassle—it is best to set the same workgroup on all of them. By default, the workgroup set on Windows XP is named "Workgroup," which is the same as with Windows 7 and many other operating systems. However, there may be cases when it is set differently for various reasons, or you just need to change it to another name.

In this exercise, you will learn how to change the workgroup in Windows XP.

→ **SET UP** On the computer running Windows XP, open the Start Menu.

1. Right-click the **My Computer** shortcut.

   The contextual menu opens, displaying options specific to My Computer.

2. Click **Properties**.

The System Properties window opens.

3. Click the **Computer Name** tab.

4. In the field labeled **Workgroup**, you can see the current workgroup that your Windows XP computer has joined. If you need to change it, click the **Change** button.

The Computer Name Changes window opens.

5. In the **Workgroup** field, type the name of the workgroup that you want your Windows XP computer to join.

6. Click **OK**.

Windows XP confirms the change.

7. Click **OK**.

Windows XP informs you that a restart must be performed in order for the work-group change to take effect.

8. Click **OK**.

You are returned to the System Properties window.

9. Click **OK**.

Windows XP asks if you want to restart your computer now.

10. Close any open applications, save any work you have open, then click **Yes**.

Your Windows XP computer reboots.

Note If you do not want to restart immediately, it's okay to click No. However, the change will not be applied until after you restart your computer.

When you log on again, the Windows XP computer joins the specified workgroup.

 CLEAN UP Repeat this procedure on all your Windows XP computers that you want as part of the same group.

Enabling Computer Browser and Print Spooler Services in Windows XP

The Computer Browser service allows your Windows XP computer to detect the computers on your network and maintain the list of active network computers continuously. The Printer Spooler service is useful if you plan to use a printer on your network because it allows you to interact with printers and use them to print your documents.

By default, these services are enabled in Windows XP. However, depending on how your Windows XP has been configured, it's possible that they are disabled. That's why it is better to check and confirm that these services are enabled and set to start automatically at each logon.

In this exercise, you will learn how to enable and set the Computer Browser and Print Spooler services to start automatically.

SET UP Open the Start Menu.

1. Right-click the **My Computer** shortcut.

   The contextual menu opens, displaying options specific to My Computer.

Tip The My Computer shortcut can also be found on your desktop, depending on how you have set up your Windows XP.

2. Click **Manage**.

   The Computer Management window opens.

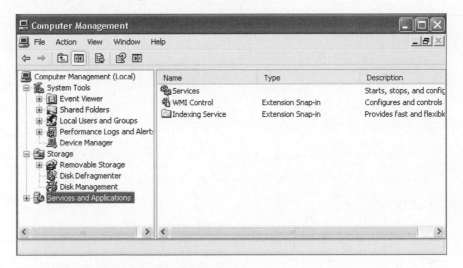

3. Go to the **Services and Applications** section.

4. Double-click **Services** to display the list of services currently on your computer.

5. Scroll until you find the **Computer Browser** service. Double-click it.

The Properties window of the service opens.

Computer Browser Properties (Local Computer) ☐ ? ☒

| General | Log On | Recovery | Dependencies |

Service name: Browser

Display name: Computer Browser

Description: Maintains an updated list of computers on the network and supplies this list to computers

Path to executable:
C:\WINDOWS\system32\svchost.exe -k netsvcs

Startup type: Automatic

Service status: Stopped

[Start] [Stop] [Pause] [Resume]

You can specify the start parameters that apply when you start the service from here.

Start parameters:

[OK] [Cancel] [Apply]

6. Look at the **Startup type** line. If it is set to **Automatic**, then things are fine. If it is not, click the **Startup type** drop-down list and select **Automatic**.

7. Look at the **Service status** line. If it indicates **Stopped**, then the service is not running. Click **Start**; if the status shows **Started**, then everything is fine.

Tip When you click Start, if you receive an error message that the computer browser service started then stopped, don't worry—everything is okay. Continue making the settings described in the next sections and everything will work out.

8. When you have finished, click **OK**.

You are returned to the list of Services.

9. Repeat steps 5 to 8 for the Print Spooler service.

The Computer Browser and Print Spooler services are enabled and set to start automatically.

✖ **CLEAN UP** Close the Computer Management window.

Enabling Sharing in Windows XP

Before you begin to share files, folders, or printers, you need to make sure sharing is enabled on your computer. While there are many ways you can do that, we will share the most simple procedure possible.

In this exercise, you will learn how to enable sharing in Windows XP and how to share folders with the computers from your home network.

 SET UP Open the My Computer shortcut.

1. Browse to a folder you would like to share with the network.
2. Right-click the folder.

   The contextual menu opens.

3. Select **Sharing and Security**.

   The Properties window of the folder opens.

Tip Another way to access this window is to right-click the folder, select Properties from the contextual menu, then go to the Sharing tab of the Properties window.

4. In the **Network sharing and security** section, click **If you understand the security risks but want to share files without running the wizard, click here**. If this message is not present, it means that sharing is already enabled. If this is the case, skip to step 7.

The Enable File Sharing window opens.

5. Select the **Just enable file sharing** check box.

6. Click **OK**.

You are returned to the Properties window of the folder you want to share.

My Music Properties   [?] [X]

General | Sharing

Local sharing and security

To share this folder with other users of this computer only, drag it to the Shared Documents folder.

To make this folder and its subfolders private so that only you have access, select the following check box.

☐ Make this folder private

Network sharing and security

To share this folder with both network users and other users of this computer, select the first check box below and type a share name.

☑ Share this folder on the network

Share name: My Music

☐ Allow network users to change my files

Learn more about sharing and security.

(i)   Windows Firewall will be configured to allow this folder to be shared with other computers on the network.

View your Windows Firewall settings

| OK | Cancel | Apply |

7. In the **Network sharing and security** section, select the **Share this folder on the network** check box. This means sharing is now enabled.

8. If you want to share the folder, select the **Share this folder on the network** check box.

9. If you want to change the name used for sharing the folder, type a new name in the **Share name** text box.

10. If you want to allow others to change the files inside the folder, select the **Allow network users to change my files** check box.

11. Click **OK**.

Sharing is now enabled and the selected folder is shared.

Tip Once sharing is enabled, you only need to use steps 1 to 3, then steps 7 to 12. Steps 4 to 6 will no longer be valid.

 CLEAN UP Share all the folders you want to make available to your network.

Accessing Shared Network Folders from Windows XP

If you have computers with multiple operating systems installed and you have set the same workgroup on all of them and configured the file sharing settings correctly, you should have no problem accessing everything that's shared on your home network from Windows XP.

In this exercise, you will learn how to access shared network folders from Windows XP.

SET UP Open the My Computer shortcut.

1. Go to the **Other Places** section, which is located on the left side of the My Computer window.

![My Computer window screenshot showing the Other Places section on the left with My Network Places circled]

2. Click **My Network Places**.

A list opens that shows the shared folders identified so far by Windows XP. The list is likely to be incomplete. Therefore, continue following the next steps.

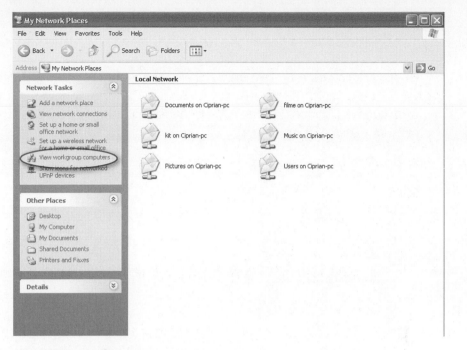

3. Click **View workgroup computers**.

A list opens that shows all the currently active computers that are a part of the same workgroup as your Windows XP computer.

4. Double-click the computer whose shared folders you want to access.

You can see all the folders and devices shared by that computer.

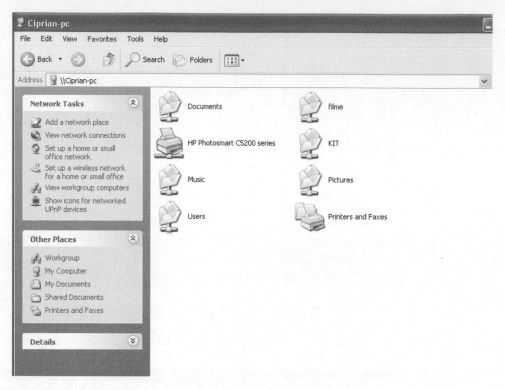

5. To access a folder, simply double-click it. If everything is set up correctly, you should be able to access the folder's contents and work with it.

Important If you receive an "access denied" error when you access a shared folder, it means the file sharing settings on the computer are not compatible with your operating system. Depending on the operating system used on that computer, refer to the appropriate chapter in this book to learn how to correctly configure the sharing settings.

CLEAN UP When you have finished accessing shared folders, close the Computer window.

Accessing Windows XP Shared Folders from Windows 7 Computers

Once you've completed setting up your Windows XP computer, your Windows 7 computers should be able to access the shared folders. This is a pretty easy task.

In this exercise, you will learn how to access your Windows XP shared folders from Windows 7.

➡ **SET UP** Open the Computer window or Windows Explorer.

1. Go to the **Network** section.

   A list opens, showing all the computers in your home network that are turned on at that moment and that Windows 7 can detect.

Note You can have additional computers turned on, but it is possible that Windows 7 will not be able to detect them due to incompatible network and sharing settings.

2. Double-click the Windows XP computer you want access.

A list opens that shows all the shared folders and devices on that computer.

3. Double-click the folder you want to open.

You can now work with the contents of the shared folder, according to the permission levels set on the Windows XP computer.

Important If you have set up your shared folder to not allow access to everyone, you will receive a network error. Make sure that you share your folders on Windows XP so that everyone has access to them.

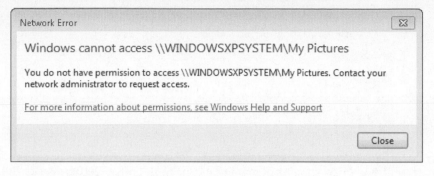

 CLEAN UP When you have finished, close the Computer or Windows Explorer window.

Installing Drivers for a Shared Network Printer in Windows XP

Installing a network printer is a process that varies greatly depending on the manufacturer of the printer. If you are using Windows XP and the printer is connected to another computer and shared with the network, you need to first install the Windows XP drivers for the printer. Some drivers allow the detection of network printers, and when you install them, you set up everything in one pass. Other drivers do not. If the driver does not allow the detection of shared network printers, you need to first install the driver, then manually add the printer using the Add a Printer Wizard.

To further complicate matters, the setup of a printer driver is different, based on the manufacturer and the model you have. Also, the number of steps is almost never the same. However, the basic principles apply to all setup programs provided by the different printer manufacturers.

In this exercise, you will learn how to install the drivers for a printer in Windows XP using the setup program provided by the manufacturer of the printer. For the purposes of this exercise, we are using the setup for the HP Photosmart C5280 printer.

SET UP Write down the manufacturer of the shared network printer and its exact model.

1. Download the Windows XP driver from the Web site of the company that manufactured your printer.

Printer drivers are typically provided as a self-extracting archive file and include the ".exe" extension in their file name.

100_235_PS_A
IO_02_Full_No
nNet_enu_NB.
exe

2. Run the printer driver setup file.

The self-extraction process starts. Usually, the driver setup displays a progress window.

8% Extracting

Cancel

Tip Some drivers ask you to choose where you want the extracted files to be placed. Others simply start the self-extraction process without asking. If you are asked for a location, select the folder where you want the driver to reside, then click the Unzip or Extract button (depending on what it is called).

3. Wait for the self-extraction process to end.

Depending on the size of the driver, the extraction can take a while to complete. Once finished, you should see the first driver installation window.

HP - Photosmart All-In-One series

Select Install to begin installing your new HP device.

Thank you for purchasing from HP!

Install

Readme

Exit

Tip Some self-extractors for printer drivers do not automatically start the first installation window. In such a case, you need to manually start it yourself. Go to the folder where the driver was extracted and run the setup.exe file.

4. Click **Install**.

After a few seconds, the installation wizard displays some information about the process that is about to start and what you need to pay attention to.

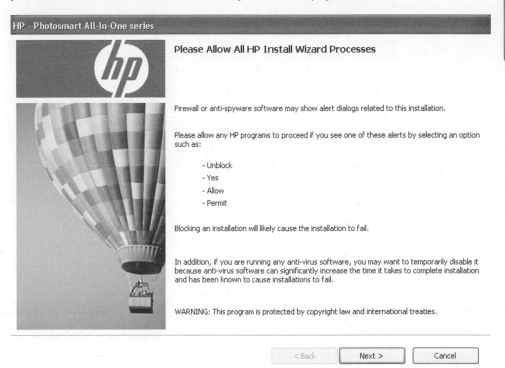

Tip This screen (or one similar to it) is shown mostly by HP printer drivers but not by other manufacturers and models. Some manufacturers prefer to start the installation immediately, with fewer preliminary windows for you to read.

5. Click **Next**.

You are asked if you want to perform an Easy Install or an Advanced Install.

6. Easy installs work only if the printer is connected to your computer. In this case, it is not, so choose **Advanced Install**, then click **Next**. In addition, using **Advanced Install** is often a better choice because **Easy Install** usually installs additional software you don't need, such as toolbars, trial versions of products you will never use, and so on.

You are asked if you want HP to check for software updates automatically.

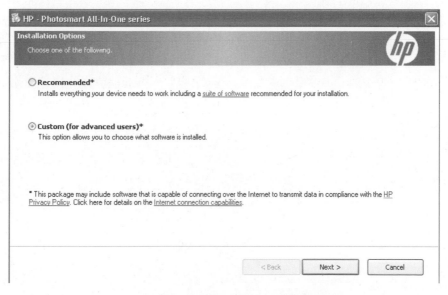

7. Choose the option you prefer, then click **Next**.

   You are asked if you want the setup to install all the software needed for your printer as well as additional elements recommended by HP, or if you want to make a custom installation of software.

8. Choose **Custom (for advanced users)**, then click **Next**.

   A list opens that shows all the software proposed for installation.

9. Clear the check boxes adjacent to the software that you don't need (for example, Yahoo! Toolbar, Shop for HP Supplies, and so on), then click **Next**.

The licensing agreement appears.

10. Click **I Agree**.

You are asked to specify where the HP Photosmart software is to be installed.

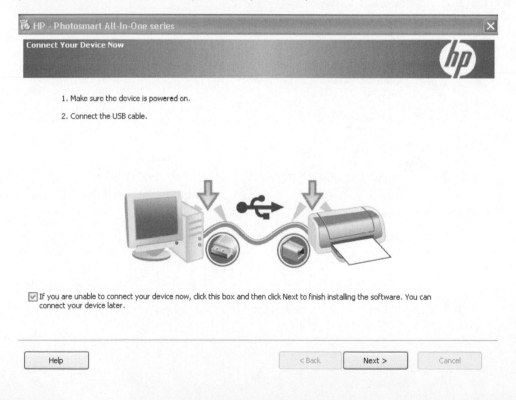

11. If you want to change the location, click **Change** and select the folder where it should be installed. Otherwise, simply click **Next**.

The setup will take a while to install the software you selected. When it has finished, you are asked to connect the printer to your computer.

12. Select the check box adjacent to **If you are unable to connect your device now, click this box and then click Next to finish installing the software.**

13. Click **Next**.

The installation process continues. After a while, a message appears telling you that the installation process has ended.

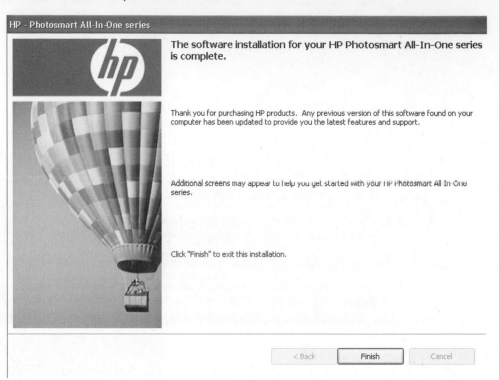

14. Click **Finish**.

The printer drivers are now installed. However, the installation process is not yet done. Be patient for a couple of moments and read the following section to learn how to finish up.

Tip Other manufacturers offer setup programs for their drivers that allow you to select a shared network printer in addition to a local one. When using such drivers, it is enough to select the shared network printer and continue the installation. When you have finished, everything works and there's no need to follow the instructions in the next section.

CLEAN UP Read the next section to learn how to complete the installation of the shared network printer.

Installing a Shared Network Printer in Windows XP

Once you've completed installing the printer driver in Windows XP, it's time to install the shared network printer. Unlike the previous procedure, in which the steps can vary greatly depending on the manufacturer and model of the printer, this procedure has the same number of steps and always progresses in the same way.

In this exercise, you will learn how to install a network shared printer in Windows XP.

SET UP Turn on the printer and the computer to which it is connected. Then, open the Control Panel.

1. Click **Printers and Other hardware**.

   The Printers And Other Hardware panel opens.

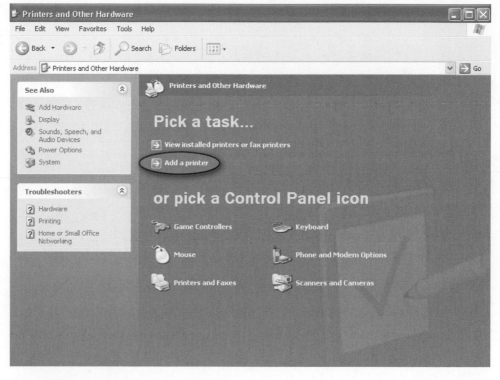

2. Click **Add a printer**.

   The Add Printer Wizard opens.

3. Click **Next**.

You are asked to select the option that best describes the printer you want to use.

4. Select **A network printer, or a printer attached to another computer**.
5. Click **Next**.

You are asked to select the printer to which you want to connect.

Add Printer Wizard

Specify a Printer
If you don't know the name or address of the printer, you can search for a printer that meets your needs.

What printer do you want to connect to?

◉ Browse for a printer

○ Connect to this printer (or to browse for a printer, select this option and click Next):

Name: [   ]

Example: \\server\printer

○ Connect to a printer on the Internet or on a home or office network:

URL: [   ]

Example: http://server/printers/myprinter/.printer

[< Back] [Next >] [Cancel]

6. You have several options. The easiest is to select **Browse for a printer**.

7. Click **Next**.

Windows XP shows a list of computers from your workgroup that have a printer installed.

Add Printer Wizard

Browse for Printer
When the list of printers appears, select the one you want to use.

Printer: [\\CIPRIAN-PC\HP Photosmart C5200 series   ]

Shared printers:

- Microsoft Windows Network
  - WORKGROUP
    - \\CIPRIAN-PC\HP Photosmart C5200 HP Photosmart C5200 series
    - CIPRIAN-PC
      - HP Photosmart C5200 series   HP Photosmart C5200 series

Printer information
Comment:
Status: Ready   Documents waiting: 0

[< Back] [Next >] [Cancel]

8. Double-click the computer to which the printer is connected, then select the printer.

9. Click **Next**.

Windows XP warns you that you are about to connect to the printer from the selected computer.

Connect to Printer

⚠ You are about to connect to a printer on CIPRIAN-PC, which will automatically install a print driver on your machine. Printer drivers may contain viruses or scripts that can be harmful to your computer. It is important to be certain that the computer sharing this printer is trustworthy. Would you like to continue?

Yes   No

10. Click **Yes**.

You are informed that the computer to which the printer is attached does not have the correct drivers installed.

Connect to Printer

⚠ The server for the 'HP Photosmart C5200 series' printer does not have the correct printer driver installed. If you want to search for the proper driver, click OK. Otherwise, click Cancel and contact your network administrator or original equipment manufacturer for the correct printer driver.

OK   Cancel

Note If the printer is connected to another computer with Windows XP installed, then you will not receive this warning. If this is the case, skip to step 12.

11. Click **OK**.

Windows XP now searches for drivers and finds those that you just installed in the previous section. When it is done searching, the Add Printer Wizard indicates that the procedure has successfully completed.

12. Click **Finish**.

The shared network printer is installed on your computer and you can now begin using it.

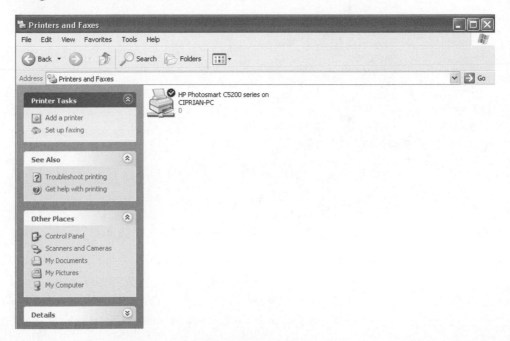

 CLEAN UP Close the Printers and Faxes window.

Setting the Workgroup on Your Windows Vista Computer

By default, the workgroup set on Windows Vista is named "Workgroup," which is the same as in Windows 7 and many other operating systems. However, there may be cases when it is set differently, or you simply want to change it to another name.

In this exercise, you will learn how to change the workgroup on your Windows Vista computer.

➡ **SET UP** On the computer running Windows Vista, open the Control Panel.

1. Click **System and Maintenance**.

   The System And Maintenance panel opens.

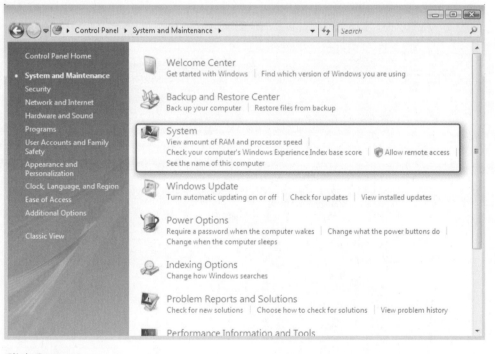

2. Click **System**.

   The System window opens, in which you can see information about your operating system and the configuration of your computer. The currently set workgroup is specified in the **Computer name, domain, and workgroup settings** section.

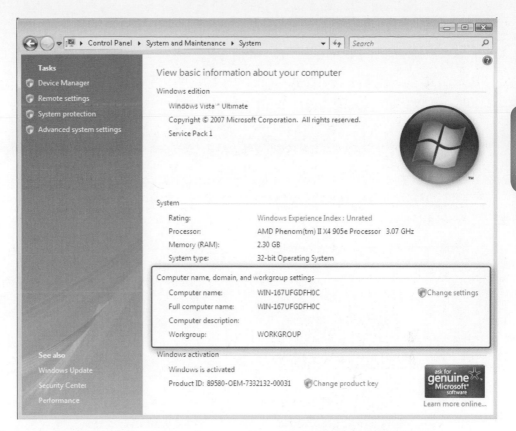

3. If you need to make changes to the workgroup, click **Change Settings**.

If you receive a UAC prompt, confirm your choice. The System Properties window opens.

4. Click the **Change** button.

The Computer Name/Domain Changes window opens.

5. In the **Workgroup** field, type the name of the workgroup that you want your Windows Vista computer to join.

6. Click **OK**.

Windows Vista confirms the change.

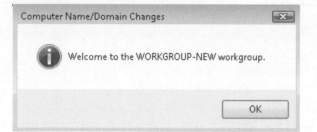

7. Click **OK**.

Windows XP informs you that a restart must be performed in order for the workgroup change to take effect.

8. Click **OK**.

You are returned to the System Properties window.

9. Click **Close**.

Windows Vista asks if you want to restart your computer now.

10. Close any open applications, save any work you have open, and then click **Restart Now**.

Your Windows Vista computer now reboots.

Note If you do not want to restart immediately, it's okay to click Restart Later. However, the change will not be applied until after you restart your computer.

When you log on again, the Windows Vista computer joins the specified workgroup.

 CLEAN UP Repeat this procedure on all of your Windows Vista computers that you want as part of the same group.

Configuring Network and Sharing Settings in Windows Vista

Before you begin to share files, folders, or printers, you need to make sure that your network and sharing settings are configured correctly so that your Windows Vista operating system can access other computers and be accessed on your home network.

In this exercise, you will learn how to correctly configure your network and sharing settings in Windows Vista so that they are compatible with other operating systems used on your home network.

 SET UP Open the Network and Sharing Center. The steps are the same as in Windows 7. See the "Opening the Network And Sharing Center" section, in Chapter 4, "Creating the Network."

1. Look at the **Network** section and check to see whether your current network profile is set as a **Public network** or **Private network**. If it is set as **Public network**, you need to change it.

Current network location

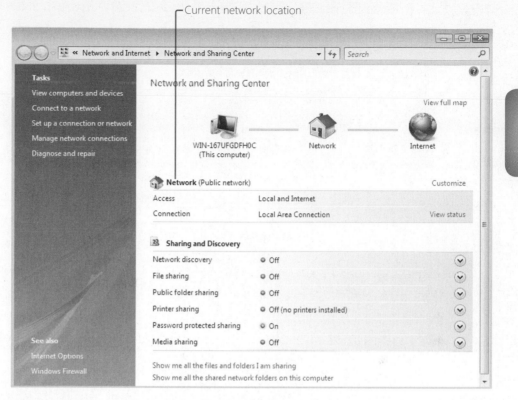

2. To change the network profile, click **Customize**. If you do not need to change it, skip to step 7.

The Set Network Location window opens.

3. Select **Private**. The Private network location is the equivalent of the Home or Work network profile in Windows 7. This allows your computer to be discovered on the network and configures many of your network and sharing settings correctly.

4. If you want to change the network icon, click **Change**, then select a new one.

5. When you have finished, click **Next**.

   If you receive a UAC prompt, confirm your choice. The Set Network Location window informs you that the network location has been successfully set.

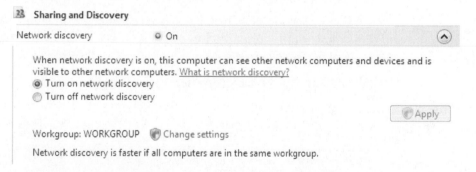

6. Click **Close**.

   You are returned to the Network And Sharing Center window.

7. Look at the **Sharing and Discovery** section to see if everything is set correctly. Let's take each setting, one by one.

   ### Sharing and Discovery

   Network discovery   ○ On   ⌃

   When network discovery is on, this computer can see other network computers and devices and is visible to other network computers. What is network discovery?
   ◉ Turn on network discovery
   ○ Turn off network discovery

             🛡 Apply

   Workgroup: WORKGROUP   🛡 Change settings
   Network discovery is faster if all computers are in the same workgroup.

8. In the **Network discovery** subsection, **Turn on network discovery** must be selected. If it is not, select it, then click **Apply**.

   Next is the **File sharing** subsection.

   File sharing   ○ On   ⌃

   When file sharing is on, files and printers that you have shared from this computer can be accessed by people on the network.
   ◉ Turn on file sharing
   ○ Turn off file sharing

             🛡 Apply

9. **Turn on file sharing** must be selected. If it is not, select it, then click **Apply**.

Next is the **Public folder sharing** subsection.

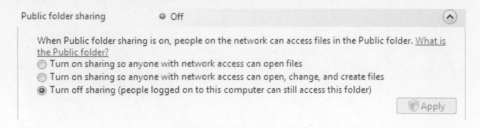

10. You should turn on the **Public folder sharing** only if you plan to use it. By default, it should be turned off. To turn it on, select one of the first two settings and click **Apply**.

Next is the **Printer sharing** subsection.

11. If there are no printers currently connected to your computer, you can simply ignore this subsection. However, if you do have printers attached, then you need to decide if you want to turn on printer sharing or keep it turned off. Select the settings you want, then click **Apply**.

Next is the **Password protected sharing** subsection.

12. To maximize compatibility with other operating systems on your network, it is best to select the **Turn off password protected sharing** option, then click **Apply**. Turning off this setting allows other computers on the network to connect to your shared files and folders without requiring the user to type the user account and password that is defined on the Windows Vista computer.

Next is the **Media sharing** subsection.

Media sharing	◉ Off	⌃

When media sharing is on, people and devices on the network can access shared music, pictures, and videos on this computer, and this computer can find those types of shared files on the network.

Change...

13. If you want to share media over the network, turn on **Media sharing**. Otherwise, there is no problem with keeping it turned off. This setting does not in any way impact your ability to share files and folders with the other computers on your network.

Your network and sharing settings are now correctly configured on your Windows Vista computer.

✖ **CLEAN UP** Close the Network and Sharing Center window. Repeat this procedure on all your Windows Vista computers, as needed.

Sharing Folders in Windows Vista

Now that the workgroup and your network and sharing settings are configured correctly on your Windows Vista computers, you can begin sharing folders with the other computers on the home network. In this exercise, you will learn how to do that.

➡ **SET UP** Open the Computer shortcut.

1. Browse to a folder you would like to share with the network.

2. Right-click the folder.

The contextual menu opens.

3. Click **Share**.

The File Sharing Wizard opens, showing the user accounts with which the selected item is already shared.

4. Click the drop-down menu.

A list appears that shows the user accounts with which you can share.

Note The drop-down menu list contains all the user accounts defined on your computer along with a user account called Everyone. This is a generic user account that stands for any of the users defined on your Windows Vista computer.

5. Select the user account with which you want to share.

6. Click **Add**.

This adds the selected user account to the list below the drop-down menu.

7. Repeat steps 4–6 until you add all the user accounts with which you want to share.

8. By default, all the added user accounts will receive **Reader** permissions to the shared item. If you want to change that, click the permission level assigned.

A list opens, displaying the available permission levels you can assign.

9. Select the desired permission level for each of the user accounts with which you want to share the item.

Reader means that the user account can only read the contents of the folder. Assigning a Permission level of **Contributor** means that a user can also modify the contents of existing files. **Co-owner** means that a user account can also add or remove files.

10. When you have finished adding user accounts and setting permission levels, click **Share**.

After a few seconds, you are informed that the selected folder has been shared.

Tip If problems occur while attempting to share the selected library or folder, you will see a message at the bottom of the screen similar to the following: "1 error(s) occurred when sharing this folder." If you click the error message, you can view details about the root cause of the problem so that you can fix it and try again.

11. Click **Done**.

The selected folder is now shared with the user accounts you specified.

CLEAN UP Repeat the procedure for all the items you want to share. When you have finished, close the Computer window.

Accessing Shared Network Folders from Windows Vista Computers

When all operating systems are configured correctly, accessing shared network folders from your Windows Vista computers is a very easy task. Simply open the Network shortcut on your Start Menu or the Network section of the Computer window.

This shows you the list of computers on your network that are turned on and a part of the same workgroup as your Windows Vista computer.

When accessing computers on your network, you might be asked to enter a user account and password.

In the User Name field, don't forget to type first the name of the computer you are connecting to, followed by a "\" (backslash character), then the user name. Next, type the password and select the Remember My Password check box. Once you click OK, you will be able to connect to that computer and its shared folders or devices.

> ### Accessing Windows Vista Shared Folders from Windows 7 Computers
>
> Accessing Windows Vista shared folders from Windows 7 computers is easy. Simply open the Network section in Windows Explorer. When you double-click the Windows Vista computer, you should be able to access its files without the need to type any user names or passwords.
>
> If you are prompted for a user name and password, don't forget to first type the computer name in the user name field, followed by "\" (backslash character), and then the user name.

Installing Drivers for a Shared Network Printer in Windows Vista

Installing a network printer is a process that varies greatly depending on the manufacturer of the printer. If you are using Windows Vista and the printer is connected to another computer and shared with the network, you need to first install the Windows Vista drivers for that printer. Some drivers allow the detection of network printers, and when you installed them, everything was set up for you in one pass. Other drivers do not. If the driver does not allow the detection of shared network printers, then you need to first install the driver and then manually add the printer using the Add a Printer Wizard.

To further complicate things, the setup of a printer driver is different, based on the manufacturer and the model. Also, the number of steps is almost never the same. However, the basic principles apply to all setup programs provided by the different printer manufacturers.

In this exercise, you will learn how to install the drivers for a printer in Windows Vista using the setup program provided by the manufacturer of the printer. For the purposes of this exercise, we will set up an HP Photosmart C5280 printer.

 SET UP Write down the manufacturer and the exact model of the shared network printer.

1. Download the Windows Vista driver from the Web site of the company that manufactured your printer.

   Printer drivers are typically provided as a self-extracting archive file and include the ".exe" extension in their file name.

2. Run the printer driver setup file. If you receive a UAC prompt, click **Continue**.

The self-extraction process starts. Usually, the driver setup displays a progress window.

> 7% Extracting
>
> [   ]
>
> [Cancel]

Tip Some drivers ask you to choose where you want the extracted files to be placed. Others simply start the self-extraction process without asking. If you are asked for a location, select the folder where you want the driver to reside, then click the Unzip or Extract button (depending on what it is called).

3. Wait for the self-extraction process to end.

Depending on the size of the driver, the extraction can take a while to complete. Once finished, you should see the first driver installation window.

> ### HP - Photosmart All-In-One series   ☒
>
> **Select Install to begin installing your new HP device.**
>
> Thank you for purchasing from HP!
>
> [Install]
>
> [Readme]
>
> Begin installing everything you need to use and enjoy your new HP device.
>
> [Exit]

Tip Some self-extractors for printer drivers do not automatically start the first installation window. In such a case, you need to manually start it yourself. Go to the folder where the driver was extracted and run the setup.exe file.

4. Click **Install**.

After a few seconds, the installation wizard displays some information about the process that is about to start and what you need to pay attention to.

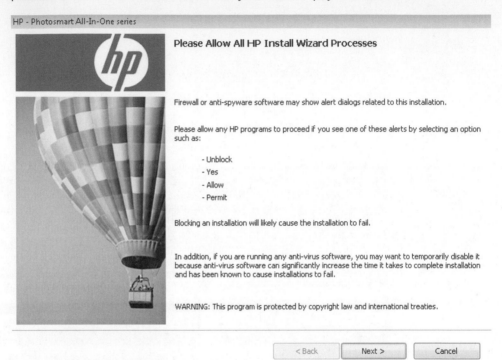

Tip This screen (or one similar to it) is shown mostly by HP printer drivers but not by other manufacturers. Some manufacturers prefer to start the installation immediately, with fewer preliminary windows for you to read.

5. Click **Next**.

You are asked if you want to perform an Easy Install or an Advanced Install.

6. Easy installs work only if the printer is connected to your computer. In this case, it is not, so choose **Advanced Install**, then click **Next**. In addition, using **Advanced Install** is often a better choice because **Easy Install** usually installs additional software you don't need, such as toolbars, trial versions to products you will never use, and so on.

You are asked if you want HP to check for software updates automatically.

7. Choose the option you prefer, then click **Next**.

You are asked if you want the setup to install all the software needed for your printer as well as additional elements recommended by HP, or if you want to make a custom installation of software.

8. Choose **Custom (for advanced users)**, then click **Next**.

A list opens that shows all the software proposed for installation.

9. Clear the check boxes adjacent to the software you don't need (for example, Yahoo! Toolbar, Shop for HP Supplies, and so on), then click **Next**.

The licensing agreement appears.

10. Click **I Agree**.

You are asked to specify where the HP Photosmart software is to be installed.

11. If you want to change the location, click **Change** and select the folder where it should be installed. Otherwise, simply click **Next**.

The setup will take a while to install the software you selected. When it has finished, you are asked to connect the printer to your computer.

12. Select the check box adjacent to **If you are unable to connect your device now, click this box and then click Next to finish installing the software.**

13. Click **Next**.

The installation process continues. After a while, a message appears telling you that the installation process has ended.

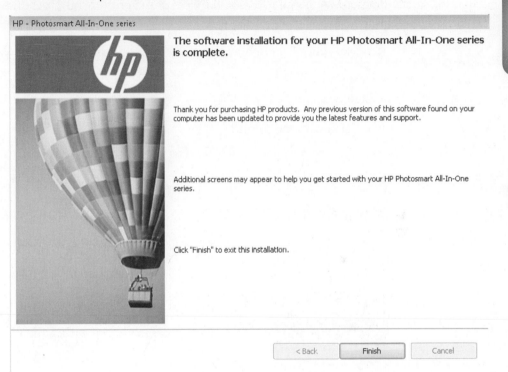

14. Click **Finish**.

The printer drivers are now installed. However, the installation process is not yet done. Be patient for a couple of moments and read the following section to learn how to finish up.

Tip Other manufacturers offer setup programs for their drivers that allow you to select a shared network printer in addition to a local one. When using such drivers, it is enough to select the shared network printer and continue the installation. When you have finished, everything works and there's no need to follow the instructions in the next section.

CLEAN UP Read the next section to learn how to complete the installation of the shared network printer.

Installing a Shared Network Printer in Windows Vista

Once you've completed installing the printer driver in Windows Vista, it's time to install the shared network printer. Unlike the previous procedure, in which the steps vary greatly depending on the manufacturer and model of the printer, this procedure has the same number of steps and always progresses in the same way.

In this exercise, you will learn how to install a network shared printer in Windows Vista.

 SET UP Turn on the printer and the computer to which it is connected. Open the Control Panel.

1. Click **Hardware and Sound**.

   The Hardware And Sound panel opens.

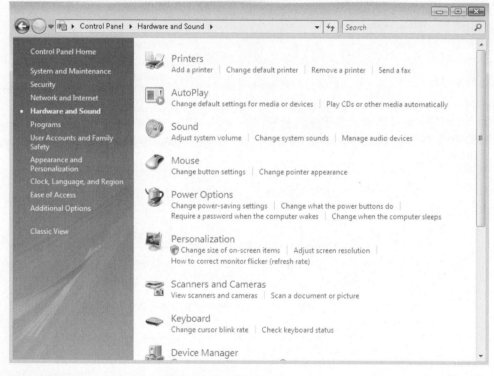

2. Under **Printers**, click the **Add a printer** link.

   The Add Printer Wizard opens.

3. Select **Add a network, wireless or Bluetooth printer**.

4. Click **Next**.

   The wizard begins searching for available printers and lists the devices that it finds.

Tip If no printer is found, verify that it is turned on and connected to the computer. Also, check that the proper drivers are installed and that your network and sharing settings are correct.

5. Select the printer you want to install, then click **Next**.

Windows Vista connects to the printer you selected. After a few seconds, you are asked to type a printer name.

For an unknown technical reason, the printer name actually cannot be changed. You can only use the name provided by the computer that shared it.

6. If you want to set the printer as your default printing device, select the **Set as the default printer** check box.

7. Click **Next**.

You are informed that the printer has been successfully added.

8. Click **Print a test page** to check if the printer works.

9. If everything is working well, click **Finish**.

The printer is now installed and you can begin to use it.

✖ **CLEAN UP** Close the Hardware and Sound panel.

Key Points

- To share files and folders between Windows XP, Windows Vista, Windows 7, and other operating systems, make sure that your home computers are in the same workgroup.

- In order to share files from Windows XP with other computers, you need to enable sharing.

- Accessing a Windows 7 shared printer from a computer running Windows XP requires that you first install the Windows XP drivers for it, then add it as a shared network printer on your Windows XP computers.

- In order to share files from Windows Vista with other computers, you need to configure your network and sharing settings correctly.

- Accessing a Windows 7 shared printer from a computer running Windows Vista requires that you first install the Windows Vista drivers for it, then add it as a shared network printer on your Windows Vista computers.

Chapter at a Glance

Set the Workgroup on
all computers, **page 338**

AirPort

| AirPort | TCP/IP | DNS | WINS | 802.1X | Proxies | Ethernet |

NetBIOS Name: MACBOOKPRO–BAC4   MACBOOKPRO–BAC4 is
                                       currently being used.
Workgroup: workgroup
WINS Servers:

+ −

?

Connect to Windows 7
shared folders, **page 348**

Connect to Server

Server Address:

smb://192.168.1.5   +   ⊙▾

Favorite Servers:

▸

?   Remove   Browse   Connect

☐ Share files and folders using AFP
File Sharing: Off

☐ Share files and folders using FTP

Warning: FTP user names and passwords are not encrypted.

☑ Share files and folders using SMB (Windows)

When you enable SMB sharing for a user account, you must enter
the password for that account. Sharing files with some Windows
computers requires storing the Windows user's account
password on this computer in a less s

Configure Mac OS X
file sharing settings,
page 339

On	Account
☑	Jack Busch
☐	jer
☐	jerry
☐	new
☑	win7

?

Add Printer

Default Fax IP Windows Advanced   Q
                                             Search

Type: LPD/LPR Host or Printer   ▢

Device: Another Device   ▢

URL: lpd://192.168.1.5/shared

Name: Shared on EEE–PC

Location:

Print Using: Generic PostScript Printer   ▢

Install a Windows 7 shared
printer in Mac OS X,
page 356

Add

11 Sharing Between Mac OS X and Windows 7 Computers

In this chapter, you will learn how to

- ✔ Set the workgroup on your Mac OS X.
- ✔ Set up Mac OS X to share with Windows 7.
- ✔ Access OS X shared folders from Windows 7 computers.
- ✔ Set up Windows 7 to share with OS X.
- ✔ Access Windows 7 shared folders from OS X computers.
- ✔ Access a Windows 7 shared printer from OS X.
- ✔ Install a Windows 7 shared printer in Mac OS X.

Sharing folders from Mac OS X with Windows 7 computers has never been easier. Thanks to OS X's built-in support for the Microsoft Server Message Block (SMB) Protocol, allowing read and write access to Windows 7 computers can be done with just a few tweaks in the Mac's System Preferences. The SMB Protocol is designed to provide easy network sharing capabilities so that people can access files, folders, printers, and other devices over the nodes of a network.

In this chapter, you will first learn how to set up Mac OS X so that you can share folders with your Windows 7 computers. Then, you will learn how to access these shared folders and how to access a Windows 7 shared printer from Mac OS X so that you can print the files you need.

> **Practice Files** You can use any of your files and folders on your Mac and Windows 7 computer to complete the exercises in this chapter. Until you get the hang of it, it is best not to use any important files. Also, back up the files and folders you are about to use, just to make sure you don't lose them by mistake.

Setting the Workgroup on Your OS X Computer

In order to share files and folders between computers running different operating systems— and without too much hassle—it is best to set the same workgroup on all of them. By default, the workgroup set on Mac OS X is named "Workgroup", which is the same as in Windows 7 and many other operating systems. However, there may be cases when it is set differently for various reasons, or you just need to change it to another name.

In this exercise, you will learn how to change the workgroup on your Mac OS X computer.

SET UP On the computer running Mac OS X, open System Preferences.

1. Open the **Network** pane.

   A window that lists your network devices opens.

2. Select the network device you are using to connect to your home network.

3. Click **Advanced**.

A window showing the properties of that device opens.

4. Click the **WINS** tab.

5. In the field labeled **Workgroup**, type the name of the workgroup that you want your Mac OS X computer to join.

6. Click **OK**.

✖ CLEAN UP Close the Network and System Preferences windows.

Setting Up Mac OS X to Share with Windows 7

Setting up network sharing settings in Mac OS X so that they work with Windows 7 computers is not a very difficult task. It involves just a few steps and, with a bit of attention, you can get it right from the first try. Just as Windows 7 has its network and sharing settings in the Network And Sharing Center, OS X has them in the System Preferences panel.

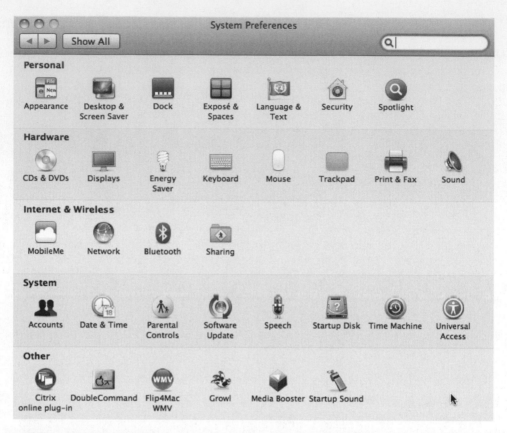

In this exercise, you will learn how to customize the network sharing settings in OS X so that they are compatible with Windows 7 computers.

SET UP Open System Preferences.

1. In the **Internet & Wireless** section, click **Sharing**.

   The Sharing window opens.

2. Select the check box next to **File Sharing**.

   With this option selected, OS X displays the IP Address for your Mac.

IP address

Sharing

Show All

Computer Name: jack-macbook

Computers on your local network can access your computer at: jack-macbook.local

Edit...

On	Service
☐	DVD or CD Sharing
☐	Screen Sharing
☑	File Sharing
☐	Printer Sharing
☐	Scanner Sharing
☐	Web Sharing
☐	Remote Login
☐	Remote Management
☐	Remote Apple Events
☐	Xgrid Sharing
☐	Internet Sharing
☐	Bluetooth Sharing

⊖ **Windows Sharing: On**

Windows users can access shared folders on this computer, and administrators all volumes, at smb://
192.168.1.6.

Options...

Shared Folders: **Users:**

+ −   + −

🔓 Click the lock to prevent further changes.   ⑦

Important Take note of the IP address of your Mac. You might need to know it in case of problems or when trying to map the Mac shared folders on other computers.

3. Click the **Options** button.

The Options window opens.

Share files and folders using AFP
File Sharing: Off

Share files and folders using FTP
Warning: FTP user names and passwords are not encrypted.

☑ Share files and folders using SMB (Windows)

When you enable SMB sharing for a user account, you must enter the password for that account. Sharing files with some Windows computers requires storing the Windows user's account password on this computer in a less secure manner.

On	Account
☑	Jack Busch
☐	jer
☐	jerry
☐	new
☑	win7

⑦   (Done)

4. Select the check box next to **Share files and folders using SMB (Windows)**.

5. Choose which accounts will have sharing enabled.

   Important You will need to be logged in under one of these accounts for Windows computers to access your Mac.

6. Click **Done**.

   You are returned to the Sharing window.

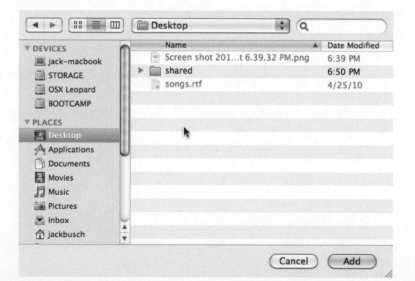

7. To add a folder for sharing, click the **+** button below **Shared Folders**.
The Finder opens.

8. Browse to the folder that you'd like to share with Windows computers, then click **Add**.

After clicking Add, you are returned to the Sharing window, in which you can set up read or write permissions to the shared folder.

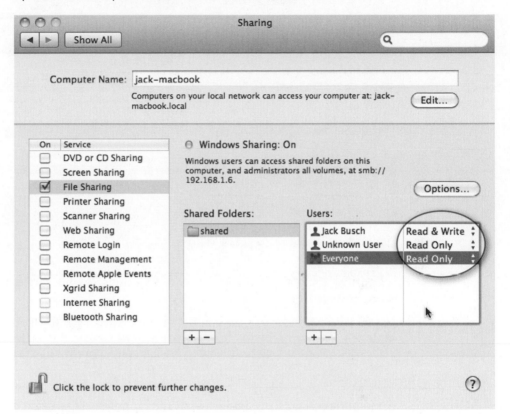

9. In the **Users** section, click in the right column, alongside the user for which you want to customize sharing permissions.

A menu opens in which you can choose one of the available sharing permissions settings for that user.

10. Select the permission level you desire for that user: **Read & Write**, **Read Only**, **Write Only (Drop Box)**, or **No Access**.

   Tip For convenience, assign Read and/or Write permissions to the Everyone user. By doing this, Windows 7 users won't need to type a user name and password to connect to the Mac shared folder. However, this means that everybody on your home network has access to your shared folder. If you don't want this, it is safer to allow access only to certain users.

11. When done adding shared folders and setting permissions, close the **Sharing** window.

   Tip You can add multiple folders, each with different read and write permissions. This is useful, for example, if you'd like to set up a Write Only drop box (where multiple users can turn in assignments or documents into a single folder but other users cannot read them) or a Read Only folder for reference.

You are now sharing the selected files with the other computers on your network.

✗ CLEAN UP Close System Preferences. If you want to access the shared folders from your Windows computers, remain logged on with one of the user accounts for which you enabled those shared folders.

Accessing OS X Shared Folders from Windows 7 Computers

Once you've completed setting up your Mac, your Windows 7 computers should be able to access the shared folders under Network In Windows Explorer. If you have allowed read/write access for everyone, or if your credentials for your Macintosh are the same as for your Windows 7 (for instance, exact same user name and password), there shouldn't be any extra steps involved. You just need to be logged on under the user account you configured for file sharing on your Macintosh. If your Mac doesn't show up immediately, wait for a few seconds, and then click the refresh button.

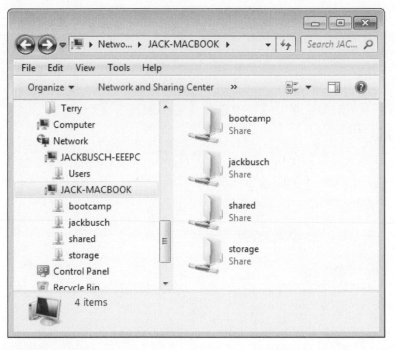

Troubleshooting If you have trouble getting the Mac to show up under Network in Windows Explorer, it is recommended to create a network drive. In most cases, this helps your Windows 7 computer to find your Mac shared folders the next time you access them. The instructions on how to map a network drive are found in the "Mapping Network Drives" section in Chapter 7, "Sharing Libraries and Folders."

Setting Up Windows 7 to Share with OS X

In order to access Windows 7 shared folders from your Mac OS X computer, you first need to set the network location in Windows 7 to Home Network.

See Also For more information on network locations and how to set them, see the "Setting the Network Location" section in Chapter 4, "Creating the Network."

Also, you need to make sure that the workgroup is set the same for both Mac OS X and Windows 7 computers.

See Also For information on how to change the Workgroup on Windows 7 computers, see the "Setting the Workgroup" section in Chapter 4.

If these settings are made, your Mac OS X should be able to easily access Windows 7 shared folders on your home network.

Accessing Windows 7 Shared Folders from OS X Computers

Once you've completed setting up your Windows 7 computer, your Mac OS X computers should pick up the shared folders. In order to access them, you need to use the Connect To Server functionality.

In this exercise, you will learn how to access Windows 7 shared folders from Mac OS X.

SET UP Open a Finder window.

1. In the **Go** menu, select **Connect to Server**.

   A Connect To Server window opens.

   ```
   ○ ○ ○              Connect to Server

   Server Address:
   ┌────────────────────────────────────┐  ┌───┐  ┌─────┐
   │ smb://192.168.1.5                  │  │ + │  │ ⊙ ▾ │
   └────────────────────────────────────┘  └───┘  └─────┘
   Favorite Servers:
   ┌────────────────────────────────────────────────────┐
   │                                                    │
   │                                                    │
   │                                                    │
   └────────────────────────────────────────────────────┘
   ┌─┐  ┌──────────┐                ┌────────┐  ┌─────────┐
   │?│  │  Remove  │                │ Browse │  │ Connect │
   └─┘  └──────────┘                └────────┘  └─────────┘
   ```

2. In the **Server Address** field, type **smb://** followed by the IP Address of the Windows 7 computer to which you want to connect.

3. Click **Connect**.

   A window opens that asks for a user name and password to connect to the Windows 7 computer.

   ```
   Enter your name and password for the server
   "192.168.1.5".

   Connect as:  ○ Guest
                ● Registered User

         Name:  7tutorials

     Password:  ••••••••

   ☐ Remember this password in my keychain

                          ┌────────┐  ┌─────────┐
                          │ Cancel │  │ Connect │
                          └────────┘  └─────────┘
   ```

4. Enter your Windows 7 user name and password.

Note These are the same credentials you would use when logging on to your Windows 7 user account.

5. Select the **Remember this password in my keychain** check box.

This will set your OS X to remember the user name and password so that it won't ask these details each time you connect to the Windows 7 shared folders.

6. Click **Connect**.

This opens a window in which you are asked which volumes you would like to mount. Your choices consist of all the shared folders on your Windows 7 computer.

7. Choose the shared folder that you'd like to mount.

Tip You can mount multiple volumes by holding the **Shift** key as you select each folder name.

8. When you're finished selecting the shared folders, click **OK**.

This opens a window in which you see your Windows 7 machine in two places: in the left sidebar under Shared, and listed with your other volumes when you click your Macintosh's name under Devices.

Tip Clicking the icon for your Windows 7 machine (under *Shared*) displays the other shared folders that you did not mount. You can browse them and access them as if they were mounted.

You can browse the contents of your Windows 7 shared folders just like they were local drives. You should also have the same read/write privileges as the user account you used to log on to the shared folders.

 CLEAN UP Close the Finder.

Automatically Mount Your Windows 7 Shared Folders on OS X

If you want to forgo the entire process of mounting your Windows 7 shared folder each time you reboot, one great trick is to add it to the login items on OS X. This saves you the trouble of having to mount it each time you want to connect to it.

In this exercise, you will learn how to set your Mac OS X computer to automatically mount your Windows 7 computer upon login.

SET UP Open System Preferences.

1. Open the **Accounts** pane.

   This opens the Accounts window. Here, you can see your account, plus any others defined on your OS X computer.

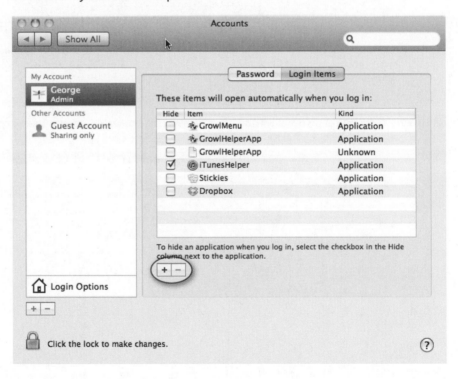

2. Click the **Login Items** tab.

3. Click the **+** sign, located roughly in the center of the window.

A Finder window appears.

4. In the **Shared** section, select the Windows 7 computer.

5. Select the shared folder you want to mount.

6. Click **Add**.

You are returned to the Accounts window.

7. Select the check box beside the Windows 7 shared folder.

8. Close the Accounts window.

The next time you reboot, Mac OS X automatically mounts the selected volume.

CLEAN UP Close System Preferences and all open documents and applications and reboot your Mac OS X computer.

Accessing a Windows 7 Shared Printer from OS X

Snow Leopard OS X 10.6 features a Windows tab in its Add A Printer dialog box. There's only one problem: It doesn't work very well, at least not for shared printers connected to Windows 7. Fortunately, you can still print to a shared Windows 7 printer from a Mac OS X computer by using a moderately simple workaround. The trick is to use the Line Printer Daemon/Line Printer Remote (LPD/LPR) protocol.

Enabling the Correct Printing Services in Windows 7

Before you can install a Windows 7 shared printer, you need to enable a few additional printing services. Otherwise, you'll have problems and won't be able to access the printer.

In this exercise, you will learn how enable the required Windows 7 printing services so that you can install your Windows 7 shared printer from Mac OS X.

 SET UP Install the printer on your Windows 7 computer and ensure that it prints correctly.

1. Type **windows features** in the **Start** menu search box.

    A list of search results displays.

    Control Panel (7)
    - Turn Windows features on or off
    - Get more features with a new edition of Windows 7
    - Find out what's new in Windows 7
    - Getting Started
    - Add gadgets to the desktop
    - Get more gadgets online

    Documents (42)
    - How-to Add No Reply All and No Forward to Outlook 2007 and...
    - batch1_reviews.docx
    - batch1_articles.docx
    - Project I_V1_092410.doc
    - Jack Reviews_V1_092410.doc
    - holidayfiestaware.xml

    Files (1)
    - pressurecooking.org and disasterpreparedness.net.zip

    See more results

    | Windows Features | ✕ | Shut down ▶ |

2. Click the **Turn Windows features on or off** search result.

    The Windows Features window opens.

Windows Features

Turn Windows features on or off

To turn a feature on, select its check box. To turn a feature off, clear its check box. A filled box means that only part of the feature is turned on.

- ⊞ ☐ 📁 Internet Information Services
- ☐ 📁 Internet Information Services Hostable Web Core
- ⊞ ☑ 📁 Media Features
- ⊞ ◼ 📁 Microsoft .NET Framework 3.5.1
- ⊞ ☐ 📁 Microsoft Message Queue (MSMQ) Server
- ⊟ ◼ 📁 Print and Document Services
  - ☑ 📁 Internet Printing Client
  - ☑ 📁 LPD Print Service
  - ☑ 📁 LPR Port Monitor
  - ☐ 📁 Scan Management
  - ☑ 📁 Windows Fax and Scan
- ☐ 📁 RAS Connection Manager Administration Kit (CMAK)

OK   Cancel

Tip Another way to display this window is to go to Control Panel -> Programs -> Programs and Features -> Turn Windows features on or off.

3. Scroll down to **Print and Document Services**, and then expand it by clicking the + sign directly beside it.

4. Select the **LPD Print Service** and **LPR Port Monitor** check boxes.

5. Click **OK**.

✖ **CLEAN UP** Wait a few seconds while Windows 7 installs these services.

Installing a Windows 7 Shared Printer in OS X

Now that you have Windows 7 set up correctly, you can finally install the network shared printer from Windows 7 on your Mac OS X computer.

In this exercise, you will learn how to install a Windows 7 shared printer in Mac OS X.

➡ **SET UP** Install the printer on your Windows 7 computer, ensure that it prints correctly, and share it with your home network.

See Also For information on how to share a printer with your network in Windows 7, read the "Sharing a Printer with Your Network" section in Chapter 8, "Sharing and Working with Devices."

1. Open **System Preferences**.

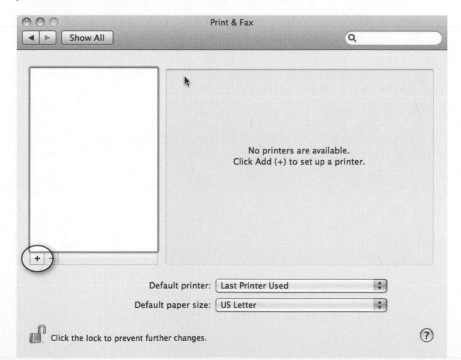

2. In the **Hardware** section, click **Print & Fax**.

This opens the Print & Fax window, which contains the list of currently installed printers and fax devices.

3. Click the **+** sign (located at the left side of the window).

The Add Printer dialog box opens.

4. Right-click the toolbar of the window.

Tip If you have a single-button mouse, right-click means you need to hold down the Ctrl key before you click your mouse button.

5. Choose **Customize Toolbar**.

This opens a window in which you can customize the items placed on the toolbar.

6. Drag the **Advanced** icon to the toolbar.

7. Click **Done**.

8. Click **Advanced**.

   A list of advanced configuration parameters opens.

9. In the **Type** field, choose **LPD/LPR Host or Printer**.

10. Leave the **Device** field set to **Another Device**.

11. In the **URL** field, type **lpd://HOSTIPADDRESS/SHARENAME**, replacing your Windows 7 computer's IP address for *HOSTIPADDRESS* and the share name of your printer for *SHARENAME*.

12. Enter anything you'd like for the **Name** field.

This can be different from the actual share name of your printer. Make it something descriptive, such as **Shared HP C4700 on Win7**.

13. Leave the **Location** field blank.

14. In the **Print Using** field, select a printer.

Important Selecting a printer is tricky. It may require some trial and error to get the best results. Ideally, you should choose the driver specific to your printer, but not all manufacturer printer drivers support LPD/LPR network printing. If the manufacturer's driver doesn't work, try a Gutenprint version for your model, if it exists. (Gutenprint comes pre-installed with OS X 10.6. You can also download Gutenprint drivers from *www.sourceforge.net*.) If those both fail, try the Generic PostScript Printer driver. The Generic PostScript Printer driver (or one of the other generic Apple drivers) works for most printers, but for some, it causes erratic behavior—for example, printing 10 blank pages for no reason.

15. Click **Add** when you have finished.

You might be asked to set printer options.

> **Installable Options**
> **192.168.1.3**
>
> ---
> Make sure your printer's options are accurately shown here so you can take full advantage of them. For information on your printer and its optional hardware, check the documentation that came with it.
> ---
>
> ☐ Duplex Printing Unit
>
>   (Cancel)   (Continue)

16. Configure the printer and click **Continue**.

 **CLEAN UP** Close the Print & Fax window, and then close System Preferences.

The Windows 7 shared printer is now installed and you can start using it from any application. It will appear just like a local printer when you bring up the Print dialog. When you click Print, the document should be printed from the Windows 7 shared printer.

This workaround is one of the easiest ways to print to a Windows 7 shared printer from a Mac OS X computer, and pending a perfect solution from either Apple or Microsoft, it's likely the best way to share a printer between a Mac OS X and Windows 7 computer.

Key Points

- To share files and folders between Mac OS X and Windows 7 with less hassle, make sure that your home computers share the same workgroup.

- In order to share files from Mac OS X with other computers, you need to configure your File Sharing settings.

- Accessing a Windows 7 shared printer from OS X requires you to install additional printing services on Windows 7.

Chapter at a Glance

Install the sharing service in Ubuntu, **page 364**

```
#   smb.conf.master  and create the "real" config file with
# testparm -s smb.conf.master >smb.conf
# This minimizes the size of the really used smb.conf file
# which, according to the Samba Team, impacts performance
# However, use this with caution if your smb.conf file contains nested
# "include" statements. See Debian bug #483187 for a case
# where using a master file is not a good idea.
#

#========================= Global Settings ==============================

[global]

## Browsing/Identification ###

# Change this to the workgroup/NT-domain name your Samba server will part of
    workgroup = WORKGROUP-NEW

# server string is the equivalent of the NT Description field
    server string = %h server (Samba, Ubuntu)

# Windows Internet Name Serving Support Section:
# WINS Support - Tells the NMBD component of Samba to enable its WINS Se
```

Change the workgroup in the Samba configuration file, **page 368**

Set the correct sharing settings for each folder you want to share, **page 370**

Type the login details correctly when accessing an Ubuntu shared folder from Windows 7, **page 373**

12 Sharing Between Ubuntu Linux and Windows 7 Computers

In this chapter, you will learn how to

✔ Install the sharing service in Ubuntu Linux.

✔ Set the Workgroup to match other computers on your home network.

✔ Share folders.

✔ Access Ubuntu Linux shared folders from Windows 7.

✔ Access Windows 7 shared folders.

✔ Access a Windows 7 shared printer.

✔ Mount a Windows 7 shared partition or folder.

Sharing files, folders, and printers between Ubuntu Linux and Windows 7 computers is a reasonably simple procedure. And even though you are required to install a special Ubuntu service to make things work, it is not difficult, and with a bit of attention, all settings can be configured correctly in one go.

In this chapter, you will first learn how to set up Ubuntu Linux so that you can share folders with your Windows 7 computers. Then, you will learn how to access these shared folders and how to access a Windows 7 shared printer from Ubuntu Linux so you can print the files you need. At the end of the chapter, you will learn how to mount a Windows 7 shared folder or partition in Ubuntu Linux to provide easy access.

> **Practice Files** You won't need any practice files to complete the exercises in this chapter. Until you get the hang of it, it is best not to use any important files. Also, back up the files and folders you are about to use, just to make sure you don't lose them by mistake.

Installing the Sharing Service in Ubuntu Linux

Before you can start exchanging files and folders between a computer running Ubuntu Linux and computers running other operating systems, you need to install the sharing service. The service is not a part of a default installation of Ubuntu Linux, and it can be installed using several methods, some more complex than others.

In this exercise, you will learn how to install the sharing service in Ubuntu Linux using the most visual and easy-to-follow procedure.

→ **SET UP** Open the Home Folder, which is located in the Places menu.

1. By default, the user account you are logged on with is selected. A list with the folders you own is opened. Right-click any folder from this list.

    This opens a contextual list of possible actions.

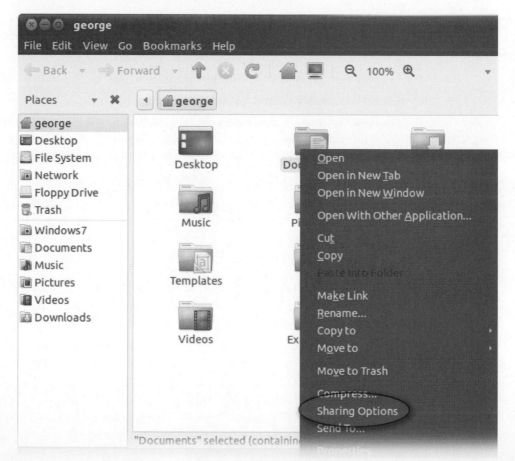

2. Click **Sharing Options**.

The Folder Sharing window opens.

3. Select the check box beside **Share this folder**.

Immediately, Ubuntu Linux displays a warning window, stating that the sharing service is not installed.

Important If you do not receive this warning, it means the sharing service is already installed. In such a scenario, close the Folder Sharing window and ignore all the other steps described in this exercise.

4. Click **Install service**.

You are asked to enter your password.

Enter your password to perform administrative tasks

The application 'Synaptic Package Manager' lets you modify essential parts of your system.

Password:

Cancel   OK

Note If you are using an Ubuntu Linux Live CD, you might not receive this prompt. In this case, simply skip step 5.

5. Type your user account password, then click **OK**.

The installation process begins. After a few seconds, you are notified that all changes have been successfully applied.

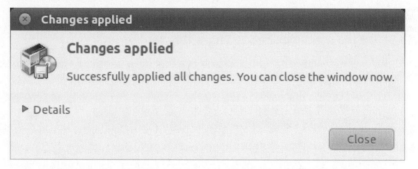

Changes applied

Changes applied

Successfully applied all changes. You can close the window now.

▶ Details

Close

6. Click the **Close** button.

Ubuntu Linux asks you to restart your session.

Restart your session

You need to restart your session in order to enable sharing.

Close   Restart session

7. Save any open files you might have, then click **Restart session**.

After the restart, the sharing service is installed and fully functioning.

 CLEAN UP The folder you tried to share at the start of this exercise was not shared. To start sharing files and folders, follow the instructions detailed in the "Sharing Folders in Ubuntu Linux" section on page 369.

Setting the Workgroup on Your Ubuntu Linux Computer

In order to share files and folders between computers running different operating systems—and without too much hassle—it is best to set the same workgroup on all of them. By default, the workgroup set on Ubuntu Linux is named "Workgroup," which is the same as in Windows 7, Mac OS X, and many other operating systems. However, there may be times when it is set differently, or you just need to change it to another name.

Important Keep in mind that you cannot change the workgroup if you have not first enabled the sharing service in Ubuntu Linux. To learn how to enable it, see the previous section, "Installing the Sharing Service in Ubuntu Linux," on page 364.

In this exercise, you will learn how to change the workgroup on your Ubuntu Linux.

➡ **SET UP** On the computer running Ubuntu Linux, open the Terminal.

1. In the Terminal window, type **sudo gedit /etc/samba/smb.conf** and press **Enter**.

Ubuntu requests that you enter your user account password.

Note If you have used the Terminal prior to this exercise, you won't be requested to enter your user account password.

2. Type your user account password and press **Enter**.

This opens the Samba configuration file in a gedit window.

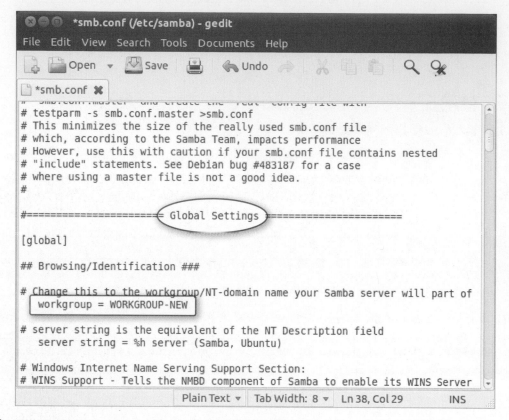

3. Find the workgroup setting in the **Global Settings** section of the configuration file.

4. Change the value of the workgroup field to match the name of the workgroup that you want your Ubuntu Linux to join.

5. Click **Save**.

 CLEAN UP Save any open files, then restart your Ubuntu Linux computer.

After the restart, Ubuntu Linux joins the specified workgroup.

Sharing Folders in Ubuntu Linux

Once you have enabled the sharing service and set up the workgroup to be the same on all your home computers, you can successfully start sharing files, folders, or printers.

In this exercise, you will learn how to share folders in Ubuntu Linux with the computers on your home network.

SET UP Open the Home Folder, which is located in the Places menu.

1. Right-click any folder.

   This opens a contextual list of possible actions.

2. Click **Sharing Options**.

   The Folder Sharing window opens.

3. Select the check box beside **Share this folder**.

4. In the **Share name** field, type the name you want to use for the shared folder.

5. In the **Comment** field, type any comments you might have. If you don't have any, there is no problem in leaving this field empty.

6. If you want to allow people who are accessing this folder to be able to add and remove files or folders within it, select the **Allow others to create and delete files in this folder** check box.

7. If you want to allow everyone to access this folder, including people without a user account defined on the Ubuntu Linux computer, select the **Guest access (for people without a user account)** check box. If this option is not selected, each time someone tries to access the shared folder, that person will be required to type a user account and password defined on the Ubuntu Linux computer.

8. When you have finished configuring all the settings, click **Create Share**.

   If you selected the **Allow others to create and delete files in this folder**, option, you will receive a prompt alerting you that Nautilus needs to add some permissions to your folder in order to share it.

9. Click **Add the permissions automatically**.

The folder is now shared with the network, based on the settings you specified.

✖ **CLEAN UP** Repeat the procedure for any other folders you want to share with the other computers on your home network.

Important This procedure for sharing folders works only if you are sharing folders found in the Home folder. If you try to use this procedure to share folders found in other locations, such as system locations, it will not work, and you will receive the following error message: "net usershare returned error 255: net usershare add: cannot share path as we are restricted to only sharing directories we own." To share folders other than the ones your user account owns, you need to go through a rather complicated procedure that involves editing configuration files. Also, doing this adds security risks. The security recommendation is to share only folders that your user account owns.

Accessing Ubuntu Shared Folders from Windows 7 Computers

Once you've completed setting up your Ubuntu Linux computer, your Windows 7 computers should pick up the shared folders. Accessing them is a pretty easy task.

In this exercise, you will learn how to access your Ubuntu shared folders from Windows 7.

SET UP Open the Computer window or Windows Explorer.

1. Go to the **Network** section.

    This opens the list with all the computers in your home network that are turned on at that moment and that Windows 7 is able to detect.

Note You can have additional computers turned on, but it is possible that Windows 7 is not able to detect them due to incompatible network and sharing settings.

2. Double-click the Ubuntu computer you want to access.

A list of all the shared folders and devices on that computer is displayed.

3. Double-click the folder you want to open.

If you have set up your shared folder to not allow Guest access, then you are prompted to enter a user account and password that is recognized and has permissions on the Ubuntu Linux computer.

4. In the top input field, first type the name of the Ubuntu computer, then type \ (backslash character) followed by the name of the user account (do not include any spaces between the name of the Ubuntu computer, the backslash character, and the name of the user account).

    As an example, if the computer name is UBUNTU and the user account is named george, you need to type **UBUNTU\george**.

5. In the second field, type the password of the user account.

6. If you don't want to be asked to type the user account and password each time you access the shared folders on this computer, select the **Remember my credentials** check box.

7. Click **OK**.

    This reveals the contents of the shared folder.

You can now work with the contents of the shared folder, according to the permission levels set on the Ubuntu Linux computer.

 CLEAN UP When done, close the Computer or Windows Explorer window.

Accessing Windows 7 Shared Folders from Ubuntu Computers

Once you've completed setting up your Windows 7 computer, your Ubuntu Linux computers should pick up the shared folders. In order to access them, you need to use the Connect To Server functionality.

In this exercise, you will learn how to access Windows 7 shared folders from Ubuntu Linux.

➡ **SET UP** Open a Connect To Server window.

1. In the **Service type** field, select **Windows share**.

2. In the **Server** field, type the name of the Windows 7 computer.

3. In the **User Name** field, type the name of a user account defined on the Windows 7 computer.

4. If you want to bookmark this computer and its shared folders, select the **Add bookmark** check box, then type the name you want to use in the **Bookmark name** field.

5. When you have finished, click the **Connect** button.

   You are now asked to type the password for the user account that you entered in step 3.

6. Type the password.

7. If you don't want to enter it each time you access the shared folders of this Windows 7 computer, choose the **Remember forever** option.

8. Click the **Connect** button.

This opens a list with all the shared folders.

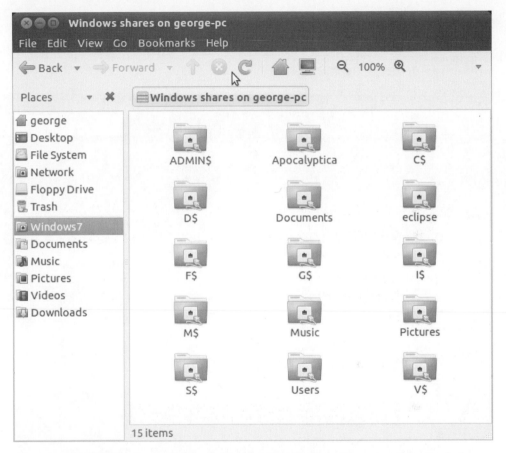

Tip You can identify the partitions defined on the Windows 7 computer by the $ sign following the letter (for example, C$, D$, E$). Unfortunately, you won't be able to access them at all. You can open only the shared folders.

You can now work with the shared folders from the Windows 7 computer.

Tip If you want to access the shared folders from the same Windows 7 computer, but you haven't made a bookmark, go to Places -> Network. You will find the shared folders there.

❌ **CLEAN UP** Repeat the procedure for all Windows 7 computers you want to access.

Accessing a Windows 7 Shared Printer from Ubuntu Computers

Accessing a network printer shared from a Windows 7 computer requires a bit of work and involves installing Ubuntu Linux drivers for the particular printer. In this exercise, you will learn how this process works.

 SET UP Start the Windows 7 computer and turn on the shared network printer that you want to share with Ubuntu Linux computers.

1. Open the **System** menu.

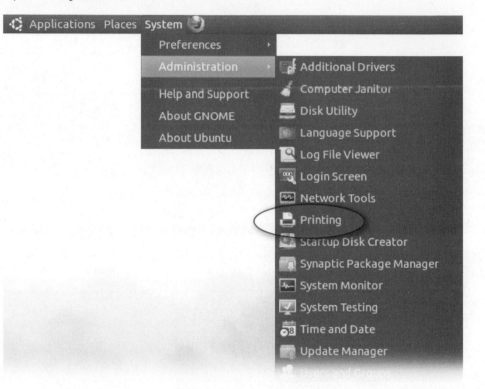

2. Go to **Administration -> Printing**.

   This opens the Printing window, in which you can see the printers identified on your computer and the home network.

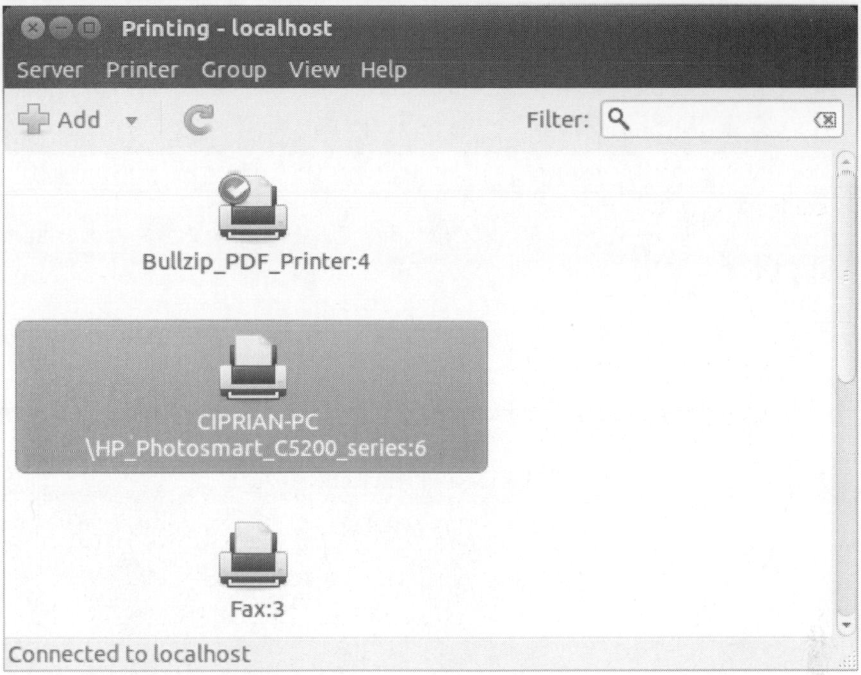

Printing - localhost

Server   Printer   Group   View   Help

Add

Filter:

Bullzip_PDF_Printer:4

CIPRIAN-PC
\HP_Photosmart_C5200_series:6

Fax:3

Connected to localhost

3. Locate and right-click the network printer that you want to access.

The contextual menu for the printer opens.

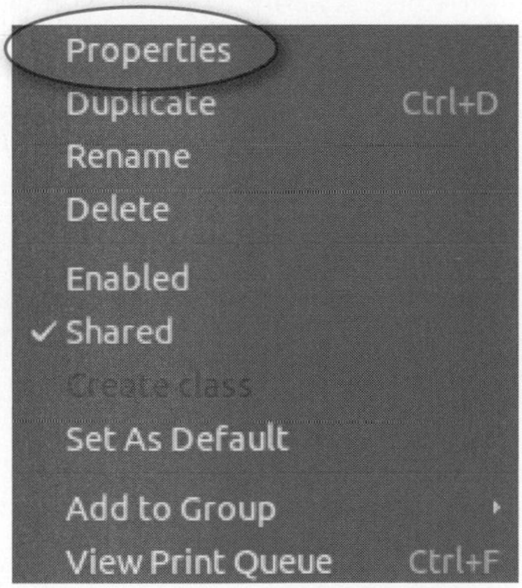

Properties

Duplicate   Ctrl+D

Rename

Delete

Enabled

✓ Shared

Create class

Set As Default

Add to Group   ▸

View Print Queue   Ctrl+F

4. Click **Properties**.

The **Printer Properties** window opens for the selected printer.

5. Look at the **Make and Model** field. If it's listed as **Local Raw Printer**, it means that the appropriate printer driver is not installed. If the printer's actual make and model information is displayed, then the driver is already present and you can ignore the following steps. The network printer will work on your Ubuntu Linux computer.

6. Click the **Change** button found on the right side of the **Make and Model** field.

The Change Driver window opens.

Change Driver

Choose Driver

- ● Select printer from database
- ○ Provide PPD file
- ○ Search for a printer driver to download

The foomatic printer database contains various manufacturer provided PostScript Printer Description (PPD) files and also can generate PPD files for a large number of (non PostScript) printers. But in general manufacturer provided PPD files provide better access to the specific features of the printer.

Makes
Gestetner
Heidelberg
Hitachi
HP
IBM
Imagen
Imagistics
InfoPrint

Cancel   Forward

7. Select the manufacturer of the printer you want to access. In our example, it is **HP**.

8. Click **Forward**.

   A list opens that shows all the models of printers for which Ubuntu Linux has drivers.

9. Find the correct model of printer and select it. For this example it is **Photosmart c5200**.

   In the drivers section, you will see another list with available drivers.

10. If you are presented with more than one version of a driver, select the one with "cups" in the name. CUPS stands for Common Unix Printing System, and these drivers generally tend to work better.

11. Click **Forward**.

    You are asked if you want to transfer the current settings.

Change Driver

Existing Settings

Try to transfer the current settings

⦿ Use the new PPD (Postscript Printer Description) as is.

This way all current option settings will be lost. The default settings of the new PPD will be used.

○ Try to copy the option settings over from the old PPD.

This is done by assuming that options with the same name do have the same meanin Settings of options that are not present in the new PPD will be lost and options only present in the new PPD will be set to default.

Back   Cancel   Forward

12. Because the printer is not yet installed, there are no true settings to transfer. Therefore, select **Use the new PPD (Postscript Printer Descriptions) as is**.

13. Click the **Forward** button.

You are now asked about additional options to enable or configure. The list depends on the printer model. For our HP Photosmart c5200 model, we are only allowed to install the Duplexer. The Duplexer is a feature which allows printing on both sides of the paper.

Change Driver

Installable Options

This driver supports additional hardware that may be installed in the printer.

☑ Duplexer Installed

Back   Cancel   Apply

14. Install and configure the options you desire. When you have finished, click **Apply**.

You are taken back to the Printer Properties window.

⊗   **Printer Properties - 'CIPRIAN-PC\HP_Photosmart_C5200_series:6' on localhost**

Settings	**Settings**
Policies	Description: \\CIPRIAN-PC\HP Photosmart C5200 series
Access Control	Location:
Installable Options	Device URI: tpvmlp://CIPRIAN-PC\HP_Photos [Change...]
Printer Options	Make and Model: HP Photosmart c5200 Series, hp... [Change...]
Job Options	Printer State: Idle
Ink/Toner Levels	**Tests and Maintenance**
	[Print Test Page] [Print Self-Test Page] [Clean Print Heads]

[Apply]   [Cancel]   [OK]

Tip If you look at the Make and Model field, you can see that now it has the name of the printer you just installed. If you have a different result, close the Printer Properties window and start again, carefully following the steps described in this exercise.

15. To test the printer, click the **Print Test Page** button.

You are informed that the test page was submitted.

⊗

ⓘ   **Submitted**

Test page submitted as job 1

[OK]

---

16. Click **OK**.

If a test page prints, your setup is correct. You can now use the network printer from Ubuntu Linux.

 CLEAN UP Close the Printer Preferences window.

Mounting Windows 7 Shared Partitions and Folders in Ubuntu

If you want to have even easier access to Windows 7 shared partitions and folders, it can be a good idea to have them mounted permanently each time you log on to Ubuntu Linux. The procedure you need to follow for mounting them is slightly more complex. However, once done, you will save time accessing shared partitions and folders, and you will find it much more convenient to do so.

In this exercise, you will learn how to mount a Windows 7 shared partition or folder in Ubuntu Linux.

➡ **SET UP** Open the Terminal.

1. In the Terminal window, type **sudo mkdir /media/*mountname*** and press **Enter**.

   Replace *mountname* with the name you want to give the folder you want to mount. In our example, we wanted to call it music; therefore, we typed **sudo mkdir /media/music**.

   Ubuntu will request that you enter your user account password.

2. Type your user account password, then press **Enter**.

3. Type **sudo gedit /etc/fstab**, then press **Enter**.

   This opens the fstab file in a gedit window.

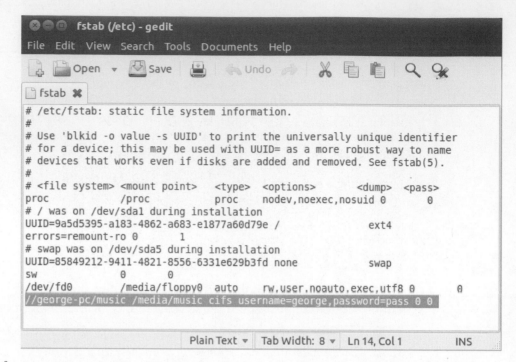

4. Go to the end of the file and type the following line: **//servername/sharename /media/mountname cifs username=myusername,password=mypassword 0 0.** Replace the following fields:

- **servername**   Type the name of the Windows 7 computer sharing the folder or partition you want to mount. In our example, it is george-pc.

- **sharename**   Supply the name of the shared folder or partition as it is on the Windows 7 system. In our example, it is named music.

- **mountname**   Provide the name of the folder you just created in step 1. The names must be the same. In our example, it is named music.

- **myusername**   This is the name of the user account defined on the Windows 7 computer. This user account must have access permissions to the shared folder or partition. In our example, it is named george.

- **mypassword**   Type the password of the user account defined on the Windows 7 computer. In our example, it is pass.

In our example, the whole line looks like this: **//george-pc/music /media/music cifs username=george,password=pass 0 0.**

Important Make sure you don't type any spaces between the username, the comma following it, and the password. The setup won't work if you don't insert the proper number of spaces in the correct locations.

5. When you have finished, click **Save**.

6. Close the gedit window.

You are now back to the Terminal window.

7. Type **sudo mount –a**, and then press **Enter**.

This causes the mounted folder or partition to appear on your Ubuntu desktop, with the name equal to the *sharename* field you entered in step 6.

The Windows 7 shared folder or partition is now mounted each time you log on to your Ubuntu Linux computer.

Tip To remove the mounted folder or partition, open the Terminal and follow step 3. Remove the line you added in step 4. Then, follow steps 5 and 6, and skip step 7. The next time you reboot your Ubuntu Linux computer, the folder or partition will no longer be mounted.

Key Points

- The sharing service is not installed by default in Ubuntu Linux; you need to manually install it yourself.

- The workgroup can be changed in the Samba configuration file.

- When sharing a folder, don't forget to set the access permissions as you want to have them.

- When accessing an Ubuntu shared folder from Windows 7, pay attention to the way you type the user account and password.

- You can access Windows 7 shared folders by using the Connect to Server functionality.

- When accessing a Windows 7 shared printer, you need to install the Ubuntu Linux printer drivers for the particular printer.

- Mounting Windows 7 shared folders or partitions makes it easier to access them when you need to work with them.

Chapter at a Glance

How UAC Works

Application wants to run & receive administrative permissions

UAC initiates elevation prompt to user

User feedback requested. Elevate permissions to administrator?

Application launches as administrator --"Yes!"--

--"No!"-- Application does not run

Application is closed and administrator privileges are gone.

Use the User Account Control (UAC) security tool that's included in Windows Vista and Windows 7, **page 393**

Set Windows Update to be turned on automatically and to check for updates regularly, **page 400**

Protect your computer from unauthorized access from other computers on the network or the Internet using Windows Firewall, **page 428**

Check the status of your system and get alerts using the Action Center, **page 457**

13 Keeping the Network Secure

In this chapter, you will learn how to

- ✔ Configure User Account Control (UAC).
- ✔ Open Windows Update.
- ✔ Configure Windows Update settings.
- ✔ Check for and install updates manually.
- ✔ Restore hidden updates.
- ✔ Review your Windows update history.
- ✔ Remove installed updates.
- ✔ Open Windows Defender.
- ✔ Use Windows Defender.
- ✔ Turn off Windows Defender.
- ✔ Open the Windows Firewall.
- ✔ Turn the Windows Firewall on and off.
- ✔ Customize the list of allowed programs.
- ✔ Add new programs to the allowed list.
- ✔ Remove programs or disable rules from the allowed list.
- ✔ Create a new rule.
- ✔ Enable, disable, or delete an existing rule.
- ✔ Restore the Windows Firewall default settings.
- ✔ Protect your computer from viruses and other security threats.
- ✔ Use the Action Center.
- ✔ Open the Action Center and review its messages.
- ✔ Configure the list of messages displayed by the Action Center.

If you arrived at this stage, your home network is fully configured. You are able to connect to the other computers on your network and share files, folders, and devices. You can also stream your media over the network and the Internet. Simply put, you can finally take full advantage of the capabilities that your home network offers.

In order for everything to keep working at optimal levels, it's time for you to learn how to keep your network secure. This means a mix of enabling and using the right security tools that Windows 7 has to offer in addition to the installation of third-party security products.

In this chapter, you will first learn how to take advantage of important security tools provided by Windows 7: the User Account Control (UAC), Windows Update, Windows Defender, Windows Firewall, and the Action Center. You will also learn how to protect your computers from viruses. We will show you where to find the best security solutions available on the market via some great Internet Web sites, which are updated on a regular basis with the latest security tools and performance patches.

> **Practice Files** You won't need any practice files to complete the exercises in this chapter.

Understanding User Account Control

When Windows Vista was launched, User Account Control (UAC) was the most criticized and misunderstood feature. Even though it was very important for security, many people chose to disable it, subsequently exposing their systems to potential security risks. Many problems could have been avoided if people understood the benefits offered by UAC. In response to that criticism, Windows 7 brings further changes to what is in reality a very good feature.

In order to avoid further misunderstanding and to prevent people from exposing their computers to security risks, this section will explain UAC in detail and present the reasons why you should always keep it turned on.

What Is UAC?

UAC is a security feature of Windows Vista and Windows 7 that helps prevent unauthorized changes to your computer. These changes can be initiated by users, applications, viruses, or other types of malware. UAC makes sure these changes are made only with the approval of the administrator of the computer. If the administrator does not approve these changes, they will never be executed, and the system will remain unchanged.

How UAC Works

Unlike Windows XP, in Windows Vista and Windows 7, applications run by default without any administrative permissions. As a result, they cannot make any changes to the operating system. When an application wants to make system changes, such as modifications that affect other user accounts, modifications of system files and folders, or installation of new software, UAC prompts the user to ask for permission.

If the user clicks **No**, the change won't be performed. If the user clicks **Yes**, the application receives administrative permissions and is able to make the system changes it is programmed to do. These permissions will be in force until the application stops running or the user closes it. The next time the application runs, it starts again without administrative permissions.

For an easier understanding, the UAC algorithm is explained in the following diagram.

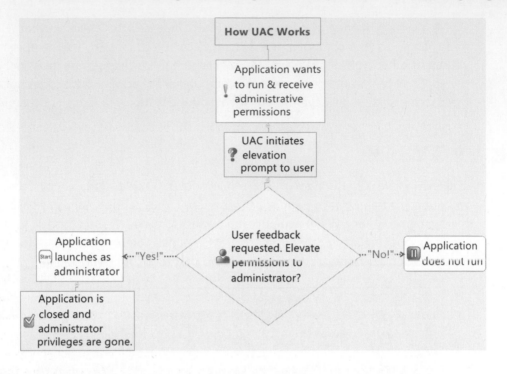

Changes Requiring Administrative Privileges

There are many changes that require administrative privileges, and depending on how UAC is configured on your computer, they can cause a UAC prompt to pop up and ask for permissions. Changes requiring administrative permission are as follows:

- Running an application as an administrator.
- Changing system-wide settings or to files in the Windows and Program Files folders.
- Installing and uninstalling drivers and applications.
- Installing ActiveX controls.
- Changing settings to the Windows Firewall.
- Changing UAC settings.
- Configuring Windows Update.
- Adding or removing user accounts.
- Changing a user's account type.
- Configuring Parental Controls.

- Running Task Scheduler.

- Restoring backed-up system files.

- Viewing or changing the folders and files of another user account.

- Changing the system date and time.

Having UAC turned off means any user and any application can make any of these changes without a prompt for permissions. This would allow viruses and other forms of malware to infect and take control of your system much easier than when UAC is turned on.

The Differences Between UAC Levels

Unlike Windows Vista, where you had only two options—UAC turned on or off—in Windows 7, there are four levels from which to choose. The differences between the levels are as follows:

- *Always notify*   At this level, you are notified before applications make changes that require administrative permissions or before you or another user change Windows 7 settings. When a UAC prompt appears, your desktop is dimmed and you must choose *Yes* or *No* before you can continue to do anything else on your computer. **Security Impact:** This is the most secure setting but also the most annoying. If you do not like the UAC implementation from Windows Vista, you won't like this level either.

- *Notify me only when programs try to make changes to my computer*   This is the default level; it notifies you only before programs make changes to your computer that require administrative permissions. If you manually make changes to Windows 7, you are not notified by UAC. This level is less annoying because it doesn't stop the user when making changes to the system; it only shows prompts if an application wants to make changes. When a UAC prompt appears, the desktop is dimmed and you must choose *Yes* or *No* before you can continue to do anything else on your computer. **Security Impact:** This is less secure because some malicious programs can simulate the keystrokes or mouse moves of a user. These programs can change Windows 7 settings. However, if you are using a good security solution, these scenarios should never occur.

- *Notify me only when programs try to make changes to my computer (do not dim my desktop)*   This level is identical to the previous level, except when a UAC prompt appears, the desktop is not dimmed and other programs might be able to interfere with the UAC dialog window. **Security Impact:** This level is even less secure because it is easier for malicious programs to simulate keystrokes or mouse moves that interfere with the UAC prompt. Again, a very good security solution can compensate for the slight decrease in security.

● *Never notify*   At this level, UAC is turned off and doesn't offer any protection against unauthorized system changes. Any user or application can make system changes without any prompts for permission. **Security Impact:** If you don't have a good security solution, you are very likely to have security problems when using this level. With UAC turned off, it is easier for malicious programs to infect your computer and take control of it and/or its settings.

Recommendation Use either of the first two levels. The third level can be used as well when you have a very good security solution in place. The fourth level should always be avoided because it negatively impacts the security of your system.

Configuring UAC

Now that you know what this feature does and how it works, it's time to show you how to configure the level of security you desire. In this exercise, you will learn how.

 SET UP Open the Control Panel.

1. Click **System and Security**.

   The System And Security window opens.

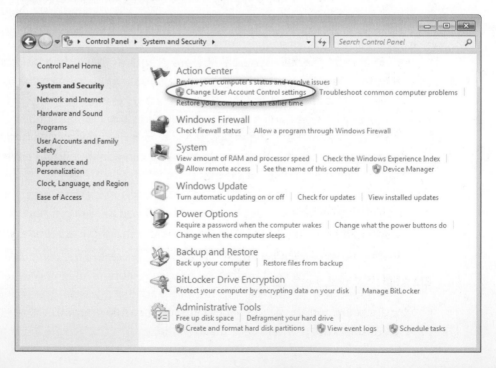

2. In the **Action Center** section, click the **Change User Account Control settings** link.

The User Account Control Settings window opens, which shows the current level set for UAC.

3. Move the slide to the UAC level you want to use on your computer.

Important Before changing the UAC level, don't forget to review the previous section, "The Differences Between UAC Levels." It is very important to first understand the differences between each level before making any changes.

4. Click the **OK** button.

5. Depending on what level UAC was set before making the change, you might receive a UAC prompt. Click **Yes** if you do.

CLEAN UP Close the System and Security window.

The UAC is set to the level you selected and will provide you with the corresponding level of security, depending on the choice you made.

Should I Disable UAC When I Install My Applications and Turn It On Afterward?

The biggest annoyance caused by UAC is when you install applications. During installation, you can receive a lot of UAC prompts (depending on how many applications you install). You might be tempted to disable it temporarily while you install all your applications and then enable it again when you're done. In some scenarios, this is a bad idea. Certain applications make lots of system changes and can fail to work if you turn on UAC after their installation, even though they work when you install them with UAC turned on. This is because when UAC is turned off, the virtualization techniques used by UAC for all applications are inactive. This causes certain user settings and files to be installed to a different place, so they no longer work when UAC is turned back on. To avoid these problems, it is better to have UAC turned on at all times.

Keeping Your System Up to Date

Keeping your system up-to-date is very important for keeping it as secure as possible. Viruses and other forms of malware that exploit security problems in Windows 7 and other operating systems appear on a daily basis. Being up-to-date means having fewer security issues and fewer chances of your computer becoming infected and exploited by unauthorized parties. Therefore, you should have Windows Update turned on at all times and configured to automatically install the most important updates.

Windows Update is one of the tools that were redesigned completely in Windows Vista. Instead of having to browse to a specific Microsoft Web page (as with Windows XP), the entire update process was managed directly by the operating system. Windows 7 keeps the same approach as Windows Vista but introduces a small number of changes to this process—mostly cosmetic.

This section will cover the important bits you need to know about this tool so that you keep your computer up-to-date with latest security and performance patches and updates for Windows 7.

Opening Windows Update

You can open the Windows Update tool using several methods. In this exercise, you will learn how to open Windows Update using two of the existing methods.

 SET UP Open the Control Panel.

1. Click **System and Security**.

   The System And Security window opens.

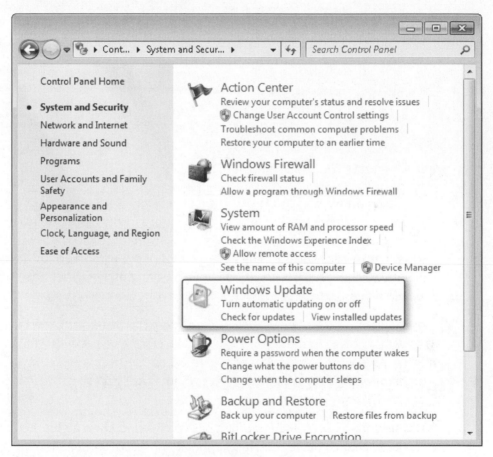

2. Scroll down and click the **Windows Update** section.

   The Windows Update window opens, which gives you a quick overview on how up-to-date your operating system is and how many updates are available.

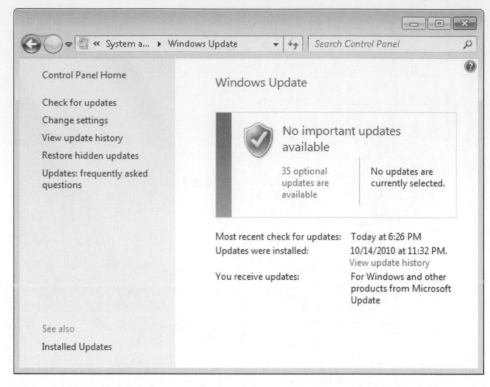

Tip Another way to open this tool is to go to Start Menu -> All Programs -> Windows Update.

You can now access all the configuration settings available in Windows Update and use the tool to check for updates, install available updates, view your update history, or restore hidden updates.

✖ **CLEAN UP** Close the Windows Update window when done working with it.

Configuring Windows Update Settings

Windows Update has a pretty good set of default settings. Without the need for you to intervene, this tool is turned on, regularly checks for updates, and automatically installs the important ones on your computer. This helps to keep your operating system as up to date and secure as possible with the most relevant updates.

Even so, it is a good idea to check these settings, understand them, and configure them to better meet your specific needs.

In this exercise, you will learn how to configure your Windows Update settings so that the tool behaves as you want it to.

SET UP Log on as administrator and open Windows Update.

1. In the left column, click **Change settings**.

   The **Change settings** window opens, which contains all the settings that you can configure for the Windows Update tool.

2. Go to the **Important updates** section. Here you can set how important updates are installed on your computer:

   ● *Install updates automatically (recommended)*   This sets Windows Update to automatically install important updates as they are available. It is also the most recommended option because it allows you to keep your computer as up to date as possible without any intervention on your part.

- *Download updates but let me choose whether to install them*   This option allows Windows Update to automatically download the important updates. Once this is done, you are notified and can choose whether to install them. This option is recommended for those who want more control over the update process.

- *Check for updates but let me choose whether to download and install them*   This option instructs Windows Update to notify you before performing any downloads and installations. When a new update is detected, you are prompted to choose what you want to do next.

- *Never check for updates (not recommended)*   This option disables any automatic update check functionality. It is highly risky because your computer will be updated only if you make manual checks for updates. It is recommended not to use this option, unless you have a regular habit of manually checking for updates.

3. Choose the option that best fits your needs.

4. If you select **Install updates automatically (recommended)**, you can also set when the new updates are installed. You can select a specific day of the week, every day, or even the hour when installations should occur.

Tip To be as up to date as possible, it is best to select Every Day, then specify an hour when your computer is generally turned on.

5. If you want recommended updates to be treated like important updates, select the **Give me recommended updates the same way I receive important updates** check box.

Recommended updates
☑ Give me recommended updates the same way I receive important updates

Who can install updates
☑ Allow all users to install updates on this computer

Microsoft Update
☑ Give me updates for Microsoft products and check for new optional Microsoft software when I update Windows

Software notifications
☑ Show me detailed notifications when new Microsoft software is available

6. If you want to allow all users to install updates on your computer, select the **Allow all users to install updates on this computer** check box. Otherwise, leave it cleared.

   Recommendation It is best to always select this option because it helps ensure that your computer is up to date at any time, independent of the user accounts using it.

7. Windows Update allows you to check for updates to other Microsoft products, such as Microsoft Office, Windows Live Essentials, Silverlight, and so on. To receive them, select the **Give me updates for Microsoft products and check for new optional Microsoft software when I update Windows** check box. Otherwise, leave it cleared.

8. If Windows Update is set to check for new optional Microsoft software, you can set it to show you detailed notifications about the update. To enable this behavior, select the **Show me detailed notifications when new Microsoft software is available** check box. Otherwise, leave it cleared.

9. When you're finished configuring all the settings, click **OK**.

   Note Depending on the model of your computer and where you bought it, you can have additional configuration options that were added by the manufacturer. To learn about the additional options, check the documentation provided with your computer.

Windows Update is now configured to work according to your needs.

 CLEAN UP Close the Windows Update window.

Checking for and Installing Updates Manually

Be default, Windows Update automatically checks for Windows 7 updates each time you log on, and it installs the updates according to the way it is configured to act. However, you can also perform manual checks and installations of updates.

In this exercise, you will learn how to manually check for updates and how to install them on your Windows 7 computer.

SET UP Open Windows Update.

1. In the left column, click **Check for updates**.

   Windows Update starts checking for the latest available Windows updates.

   ![Windows Update window showing "Checking for updates..." with a progress bar. The left column shows Control Panel Home, Check for updates, Change settings, View update history, Restore hidden updates, Updates: frequently asked questions, See also, Installed Updates. Address bar shows Control Panel ▸ System and Security ▸ Windows Update. Below the progress area: Most recent check for updates: Today at 16:51; Updates were installed: Today at 16:28. View update history; You receive updates: For Windows and other products from Microsoft Update.]

2. After a while, a summary of the findings appears. If there are updates available, they are separated into two categories: important updates and optional updates.

Windows Update

Download and install your selected updates

2 important updates are available

1 optional update is available

2 important updates selected, 45,3 MB

1 optional update selected, 2,8 MB

Install updates

Most recent check for updates: Today at 16:29

Updates were installed: 29.09.2010 at 20:36.
View update history

You receive updates: For Windows and other products from Microsoft Update

Find out more about free software from Microsoft Update.
Click here for details.

Important Do not click the Install Updates button yet. Follow the steps recommended below.

3. Click the updates summary to review the list of available updates.

This opens the list of available updates, separated by category:

- Important updates are those that fix security, stability, and compatibility problems in Windows 7. They can also add functionality. One good example is Service Packs. They are labeled as important because they help maintain your security and keep your performance up to date. Within this section is a subsection called Recommended Updates. These updates can fix stability and compatibility problems for applications that are installed on your computer, such as compatibility fixes for Windows Media Center or Internet Explorer, Definition Updates for Windows Defender or Microsoft Security Essentials, and updates for Microsoft Office.

- Optional updates are extras that consist of language packs, additional software, or drivers for your computer's components. Most of these updates can be skipped unless they provide some specific functionality or drivers that you need.

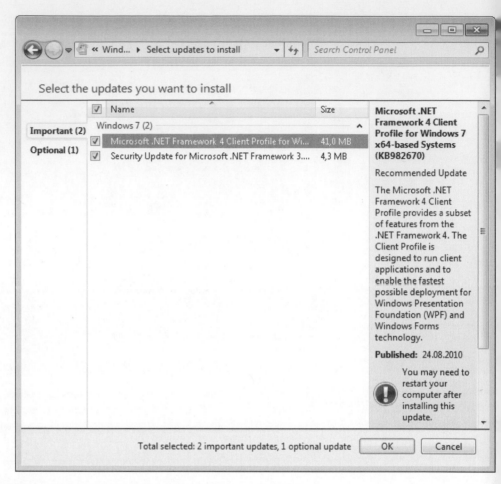

4. Click each update to learn more about it.

   A description of the update will appear that gives you information about what it does and when it was published. You are also notified if it will require a restart of your computer after it is installed.

5. Select the updates you want to install on your computer by selecting the check boxes beside their names.

6. For updates that you do not want installed, clear the check boxes beside their names.

7. When you have finished, click **OK**.

   Windows Update starts to download and install the selected updates.

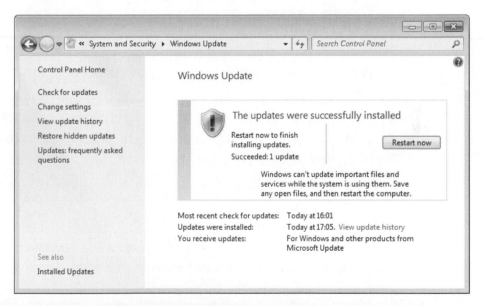

Note If for any reason you want to cancel the download process, you can always press the Stop Download button.

8. When done, Windows Update informs you that the updates were successfully installed.

9. If the **Restart now** button is displayed, it means you need to restart your computer in order for the updates to be applied. Close any applications and documents you have open, then click **Restart now**.

Tip You can use your computer without restarting it. If you want to do so, simply do not click the Restart Now button. The update process will finish the next time you restart your computer.

Your computer is now updated and secure.

✖ CLEAN UP If you did not need to restart your computer, close the Windows Update window.

Postponing Restarts Required by Windows Updates

Some of the updates automatically installed by Windows Update require a restart in order for them to be applied to the operating system. In such cases, you receive a notification to restart your computer.

Windows Update

⚠ Restart your computer to finish installing important updates

Windows can't update important files and services while the system is using them. Make sure to save your files before restarting.

Remind me in: 10 minutes   ▼

Restart now   Postpone

If you want to restart when you receive the notification, first save any work you have in progress, close all your applications, then click Restart Now. This restarts your computer and finalizes the update installation process.

If you do not wish to restart, go to the **Remind me in** drop-down menu, select when you want to be reminded again, and then click Postpone. You will be notified again when the selected time is up, and you will be able to choose the most convenient option again.

Hiding or Preventing Updates from Installing

There are scenarios for which you might not want a certain update to be installed on your computer. A scenario that we have encountered on several occasions is Windows 7 proposing an update for an outdated or bad driver for one of the computer's components. This happens especially when it comes to video cards. If you download the latest driver for your video card directly from the Web site of its manufacturer (AMD, ATI, Intel, NVIDIA, and so on), you will notice that the one proposed by Windows Update is, most of the time, an older version.

Another scenario is when you do not require the functionality added by an update, such as Microsoft's browser ballot, which was imposed by the European Union. You might not need to install this update because you might have already installed the browsers you need.

To avoid these issues, it is better to review the available updates before installing them. Therefore, check for updates, but also check the available updates and what they offer. When you click an update, Windows Update presents some information about what it does. If you don't want the update, right-click it, and then select Hide Update.

The upgrade is dimmed and it will not be installed or shown by future update checks.

Restoring Hidden Updates

Once you hide an update, it is not installed on your computer and is never shown in future update checks. If you want to restore it and make it available again, you need to go through a series of steps.

In this exercise, you will learn how to restore the updates that you have previously hidden.

SET UP Open Windows Update.

1. In the left column, click **Restore hidden updates**.

   The Restore Hidden Updates window opens.

2. To view information about an update, right-click it, then choose **View details**.

	Name	Importance	Size
	Windows 7 (2)		
☐	Canon - Printer... ~~View details~~ (KB...)	Optional	14.7 MB
☐	Update for Wind... ~~Copy details~~ (KB971033)	Important	1.2 MB
	Windows 7 Langua...		
☐	Arabic Language Pack - Windows 7 for x64-based Systems (KB972813)	Optional	50.1 MB
☐	Bulgarian Language Pack - Windows 7 for x64-based Systems (KB9728...	Optional	39.7 MB
☐	Chinese (Simplified) Language Pack - Windows 7 for x64-based Syste...	Optional	152.8 MB
☐	Chinese (Traditional) Language Pack - Windows 7 for x64-based Syste...	Optional	174.1 MB
☐	Croatian Language Pack - Windows 7 for x64-based Systems (KB972813)	Optional	45.0 MB
☐	Czech Language Pack - Windows 7 for x64-based Systems (KB972813)	Optional	52.5 MB
☐	Danish Language Pack - Windows 7 for x64-based Systems (KB972813)	Optional	47.4 MB
☐	Dutch Language Pack - Windows 7 for x64-based Systems (KB972813)	Optional	50.6 MB
☐	Estonian Language Pack - Windows 7 for x64-based Systems (KB972813)	Optional	37.8 MB
☐	Finnish Language Pack - Windows 7 for x64-based Systems (KB972813)	Optional	52.2 MB
☐	French Language Pack - Windows 7 for x64-based Systems (KB972813)	Optional	90.6 MB

Restore hidden updates

After restoring updates, you can choose to install them. We suggest you restore all important updates.
Restoring and installing hidden updates

This opens a Windows Update window that shows information about the update.

Windows Update

Canon - Printers - Canon MP270 series Printer

Download size: 14.7 MB

Update type: Optional

Canon Printers software update released in May, 2010

More information:
http://winqual.microsoft.com/support/?driverid=20359753

Help and Support:
http://support.microsoft.com/select/?target=hub

Close

3. When you're done reading the information, click **Close**.

4. Read the information available about the hidden updates until you find the one(s) that you want to restore.

5. Select the check box beside the name of the update you want to restore.

> **Note** If you want to restore more than one update, select the corresponding check boxes for each of them.

6. Click **Restore**.

Windows Update checks again for available updates and shows you a quick report.

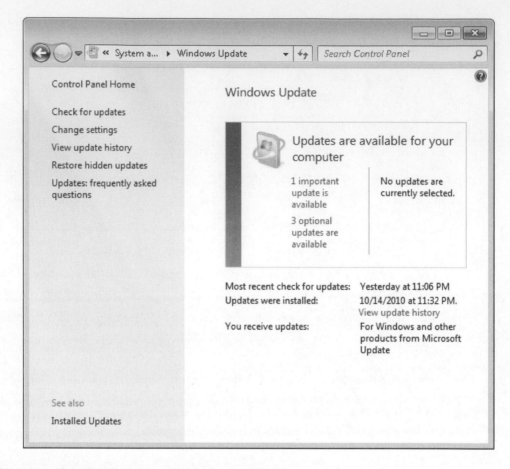

The restored update is now available for installation.

See Also To learn how to manually check for updates and how to install them, see the "Checking for and Installing Updates Manually" section on page 404.

✖ **CLEAN UP** Close the Windows Update window.

Reviewing Your Windows Update History

Windows Update stores a complete log of its activities. This log contains information such as which updates were installed and when, the status of the installation process, and the importance of each update. There are times when you might be interested to know such details. Luckily, making this check is very easy.

In this exercise, you will learn how to review your Windows Update history and view complete information about the updates installed on your computer.

SET UP Open Windows Update.

1. In the left column, click **View update history**.

    The View Update History window opens.

2. To easily find more of the updates you're interested in, it is best to use the column sort option.

    For example, if you click the Name column, it will sort all updates by name, in ascending order. If you click it again, it will sort them in descending order. You can do the same with the other columns (Status, Importance, and Date Installed).

3. Right-click the update you are interested in knowing more about.

    This opens a contextual menu that contains two options: View Details and Copy Details.

Name	Status	Importance	Date Installed
Definition Update for Microsoft Security Essentials - KB97...	Successful	Optional	08.10.2010
Definition Update for Microsoft Security Essentials - KB97...	Successful	Optional	06.10.2010
Definition Update for Microsoft Security Essentials - KB97...	Successful	Optional	04.10.2010
Security Update for Microsoft .NET Framework 3.5.1, Win...	Successful	Important	03.10.2010
Security Update for Microsoft .NET Framework 4 on Wind...	Successful	**View details**	.2010
Definition Update for Microsoft Security Essentials - KB97...	Successful	Copy details	.2010
Update for Windows 7 for x64-based Systems (KB2158563)	Successful	Important	02.10.2010
Definition Update for Microsoft Security Essentials - KB97...	Successful	Optional	01.10.2010
Update for Windows 7 for x64-based Systems (KB979538)	Successful	Recommended	01.10.2010
Update for Windows 7 for x64-based Systems (KB2158563)	Failed	Important	30.09.2010
Update for Microsoft Silverlight (KB2416427)	Successful	Important	30.09.2010
Update for Windows 7 for x64-based Systems (KB979538)	Successful	Recommended	30.09.2010
Definition Update for Microsoft Security Essentials - KB97...	Successful	Optional	28.09.2010
Definition Update for Microsoft Security Essentials - KB97...	Successful	Optional	26.09.2010
Definition Update for Microsoft Security Essentials - KB97...	Successful	Optional	25.09.2010

4. Select **View details** if you want to learn more about that specific update.

   This opens a window containing complete details about the update, such as installation date and time, installation status, the type of update, what the update does, where to find more information about it, and a help and support link.

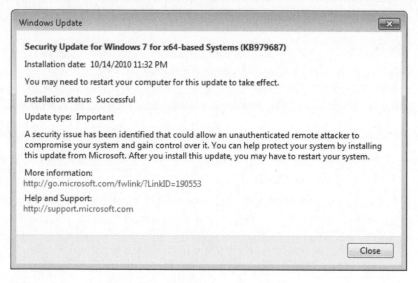

5. When done reading the information, click **Close**.

6. If you want to copy the information about the update to another application, select **Copy details** in the contextual menu shown in step 3. You can then use the **Paste** option to transfer the information to its destination.

7. When you're done reviewing the history of updates, close the **View update history** window.

✖ **CLEAN UP** Close the Windows Update window.

Removing Installed Updates

If you mistakenly installed a Windows Update, such as an incorrect or old driver, or simply an update that you do not really need, you can uninstall it at any time.

In this exercise you will learn how to remove installed updates from your computer.

SET UP Open Windows Update.

1. Click **Installed Updates**, which is located at the bottom of the left column.

   The Installed Updates window opens. Here you can see all the installed updates, separated by category.

   ![Installed Updates window screenshot showing "Uninstall an update" with a list of Microsoft Windows security updates]

2. Scroll through the list and click the update you want to remove.

   Tip To find the update you want to remove more quickly, use the sorting function for each of the available columns. For example, if you click the Name column, all updates will be sorted by name, in ascending order. If you click it again, the names will be sorted in descending order. You can do the same with the other columns.

3. Click **Uninstall**.

   You are asked to confirm the uninstall operation.

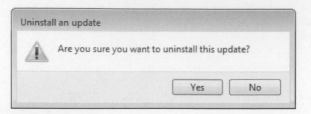

4. Click **Yes**.

The uninstallation process now starts.

Microsoft Windows

Please wait while the updates are being uninstalled. This might take several minutes.

Cancel

5. When finished, you are taken back to the **Installed Updates** window.

6. Repeat steps 2 to 5 for all the updates that you want to remove.

The update you selected is now removed from your computer, and it will be available again for selection during the next update check.

 CLEAN UP Close the Windows Update window.

What Is Windows Defender?

Windows Defender is an application built to detect and remove spyware and other similarly harmful programs. It is included by default in all versions of Windows 7, and it can be used to protect your system. However, there are better alternatives available, including some that are free, such as Microsoft Security Essentials, which provide both spyware and virus protection.

If you choose to use Windows Defender, this section will cover the basics you need to know about how this application works and how to use it.

Opening Windows Defender

Due to the fact that Windows Defender doesn't offer a lot of security features (it sticks only to spyware protection), Microsoft has chosen to hide it somewhat within the Windows 7 operating system. Unfortunately, it doesn't have a direct application shortcut in the Start menu. You need to search a bit in order to access it.

In this exercise, you will learn how to open Windows Defender.

 SET UP Open the Control Panel.

1. On the upper-right side of the Control Panel window, look for a line that says **View by**. Click the menu near it, then select **Large icons**.

   This displays your Control Panel items alphabetically, similar to the way they were presented in Windows XP.

2. Scroll down until you find the items that begin with the letter W.

3. Click the **Windows Defender** shortcut.

   The Windows Defender window opens.

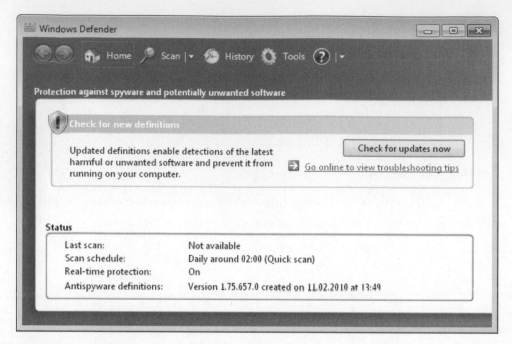

Tip Another way to launch Windows Defender is to type the word **defender** in the Start menu search box, then click the Windows Defender search result.

 CLEAN UP In the Control Panel window, click the View By menu again, then select Category. This will revert your Control Panel to its original appearance. If you don't make this change, you might have issues completing other exercises, because the Control Panel structure will be different from the default view.

Using Windows Defender

The Windows Defender interface is pretty easy to understand and use. There are no sophisticated options, but only the things you would expect from a spyware protection solution.

In this exercise, you will learn the basics of how to use Windows Defender.

SET UP Open Windows Defender.

1. The Windows Defender window has five application areas: **Home**, **Scan**, **History**, **Tools**, and **Help**. You also have **Back** and **Forward** buttons to help you navigate through the different application areas you access.

Back
Forward

	Windows Defender		
Home	Scan	History	Tools	?

Protection against spyware and potentially unwanted software

Check for new definitions

Updated definitions enable detections of the latest harmful or unwanted software and prevent it from running on your computer.

Check for updates now

→ Go online to view troubleshooting tips

Status

Last scan:	Not available
Scan schedule:	Daily around 02:00 (Quick scan)
Real-time protection:	On
Antispyware definitions:	Version 1.75.657.0 created on 11.02.2010 at 13:49

2. When you start the application, you are brought to window called **Home**. This window shows details such as the date of the last system scan, the status of the Real-Time Protection offered by the application, the version of the definitions used to identify spyware, plus different application messages, such as the need for new definitions. If you are in a different area and you want to access these statistics, click **Home**.

3. If you want to run a quick scan for spyware, click **Scan**.

The scan process begins. After a few minutes, the results are displayed.

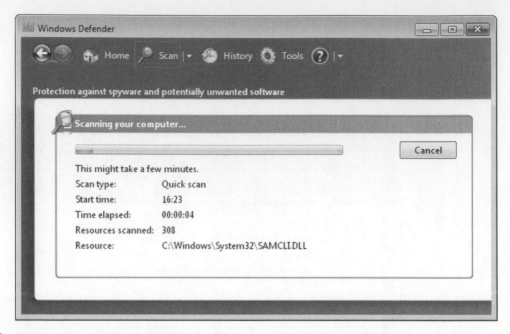

4. If you want to make a full system scan for spyware or a custom one, click the arrow beside **Scan**, then choose the option you want. If you select **Custom scan**, you are asked to define the parameters (which drives or folders should be included) of the custom scan before starting the process.

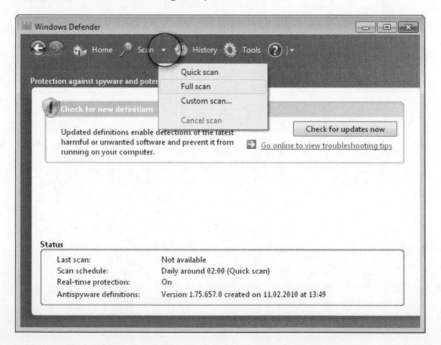

5. If you want to check the activities performed by Windows Defender in the past, click **History**.

This loads a quick report with the alerts you received during the time you used this application and the actions you selected for it to perform.

6. If you want to configure different aspects of Windows Defender, click **Tools**.

This opens the Tools And Settings section. Here you can configure the way you want Windows Defender to run. Also, you can join the Microsoft SpyNet community and help identify spyware infections. You can view all the Quarantined items, the Allowed Items list, and access the Windows Defender Web site or the Microsoft Malware Protection Center portal.

7. If you want to get help regarding Windows Defender and learn how to use it, click the **Help** icon (the question mark).

This opens the Windows Help And Support window, which contains help information about Windows Defender.

8. If you want to access other options beside Help, click the arrow adjacent to the **Help** icon. This opens a menu with additional options: **View Help**, **Check for updates**, **View privacy statement online**, and **About Windows Defender** (this shows information such as client version, engine version, and antispyware definitions).

These are all the interface elements and functionalities of the Windows Defender application.

✖ **CLEAN UP** When you're done working with the tool, close Windows Defender.

Turning Off Windows Defender

If you decide to install a complete Internet security solution or security products other than Windows Defender, it is best to first turn it off. Having multiple security solutions with similar features enabled is not good idea, as it can create problems between the different security applications and cause them to malfunction.

In this exercise, you will learn how to turn off Windows Defender.

 SET UP Open Windows Defender.

 1. Click **Tools**.

The Tools And Settings window opens.

2. Click **Options**.

This opens a list of configuration options, organized by type.

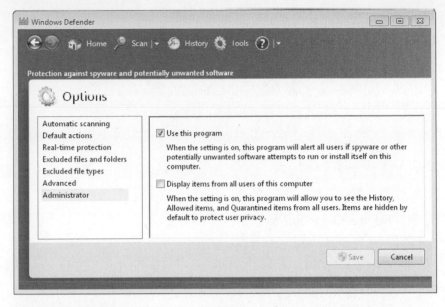

3. Click **Administrator**.

This opens the list of administrative settings that are available for this tool.

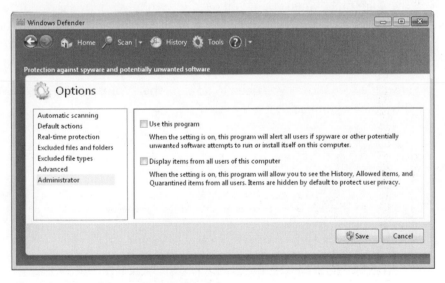

4. Clear the **Use this program** check box.

5. Click the **Save** button.

This disables Windows Defender. A confirmation window pops up to tell you the tool is turned off.

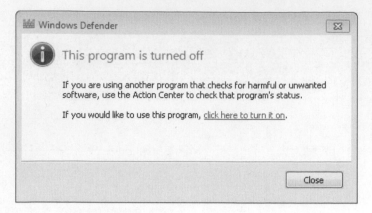

6. Click the **Close** button.

CLEAN UP Now that Windows Defender is turned off, don't forget to install a more complete security solution. It is not safe to use your computer without a security solution that provides anti-spyware protection.

Turning On Windows Defender

There are times when you might need to turn on Windows Defender again. One such scenario might be if you want to run a quick scan to see if your other security solution hasn't escaped any threats. Having Windows Defender run a quick scan can be a good idea.

In such a scenario, all you need to do is to open Windows Defender. When you do this, you are notified that it is turned off.

Click the **click here to turn it on** link. The application starts automatically, and you can now use it again.

Important If you have other security products installed, don't leave Windows Defender turned on as well, unless you are absolutely sure it doesn't conflict with the other solutions. It is best to run a quick double-check scan, make sure no spyware threats are left unidentified on your computer, and then turn it off again.

What Is the Windows Firewall?

The Windows Firewall is a security application that is built into Windows 7. It helps block unauthorized access to your computer while permitting authorized communications to and from your computer. This application has been improved with each new version of Windows.

Windows 7 now allows this tool to filter both inbound and outbound traffic or set rules and exceptions depending on the type of network you are connected to. If you are not using a third-party security suite that includes a firewall, then it is highly recommended that you use the Windows Firewall; it does provide a good level of security.

This section will detail all there is to know about the Windows Firewall and how to use it.

Understanding How the Windows Firewall Works

Windows Firewall has a predefined set of rules that is applied as soon as it is turned on. By default, it allows you to do many things: browse the Internet; use instant messaging applications; connect to a Homegroup; share files, folders, and devices with other computers; and so on. The rules are applied differently depending on the network location set for your current network connection.

See Also For more information about network locations, see the "Setting the Network Location" section in Chapter 4, "Creating the Network."

Some of the applications that you install on your computer (such as uTorrent, for example), automatically add an exception to the Windows Firewall so that they work as soon as you launch them. However, if they don't add such an exception, Windows Firewall asks you to allow them access to the Internet. At this point, you receive a security alert (similar to the one shown in the image that follows), in which you are asked to select the network locations that you will allow to access the application: private networks (such as home or work networks), or public networks (such as airports, coffee shops, etc.).

By default, Windows Firewall selects the appropriate check box for the network that you are currently using. However, you can select either of the two options or both, depending on what you want to do. When you're done, click Allow Access to allow the application to communicate on the selected type(s) of network. To block access, simply click Cancel.

Note If you do not have administrator access, you are not able set any exceptions, and the programs that do not comply with the standard set of rules are automatically blocked.

Opening the Windows Firewall

The Windows Firewall is turned on by default in Windows 7, and it runs silently in the background, as a service. The application prompts you whenever you need to make a decision, and you don't need to open it unless you want to see its status or configure it to better meet your needs.

In this exercise, you will learn how to open the Windows Firewall.

SET UP Open the Control Panel.

1. Click **System and Security**.

   The System And Security panel opens, with all tools and configuration options available for this category.

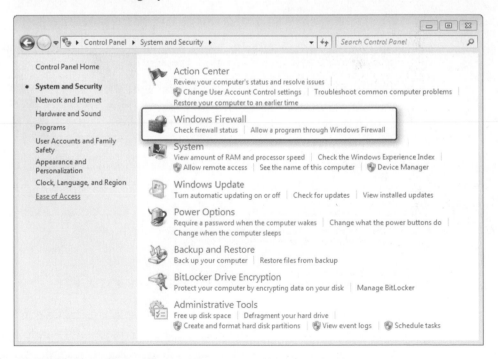

2. Click **Windows Firewall**.

   The Windows Firewall application opens to its main window.

Tip Another way to launch Windows Firewall is to type the word **firewall** in the Start Menu search box, and then click the Windows Firewall search result.

3. In the center of the window, you can see information about the status of your network connections and how the Windows Firewall is set for each type of connection. In the left column, there are links to different configuration options for the Windows Firewall and other tools such as the Action Center.

See Also To learn more about how to configure the Windows Firewall and how to work with it, see the following sections.

CLEAN UP When you are done working with the tool, close the Windows Firewall window.

Turning the Windows Firewall On or Off

If you choose to install a third-party security application, such as a complete Internet security suite or simply another firewall, it is best to disable the Windows Firewall so that it doesn't create conflicts and problems.

In this exercise, you will learn how to disable the Windows Firewall and how to enable it again, when needed.

SET UP Log on as administrator and open the Windows Firewall.

1. Click the **Turn Windows Firewall on or off** link, which is located in the left column.

This opens the Customize Settings window, which shows if the application is turned on. By default, the Windows Firewall is turned on for both types of network locations: Home Or Work (Private) and Public. You can choose to turn it on or off for both or just for one of the locations.

2. If you want to turn it off for a network location, select the **Turn off Windows Firewall (not recommended)** option. If you select this option for both network locations, the Windows Firewall will be turned off completely. If you choose it for one, Windows Firewall will be turned off only when you connect to that type of network location.

3. To turn the Windows Firewall on for a network location, select the **Turn on Windows Firewall** option.

4. Beneath the **Turn on Windows Firewall** option, there are two other settings you can make.

   The first blocks all incoming connections to your computer. We do not advise enabling this unless you want your computer to not be available to anyone or any application. The second addresses receiving notifications when the Windows Firewall blocks a new program. We advise that you enable this option; otherwise, if an application doesn't access the network or the Internet correctly, you won't know why. Check any of these options that you want to enable.

5. When you have finished, click **OK**.

   You are returned to the Windows Firewall window.

✖ **CLEAN UP** Close the Windows Firewall window.

Important You can turn Windows Firewall on or off only if you are logged on as an administrator. This setting will apply to all users defined on your computer. Also, if you disable the Windows Firewall, make sure that your user and others have proper security alternatives installed.

Customizing the List of Allowed Programs

The Windows Firewall allows you to edit its communication rules so that you can permit or deny network access for certain applications or services. In this exercise, you will learn how.

 SET UP Log on as administrator and open the Windows Firewall.

 1. Click the **Allow a program or feature through Windows Firewall** link.

   The Allowed Programs window opens, which contains all the programs that are allowed to go through the Windows Firewall. By default, the list is not editable—you can use it for viewing purposes only.

Important When the Allowed Programs window opens, some of the program name check boxes are selected. This means that the rules defined for those programs are active and used by the Windows Firewall. The programs that are not selected don't have any active rules used by the Windows Firewall. There are also some selected check boxes in the Home/Work (Private) and Public columns. If a check box is selected in any of these columns, it means that the rule defined for that program is applied to the selected network location. Some programs have rules for one network location, while others have rules for both. The rules are active only for the network locations that are selected.

2. To view details about any allowed program, select it, then click **Details**.

A window opens that presents the properties for the selected application.

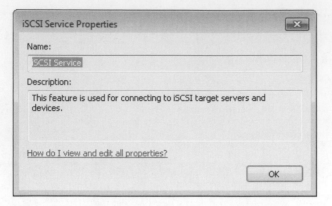

3. When done reading the information, click **OK**.

   This closes the properties window of the application and returns you to the list of allowed programs.

4. To modify any of these settings, click **Change settings**.

   This causes the Change Settings button to become dimmed and the list of allowed programs and features to become editable.

5. You can now edit the list of active rules, add new programs and features to the list, or remove existing rules. When you're done making changes, click **OK**.

The changes you made are now applied.

See Also To learn how to edit the list of active rules, read the following sections in this chapter.

 CLEAN UP Close the Windows Firewall window.

Adding New Programs to the Allowed List

You can easily add new programs to the list of allowed programs through Windows Firewall. In this exercise, you will learn how.

 SET UP Log on as administrator and open the Windows Firewall. Go to the Allowed Programs window and make the list of allowed programs and features editable, as described in the previous section.

 1. Click **Allow another program**.

The Add A Program window opens, in which you see a list with some of the programs installed on your computer.

Add a Program

Select the program you want to add, or click Browse to find one that is not listed, and then click OK.

Programs:

- Create a System Repair Disc
- Internet Explorer
- Uninstall Google Talk
- Windows DVD Maker
- Windows Fax and Scan
- Windows Media Center
- Windows Remote Assistance
- XPS Viewer

Path: C:\Windows\system32\recdisc.exe   Browse...

What are the risks of unblocking a program?

You can choose which network location types to add this program to.

Network location types...   Add   Cancel

2. If you can find the program you want to add, skip to step 4. If you cannot find it, click **Browse**.

This opens the Browse window.

3. Find the location where the program is installed, select its main executable file, then click **Open**.

This adds it to the list of Programs that can be selected for inclusion into the allowed programs list.

Add a Program   ✕

Select the program you want to add, or click Browse to find one that is not listed, and then click OK.

Programs:

- μTorrent
- Create a System Repair Disc
- Internet Explorer
- Uninstall Google Talk
- Windows DVD Maker
- Windows Fax and Scan
- Windows Media Center
- Windows Remote Assistance
- XPS Viewer

Path: C:\Program Files\uTorrent\uTorrent.exe   Browse...

What are the risks of unblocking a program?

You can choose which network location types to add this program to.

Network location types...   Add   Cancel

4. Select the program you want to add, then click **Network location types.**

This opens the Network Location Types window, in which you can select through which type of network location you allow the program to communicate.

Choose Network Location Types   ✕

Allow this program or port to communicate through Windows Firewall for the selected network locations:

☑ Home/Work (Private): Networks at home or work where you know and trust the people and devices on the network

☐ Public: Networks in public places such as airports or coffee shops

What are network locations?

OK   Cancel

5. Select the network locations through which you want to allow the program to communicate then click **OK**.

    This brings you back to the Add a Program window.

6. Make sure the program that you just configured is selected, then click **Add**.

    This brings you back to the Allowed Programs window. Notice that the newly added program appears on the list.

7. Click **OK**.

The change is now applied to the list of active rules used by the Windows Firewall.

✖ CLEAN UP Repeat this procedure for all the programs that you want to add. When you have finished, close the Windows Firewall window.

Removing Programs or Disabling Rules from the Allowed List

Removing programs from the list of allowed programs through the Windows Firewall or disabling active rules can be done just as easily as adding them. In this exercise, you will learn how.

SET UP Log on as administrator and open the Windows Firewall. Go to the Allowed Programs window and make the list of allowed programs and features editable, as shown in the "Customizing the List of Allowed Programs" section.

1. Select the rule you want to disable or remove.

Allowed programs and features:		
Name	**Home/Work (Private)**	**Public**
☑ Network Discovery	☑	☐
☑ octoshape.exe	☑	☐
☐ Performance Logs and Alerts	☐	☐
☑ Remote Assistance	☑	☑
☐ Remote Desktop	☐	☐
☐ Remote Event Log Management	☐	☐
☐ Remote Scheduled Tasks Management	☐	☐
☐ Remote Service Management	☐	☐
☐ Remote Volume Management	☐	☐
☐ Routing and Remote Access	☐	☐
☐ Secure Socket Tunneling Protocol	☐	☐
☐ SNMP Trap	☐	☐

[Details...] [Remove]

2. If you want to disable the rule, simply clear the check box on the left side of the rule name. It will no longer be used by the Windows Firewall.

3. If you want to disable the rule for a certain network location only, clear the corresponding check box found in the column of that network location.

   For example, if you want a rule to not be applied to the program when you are connected to a public network, clear the check box from the Public column. The same applies for Home/Work (Private) network locations.

4. If you want to remove the program from the list of allowed programs, click **Remove**.

   You are asked to confirm the removal.

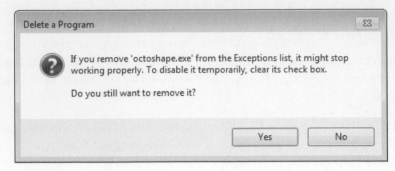

5. Click **Yes**.

   This brings you back to the Allowed Programs window. Notice that the program was removed from the list.

6. Click **OK**.

The change is now applied to the list of active rules used by the Windows Firewall.

✖ **CLEAN UP** Repeat this procedure for all the programs that you want to remove or for the rules you want to disable. When you have finished, close the Windows Firewall window.

Gaining Additional Control by Using the Windows Firewall with Advanced Security

The Windows Firewall with Advanced Security is a tool that allows a lot more control over the rules applied by the Windows Firewall to protect your computer. With it, you can tweak all properties of every security rule, define new rules, or disable undesired ones. This tool is quite advanced, so if you just want to stick to the basics, it is best not to fiddle with it. However, if you want to be more hands-on regarding the security rules applied to your computer, then this tool is of great utility.

This section will give you an overview of the Windows Firewall with Advanced Security and its major capabilities.

Opening the Windows Firewall with Advanced Security

The Windows Firewall with Advanced Security is simply a more advanced way of showing the rules that govern the functioning of the Window Firewall. The same settings are shown in a different and complex way, each with the complete set of parameters applied to it.

To access it, first open the Windows Firewall. Then, click **Advanced Settings**. This opens the Windows Firewall with Advanced Security window.

Tip Another way to access this is to search for the word **firewall** in the Start menu search, and then click the Windows Firewall With Advanced Security shortcut.

In the center of this window, you can see the status of the Windows Firewall.

On the left side, there is panel in which you can access the currently defined rules (inbound, outbound, and connection security rules) and monitor what is going on with the Windows Firewall.

On the right side, there is the Actions panel, in which you can define actions to take. This panel changes dynamically, presenting varying options based on the items you access in the left panel.

Understanding Inbound, Outbound, and Connection Security Rules

In order to provide the security you need, the Windows Firewall has a standard set of rules that are used depending on the location of the network to which you are connected. These rules are split into three categories:

- *Inbound rules* These rules are applied to the traffic that is coming from the network or the Internet to your computer. Inbound traffic includes: files that you are copying from another computer to yours, files downloaded from a Web page, e-mails received, remote connections made to your computer over the network or the Internet, and so on. These rules can be configured so that they are specific to computers, users, programs, services, ports, or protocols. You can also specify to which type of network adapter (for example, wireless, cable, virtual private network) or user profile they are applied.

- *Outbound rules* These are rules that apply to the traffic going from your computer to the network or the Internet. Outbound traffic includes: connecting to a Web site to browse its contents, uploading files to a Web page, sending an e-mail, remote connections made from your computer to another over the network or the Internet, and so on. These rules can be configured so that they are specific to computers, users, programs, services, ports, or protocols. You can also specify to which type of network adapter (for example, wireless, cable, virtual private network) or user profile they are applied.

- *Connection Security rules* These rules are used to secure traffic between two computers while it crosses the network. One example would be a rule specifying that connections between specific computers must be encrypted. Unlike the inbound or outbound rules, which are applied only to one computer, connection security rules require that both computers have the same rules defined and enabled. By default, there are none defined for Windows 7 or Windows Vista computers. They are generally defined by users or a network administrator (in business networks). For the typical activities done over a home network, such rules are not required to be defined. There's no need for you to implement them on your home network.

You can access the rules defined in each category by clicking the appropriate section on the left panel of the Windows Firewall with Advanced Security window. In each section, there are rules marked with either a green check mark or a gray one. The green check marks represent active rules, and gray check marks represent disabled rules that are not used by the Windows Firewall.

Viewing and Modifying the Properties of a Rule

You can easily view the properties of a rule (inbound, outbound, or connection security). To do so, simply right-click the rule in which you're interested, then select Properties. This opens the Properties window for the selected rule.

The properties are organized by category, each with its own tab:

- *General*   This includes the name of the rule, a description of the rule, whether it is enabled or not, and if it allows or blocks a connection.

- *Programs and Services*   This tab shows which programs and Windows services the rule applies to.

- *Computers*   On this tab, you can see whether or not this rule applies to specific computers. If no computer is specified, then the rule applies to connections to all computers.

- *Protocols and Ports* On this tab, you see the list of protocols and ports to which the rule applies.

- *Scope* This tab shows if the rule applies to specific IP addresses or to any address.

- *Advanced* On this tab, you can see which type of network location and network adapter (network device) the rule applies to and if it allows the computer to accept unsolicited inbound traffic that has passed through other devices such as routers or firewalls.

- *Users* On this tab, you see the user accounts to which the rule applies and the ones to which it doesn't apply. If no specific user account is listed, it means it applies to all user accounts.

To modify the properties of the rule, you can simply use the available options in each of the tabs. Once you have set up the configuration you need, simply click OK and the changes are applied.

Monitoring with Windows Firewall with Advanced Security Monitor

The Windows Firewall with Advanced Security also offers some monitoring features. If you click on the Monitoring section in the left panel, you can access several monitoring reports, organized by category.

This is what is shown in each category:

- *Firewall* This category shows all the active inbound and outbound rules used by the Windows Firewall to function.
- *Connection Security Rules* This shows all active Connection Security rules.
- *Security Associations* This category shows the security associations currently established on your computer, including detailed information about their settings and endpoints. A security association defines the shared security information used to protect the communications between two computers: your computer and another one.

Note Security associations are generally used in business networks where computers need to share information in a more secure environment. They don't generally apply to home networks.

Creating a New Rule

As you can imagine, the Windows Firewall with Advanced Security allows you to create your own custom rules that include even more advanced settings than the default version of the Windows Firewall.

In this exercise, you will learn how to create your own rules in the Windows Firewall with Advanced Security.

For this exercise, we will use as an example creating a rule for the ActiveSync application included in Windows operating systems. ActiveSync is the client used to connect and synchronize Windows Mobile phones to Windows computers. This application is useful for many owners of Windows Mobile smartphones. In order for the application to function properly, it uses the following inbound TPC ports: 990, 999, 5678, 5721, 26675, and outbound UDP port 5679. Let's create a rule for the inbound ports.

 SET UP Log on as administrator and open the Windows Firewall with Advanced Security.

 1. Go to the **Action** menu, then click **New Rule**.

   The New Inbound Rule Wizard opens. You will use this to create the new rule.

2. Select the type of rule you want to create. Your options are: **Program**, **Port**, **Predefined**, and **Custom**. For our exercise, select **Port**.

3. Click the **Next** button.

   You are asked to select the type of protocols and provide the actual ports to which the rule applies.

4. ActiveSync uses TCP inbound ports 990, 999, 5678, 5721, and 26675. Therefore, select **TCP**.

5. Select **Specific local ports** and type **990,999,5678,5721,26675**.

   If you need to add a rule to all ports, select All Local Ports.

6. Click **Next**.

   You are asked to select which type of action the rule will take: allow or block.

7. For our exercise, we need to allow traffic through the TCP protocol and the ports mentioned in step 4. Therefore, select **Allow the connection**.

8. Click **Next**.

   You are asked to select to which type of network location the rule applies.

See Also For more information about network locations, see the "Setting the Network Location" section of Chapter 4, "Creating the Network."

9. Select the type of network locations where the rule should be applied. For our exercise, it is best to have this rule enabled for safer locations such as Domain and Private. Select the **Domain** and **Private** check boxes and clear the **Public** check box.

10. Click **Next**.

You are now at the last step in the wizard.

11. Type the name you want your rule to have. Make it something descriptive so that it gives you a good idea about what the rule does.

New Inbound Rule Wizard

Name

Specify the name and description of this rule.

Steps:

- Rule Type
- Protocol and Ports
- Action
- Profile
- Name

Name:

Inbound Ports for ActiveSync

Description (optional):

Allow ports 990, 999, 5678, 5721, 26675

< Back   Finish   Cancel

12. Type the description for the rule that provides a bit more detail.

13. Click **Finish**.

The rule is now created and allows TCP inbound traffic for ports 990, 999, 5678, 5721, and 26675.

✖ CLEAN UP To create a rule for the outbound traffic used by ActiveSync, follow the same steps. At step 4, you need to select UDP and then type the port 5679. The rest of the procedure is the same. When done, you can close Windows Firewall with Advanced Security.

Important The principles in the New Inbound Rule Wizard are the same for all types of rules. Only certain configuration options differ, based on the type of rule you define: program, port, predefined, or custom. For all rules, you need to specify the action to be taken, the network profile to which it applies, and the rule name and description.

Enabling, Disabling, or Deleting an Existing Rule

Just like with the standard Windows Firewall, the Windows Firewall with Advanced Security allows you to enable inactive rules, disable active ones, or simply delete rules you no longer need. In this exercise, you will learn how to do this.

 SET UP Log in as administrator and open the Windows Firewall with Advanced Security.

1. Open the category of the rule that you want to disable (inbound, outbound, or connection security) and select the rule that you want to enable, disable, or delete.

2. Right-click the rule to open the contextual menu.

ActiveSync Inbound Hosts

BranchCache Co

BranchCache Ho   Disable Rule

BranchCache Pee   Cut

Connect to a Net   Copy

Connect to a Net   Delete

Connect to a Net

Connect to a Net   Properties

Connect to a Net   Help

Tip You can select multiple rules by pressing and holding the **Ctrl** key on your keyboard and selecting the rules with the mouse.

3. If the rule is active and you want to disable it, select **Disable Rule**.

4. If the rule is inactive and you want to enable it, select **Enable Rule**.

5. If you want to remove the rule, select **Delete**.

   You are asked to confirm your choice.

   Windows Firewall with Advanced Security

   ⚠ Are you sure you want to delete these rules?

   Yes   No

6. Click **Yes**.

The rule is now enabled, disabled, or deleted, according to your selection.

CLEAN UP Repeat the procedure for all the rules you want to enable, disable, or delete. When done, you can close Windows Firewall with Advanced Security.

Important Before disabling or deleting a rule, make sure that you understand what it does and what this change means to the security of your system. If you are not sure about what its impact will be, it is best not to fiddle with it. Also, if your Windows Firewall seems to be acting out of your control, it is best to reset its settings by using the instructions found in the following section.

Restoring the Windows Firewall Default Settings

If you have been using this tool for a long time and have made many changes to its settings, chances are that some things might stop working. For such cases, it is best to reset all rules to the default settings and values created by Microsoft. Then you can start from scratch and define the rules that apply to your programs so that everything works again as it should.

In this exercise, you will learn how to restore the default settings of the Windows Firewall.

SET UP Log on as administrator and open the Windows Firewall.

1. Click **Restore defaults**.

    The Restore Defaults Window opens, in which you are warned about the consequences of the change you are about to make.

    ![Restore default settings window showing Windows Firewall control panel]

    Restore default settings

    Restoring default settings will remove all Windows Firewall settings that you have configured for all network locations. This might cause some programs to stop working.

    [Restore defaults]

    [Cancel]

2. Read the information shown and click **Restore defaults**.

    You are asked to confirm your action.

Restore Defaults Confirmation

⚠ Restoring the default settings will delete all settings of Windows Firewall that you have made since Windows was installed. This may cause some programs to stop working

Do you want to continue?

Yes   No

3. Click **Yes**.

You are returned to the Windows Firewall window, and all the settings you created are deleted. Everything is now reset to the initial settings and values existing at the time when Windows 7 installed on your computer.

 CLEAN UP When you have finished, close the Windows Firewall window.

Protecting Your Computer from Viruses and Other Security Threats

In order to have a safe and pleasant computing experience, it is highly recommended to install complete security solutions such as Internet security suites (which include antivirus, anti-spyware, firewall, and other protection features) or individual antivirus, anti-spyware and firewall solutions.

Windows 7 offers by default built-in firewall and anti-spyware solutions, which were covered in the prior sections of this chapter. However, they are not enough to completely secure your system.

Why Should I Install Additional Security Solutions in Windows 7?

This is a question many people ask. Windows 7 offers by default a pretty good protection level. The Windows firewall protects from network and Internet threats, while Windows Defender protects your computer from spyware. Unfortunately, this is not enough. With only these solutions enabled, you won't have any form of protection from computer viruses and other more advanced threats such as rootkits (a form of "virus" which is able to hide its presence by concealing its processes from the monitoring mechanisms of your operating system).

In order to be completely protected, you need to install at least an antivirus solution on top of the Windows Firewall and Windows Defender.

The best way to remain protected is to use a complete security package, generally called an Internet Security Suite. These packages include antivirus, anti-spyware, and firewall protection, plus other security modules, such as spam filters for your e-mail client, monitors for your Internet browser, parental controls, and so on.

Finding Security Solutions Compatible with Windows 7

There are many security solutions on the market, most of them commercial. However, there are also free solutions available. Before making a choice, it is best to see which options are available on the market. In order to make an informed decision, we recommend that you check the following Internet sources:

- **Consumer security software providers** (*http://www.microsoft.com/windows /antivirus-partners/windows-7.aspx*)   This Microsoft page lists all of the security software providers that offer solutions compatible with Windows 7, Windows Vista, and Windows XP.

- **Security for Everyone at 7 Tutorials** (*http://www.7tutorials.com /security-everyone*)   The 7 Tutorials Web site provides a series of reviews for the latest Internet Security Suites. The 7 Tutorials team regularly tests the latest offerings from both a security and usability perspective. The aim of the reviews is to highlight those solutions that provide the best mix of security and user friendliness.

- **AV Comparatives** (*http://av-comparatives.org*)   This is the Web site of an independent security organization that regularly tests the quality of security provided by antivirus products. Their tests are very professional and evaluate all the important security aspects of an antivirus solution. If you want to know which security company has the best detection engine for viruses, this Web site is the place to visit.

- **AV Test** (*http://www.av-test.org*)   This Web site is run by the AV-Test GmbH company, which offers security testing and consultancy services. They run regular reviews of the latest security products on the market and publish the results of their evaluations. Just like AV Comparatives, this Web site is a great destination for learning how effective the latest security offerings on the market are.

- **Home PC Firewall Guide** (*http://www.firewallguide.com/*)   This Web site provides test results for firewall products and also links to the latest reviews published by other Web sites for firewalls, antivirus products, and Internet security suites. It's a good destination, especially for those interested in knowing how firewall products or modules rank.

- **Internet Security Suites Software Reviews at TopTenReviews** (*http://Internet-security-suite-review.toptenreviews.com*)   This Web site regularly reviews all kinds of software, including antivirus solutions and complete Internet security solutions. If you want to know the latest top 10 together with a complete feature comparison table, this Web site is a good destination.

Using the Action Center

Windows 7 comes with a convenient way to help you review the state of your system and find solutions to security and maintenance issues. The feature that facilitates this is called the **Action Center**, and it is built upon the foundation set by the Windows Security Center, which was first introduced by Windows XP Service Pack 2 and then tweaked by Windows Vista. This section will explain all the functionality of the Action Center and show how to configure it so that you receive only the notifications that are relevant to you.

Explaining the Action Center

Action Center continuously monitors the state of your system's security. If it notices any kind of problem, such as your antivirus being disabled, it immediately notifies you so that you can take corrective action. It also monitors a series of maintenance-related items, including checking whether you have any scheduled system backups, trying to find solutions to recent computer issues, and checking for any maintenance problems, and so on.

When a problem is detected, the user is notified and guided to what he can do to fix it.

Messages Displayed by the Action Center

In the notification area of the Windows 7 taskbar, there's always a little white flag icon. This is the icon of the Action Center. When there are messages for the user, the white flag is overlaid by one of two icons: a red x, and a black clock. The red x overlay indicates that there is at least one important message, so you need to pay attention. The black clock overlay means that there is a scheduled task running in the background (for example, a scheduled Windows Defender scan).

Hover the mouse cursor over the flag icon and you see a tooltip, giving you some brief information about what is happening with your system.

To see the list of messages that you need to pay attention to, click the Action Center icon (the white flag).

Opening the Action Center and Reviewing Its Messages

Reviewing the list of messages displayed by the Action Center is a simple task. There are few steps to follow, and the way the tool communicates with the user is very easy to understand. There's no complicated jargon involved, and typically, you can intuitively understand what the tool recommends for you to do to keep your computer secure and your data backed up properly.

In this exercise, you will learn how to open the Action Center and review its messages.

SET UP Go to the notification area of the taskbar (the lower-right side of the screen).

1. Click the Action Center **white flag** icon.

   This shows a summary of the current active messages.

2. Click the **Open Action Center** link.

   The Action Center window opens. In this window, you can see the current status of your system and all the recommendations the tool has to offer.

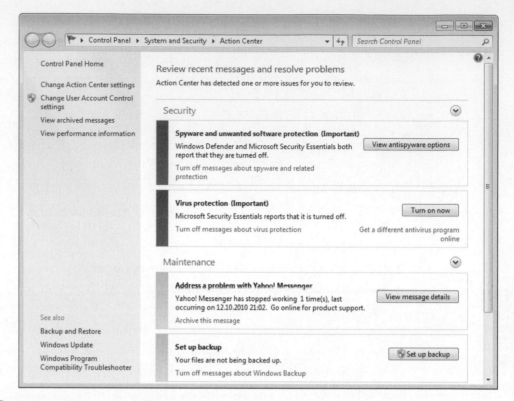

3. The messages shown by the Action Center are split into two categories: Security and Maintenance. To maximize or minimize either of these two categories, click the arrow to the right of the category name.

Tip All messages shown by the Action Center use the following color coding: Red means it is a very important message that you should not ignore, and yellow indicates that it is a recommendation that can be ignored if you do not consider it important.

You can check all the messages and recommendations shown by the tool and decide what you want to do about them. To learn more about the possible messages you can receive, read the sidebar "Explaining the Action Center Messages" that follows the Clean Up instructions.

✖ CLEAN UP When you have finished working with the tool, close the Action Center.

Explaining the Action Center Messages

The Action Center informs you when the following problems are identified:

- **Windows Update (Important)**   This message warns you that Windows Update is set to never check for updates, leaving your computer exposed to all sorts of security risks. The recommended setting is to automatically download and install updates. To review the available options, click the Change Settings button, then select the appropriate update option.

- **Spyware and unwanted software protection (Important)**   This message warns you that Windows Defender or any other anti-spyware solution you installed is turned off. To see a list of available options, click View Antispyware Programs.

- **Virus protection (Important)**   This message occurs when your antivirus is not installed, is disabled, or uses outdated definitions. It is strongly recommended to either install an antivirus application, turn on your antivirus (if you already have one), or update your antivirus definitions.

- **User Account Control (Important)**   This message warns you that the User Account Control is disabled.

- **Network firewall (Important)**   This message warns you that Windows Firewall or the firewall you installed (for example, ESET, ZoneAlarm, Symantec, Kaspersky, and so on) is turned off. You should always have a firewall turned on. To see the available options, click View Firewall Options.

- **Internet security settings (Important)**   This message occurs when certain Internet Explorer security settings are configured lower than their default level. You can easily reset them to the desired level by clicking the Restore Settings button in the *Action Center* message about Internet security.

- **Network Access Protection**   This message refers to a security feature deployed in corporate environments to manage health information for client computers in a centralized manner. This setting depends on the Network Access Protection Agent service and further software settings; it will not be an issue for home users.

- **Set up backup**   This message notifies you that you should set up a backup task. This is not as important as the preceding security issues, although if you have enough available storage space, you could set your system to perform regular backups of your files and settings.

- **Check for solutions to problem reports** This message notifies you about reported problems with your software and hardware and checks for solutions online.

- **Check for updates** This message notifies you about noncritical software updates, either for Windows components or for other Microsoft products.

- **Troubleshooting: System Maintenance** This message notifies you about any maintenance routines that need to be carried out in order to help your computer run more smoothly.

Configuring the List of Messages Displayed by the Action Center

The great thing about the Action Center is that it is a very configurable application. You can easily customize which type of alerts and messages you want to receive, depending on how you have configured your Windows 7 installation and the additional software you installed.

In this exercise, you will learn how to configure the list of messages that is displayed by the Action Center.

SET UP Open the Action Center.

1. Click the **Change Action Center settings** link on the upper-left side of the Action Center window.

   This shows a summary of the currently active messages, grouped by category.

Turn messages on or off

For each selected item, Windows will check for problems and send you a message if problems are found.
How does Action Center check for problems?

Security messages

☑ Windows Update   ☑ Spyware and related protection

☑ Internet security settings   ☑ User Account Control

☑ Network firewall   ☑ Virus protection

Maintenance messages

☑ Windows Backup   ☑ Check for updates

☑ Windows Troubleshooting

Related settings

Customer Experience Improvement Program settings

Problem reporting settings

Windows Update settings

[OK]   [Cancel]

Note A message is an area that Action Center regularly checks for problems. If a problem is identified, Action Center informs you through a message.

2. Select the check boxes for the messages that you want to receive.

3. Clear the check boxes for the messages that you do not want to receive.

Recommendation We strongly recommend that you do not disable the messages from the Security category. If there are security issues with your computer, you would miss important alerts that could help you fix them promptly.

4. When you have finished, click **OK**.

   Action Center will now show only the messages you selected.

 **CLEAN UP** Close Action Center.

Key Points

- The User Account Control should be turned on at all times.

- Keep Windows Update turned on, and use it actively to keep your system up to date with the latest patches from Microsoft.

- Using Windows Defender can be a useful security measure if you do not use more complete security suites. If you do have more complete security solutions installed, it is best to disable Windows Defender so that it doesn't create conflicts.

- The Windows Firewall is a great security tool you can use to protect against unauthorized connections to your computer.

- The Windows Firewall with Advanced Security is a special view of the Windows Firewall with which you can create advanced security rules.

- It is very important for you to have antivirus protection on your system. Don't hesitate to read the Web sites we recommend so that you can find the best security solution that works for you.

- By using the Action Center, you get a good perspective on the status of your system, and you are always notified when Windows 7 identifies problems.

Chapter at a Glance

Turn on Parental Controls, **page 466**

Set time limits and application restrictions, **page 468**

Define restrictions for games, **page 472**

Receive notifications from Parental Controls, **page 478**

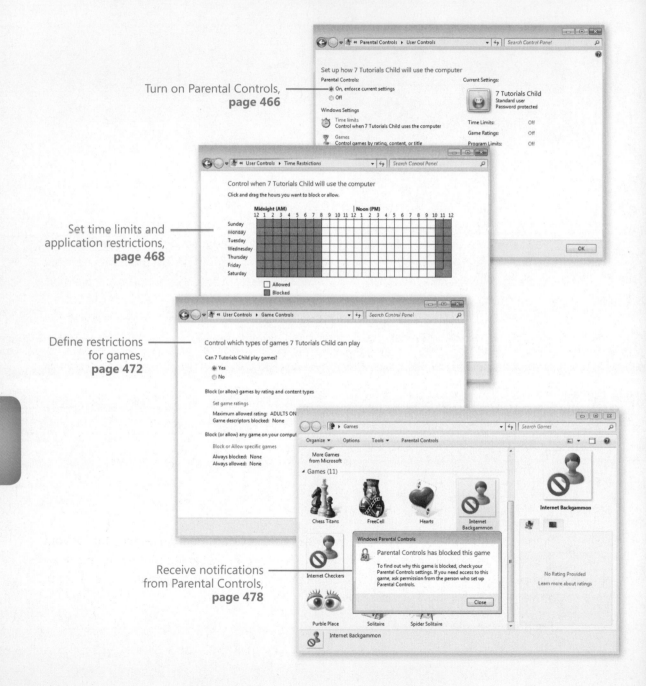

14 Setting Up Parental Controls

In this chapter, you will learn how to

✔ Turn on Parental Controls.

✔ Set time limits and application restrictions.

✔ Set up restrictions for games.

Your home network is now up and running. Everything is correctly set and you can share media, libraries, folders, and devices between the computers on your network. But there's one more thing to consider: If you have children using computers on the home network, it's a good idea to use Parental Controls. This feature of Windows 7 allows you to define when children can use the computer (during which days of the week and at what time intervals in each day), which games they are allowed to play, and which programs they are allowed to use.

In this chapter, you will learn how to turn on Parental Controls, how to define time limits, and how to apply restrictions for games and applications.

> **Practice Files** You do not need any practice files to complete the exercises in this chapter.

Turning On Parental Controls

Before setting up Parental Controls, you need to create a standard user account for your child that has no administrative permissions. If your child's user account has administrative permissions, he will have all the required rights to override any controls you want to apply.

See Also To learn more about user accounts and how to set them up, see Chapter 2, "Setting User Accounts on All Computers."

Once you have created a user account for your child, you can begin enabling Parental Controls. In this exercise, you will learn how to do that.

 SET UP Open the Control Panel.

1. Click **User Accounts and Family Safety**.

   The User Accounts And Family Safety panel opens, which contains all the settings related to user accounts.

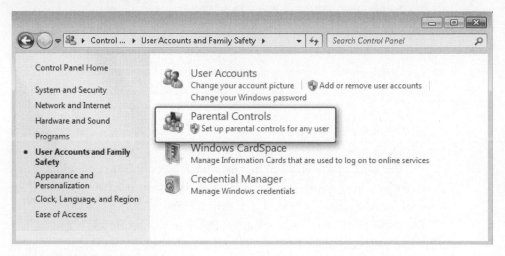

2. Click **Parental Controls**.

   The Parental Controls panel opens. You are asked to which user account you want to apply Parental Controls.

3. Select your child's user account (which, for the purposes of this exercise, is named
7 Tutorials Child).

The User Controls window opens. Here you can see if Parental Controls are enabled
for the selected user account, and if they are enabled, what types of limits are
defined (time limits, game ratings, or program limits).

Set up how 7 Tutorials Child will use the computer

Parental Controls:
- ● On, enforce current settings
- ○ Off

Windows Settings

⏱ Time limits
Control when 7 Tutorials Child uses the computer

🏆 Games
Control games by rating, content, or title

Allow and block specific programs
Allow and block any programs on your computer

Current Settings:

7 Tutorials Child
Standard user
Password protected

Time Limits:	Off
Game Ratings:	Off
Program Limits:	Off

OK

4. Select the **On, enforce current settings** option.

5. Click the **OK** button.

Parental Controls are now enabled, using the default settings. Note that the default settings do not apply any limits to your child's user account. To learn how to define limits, read the following sections.

✖ **CLEAN UP** There is no cleanup required.

Setting Time Limits and Application Restrictions

Now that Parental Controls are enabled, it's time to define the restrictions you want applied. The easiest restrictions you can define are related to the time when the computer can be used by your child and which applications she is allowed to use.

In this exercise, you will learn how to set restrictions.

➡ **SET UP** Open Parental Controls.

1. Select your child's user account.

The User Controls window opens. On the right side of the window, you can see if any limitations are currently applied.

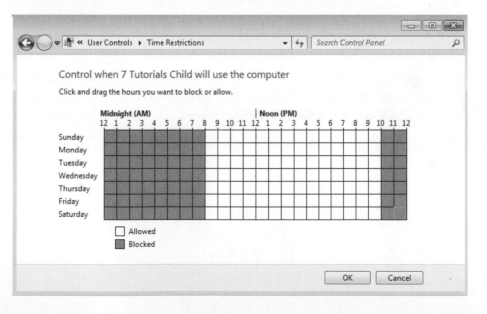

2. First, let's apply limits to when your child can use her account. Click **Time Limits**.

Note If you are not interested in setting time limits, skip to step 7.

The Time Restrictions window opens, in which you can see a table comprised of the days of the week and the hours in a day. By default, the table is empty (the squares are all white), which means no time restrictions are defined.

3. To block a certain hour in a day, simply click the appropriate square.

   The square turns blue, which indicates that you child cannot use the computer at that particular hour during that particular day of the week.

4. Click all the squares that correspond to the hours and days for which you want to block access.

   The previous image shows how the table needs to be completed if you want to block access each day (between 10 P.M. and 8 A.M.) so that your child doesn't stay up late at night playing on the computer.

5. If you want to cancel blocking a time slot, simply click it again and it will turn white.

6. When you have finished setting the time slots, click **OK**.

   You are returned to the User Controls window.

7. To set applications restrictions, click **Allow and block specific programs**.

   You are asked to decide which programs your child's user account can use.

8. Select the second option, which is the one that has **can only use the programs I allow** appended to the name of the user account (in this exercise, **7 Tutorials Child can only use the programs I allow)**.

   A list appears that shows the currently installed applications on your computer.

9. Select the check boxes adjacent to the programs that your child can use and leave the check boxes cleared for the ones that you don't want him to use.

10. If a program is not on the list, click **Browse**, navigate to its location, and then select it.

11. When you have finished selecting the programs your child can access, click **OK**.

    You are returned to the User Controls window.

12. Click **OK**.

✖ **CLEAN UP** Close the Parental Controls window.

Setting Restrictions for Games

Another important parental control option you might want to take advantage of is setting up restrictions for the kinds of games your child can play. This can be very important to you, especially if he is very young. Fortunately, Parental Controls makes it very easy for you to set such restrictions.

In this exercise, you will learn how to set restrictions for the games your child is allowed to play.

SET UP Open Parental Controls.

1. Select your child's user account.

   The User Controls window opens.

2. Click **Games**.

   The Game Controls window, in which you can block and allow games based on a variety of criteria, opens.

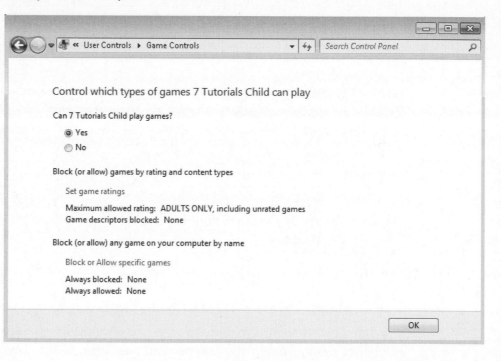

3. You are asked if you allow your child to participate in computer games. Select **No** if you don't want your child to play any games at all. Select **Yes** if you want to allow game play.

If you select **No**, all the other options are grayed out and you can end the exercise at this step (there are no other settings to be made).

4. If you want to block or allow games by rating and content type, click **Set game ratings**.

The Game Restrictions window opens, displaying a long list of restrictions you can define.

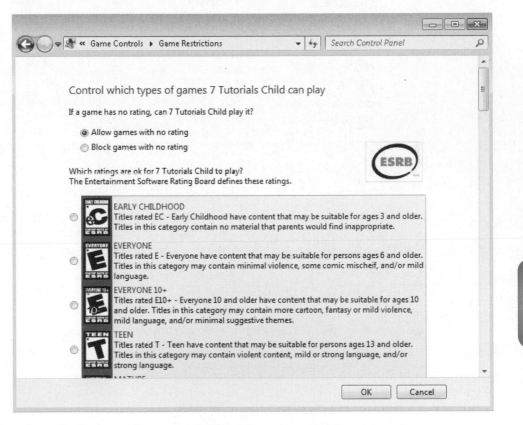

5. Select whether you allow your child to play games that have no rating.

Unrated games are usually casual games. They can be downloaded from the Internet, mostly from smaller independent publishers. Select Allow Games With No Rating or Block Games With No Rating, depending on your preference.

Which ratings are ok for 7 Tutorials Child to play?
The Entertainment Software Rating Board defines these ratings.

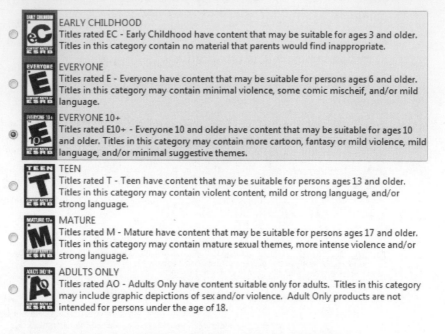

EARLY CHILDHOOD
Titles rated EC - Early Childhood have content that may be suitable for ages 3 and older.
Titles in this category contain no material that parents would find inappropriate.

EVERYONE
Titles rated E - Everyone have content that may be suitable for persons ages 6 and older.
Titles in this category may contain minimal violence, some comic mischief, and/or mild
language.

EVERYONE 10+
Titles rated E10+ - Everyone 10 and older have content that may be suitable for ages 10
and older. Titles in this category may contain more cartoon, fantasy or mild violence, mild
language, and/or minimal suggestive themes.

TEEN
Titles rated T - Teen have content that may be suitable for persons ages 13 and older.
Titles in this category may contain violent content, mild or strong language, and/or
strong language.

MATURE
Titles rated M - Mature have content that may be suitable for persons ages 17 and older.
Titles in this category may contain mature sexual themes, more intense violence and/or
strong language.

ADULTS ONLY
Titles rated AO - Adults Only have content suitable only for adults. Titles in this category
may include graphic depictions of sex and/or violence. Adult Only products are not
intended for persons under the age of 18.

6. You are asked to select the acceptable ratings for your child.

The list contains the standard ratings as defined by the Entertainment Software Rating Board: Early Childhood, Everyone, Everyone 10+, Teen, Mature, and Adults Only. Read carefully what each rating means and select the maximum rating allowed for your child, depending on his or her age—and your personal preference.

Scroll down a bit farther and you find another list that contains more specific types of content that you can block. These restrictions will be applied in addition to the general rating you just set. The list of content that can be blocked is comprehensive. It includes anything from intense violence to mild language. Select the types of content that you want to block.

Block these types of content

Even if a game has an allowed rating, you can block it for the type of content it contains.

☑	Online Rating Notice	Online Interactions Are Not Rated by the ESRB
☑	Alcohol and Tobacco Reference	Alcohol and Tobacco Reference
☐	Alcohol Reference	Reference to and/or images of alcoholic beverages
☐	Animated Blood	Discolored and/or unrealistic depictions of blood
☑	Blood	Depictions of blood
☑	Blood and Gore	Depictions of blood or the mutilation of body parts
☐	Cartoon Violence	Violent actions involving cartoon-like situations and characters. May include violence where a character is unharmed after the action has been inflicted
☐	Comic Mischief	Depictions or dialogue involving slapstick or suggestive humor
☐	Crude Humor	Depictions or dialogue involving vulgar antics, including 'bathroom' humor
☑	Drug and Alchohol Reference	Drug and Alchohol Reference
☑	Drug and Tobacco Reference	Drug and Tobacco Reference
☑	Drug Reference	Reference to and/or images of illegal drugs
☑	Edutainment	Content of product provides user with specific skills development or reinforcement learning within an entertainment setting. Skill development is an integral part of product
☐	Fantasy Violence	Violent actions of a fantasy nature, involving human or non-human characters in situations easily distinguishable from real life
☐	Informational	Overall content of product contains data, facts, resource information, reference materials or instructional text
☑	Intense Violence	Graphic and realistic-looking depictions of physical conflict. May involve extreme and/or realistic blood, gore, weapons and depictions of human injury and death

7. When you have finished setting restrictions, click **OK**.

You are returned to the Game Controls window.

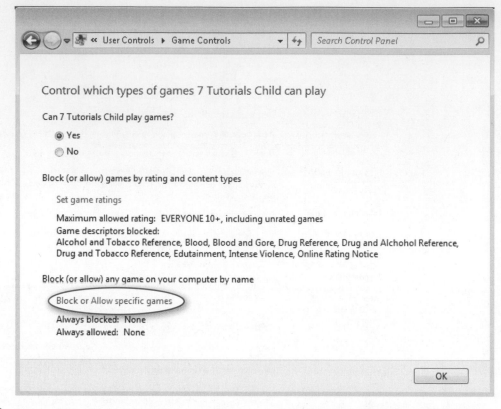

8. To block or allow games by a specific name, click **Block or Allow specific games**.

The Game Overrides window opens, in which you can individually choose the games (from those installed on your computer) that your child is allowed to play.

9. For each game installed on the computer, you have three choices:

- **User Rating Setting**   The game will be allowed or blocked, based on the game rating and the rules you defined.

- **Always Allow**   The game is allowed, independent of the other restrictions that you have set (rating or type of content).

- **Always Block**   The game is always blocked, independent of other defined restrictions.

For each of the games on your computer, select your desired setting.

10. When you have finished setting the games from the list, click **OK**.

You are returned to the Game Controls window.

11. Click **OK**.

The Game Controls window closes and you are returned to the User Controls window.

12. Click **OK**.

The game restrictions you have defined are now applied to your child's user account.

 **CLEAN UP** Close the Parental Controls window.

Understanding Messages from Parental Controls When Restrictions Are Applied

When your child wants to log on to the computer during a day and hour that is set as blocked, she will receive the following message: "Your account has time restrictions that prevent you from logging on at this time. Please try again later."

Your child will be unable to log on unless you set that specific slot as allowed.

If you have set restrictions for games, those games that are restricted display an icon (the well-recognized red circle with a diagonal line through its center) to indicate the restricted status. Also, if your child tried to play a restricted game, a pop-up window appears with the message, "Parental Controls has blocked this game."

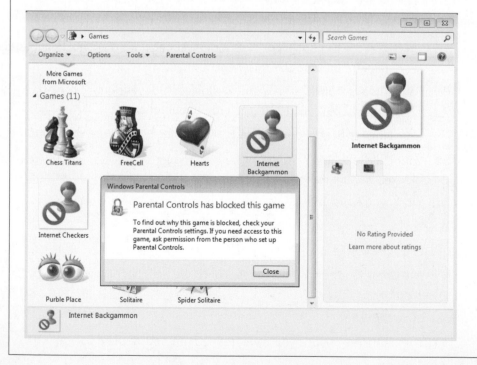

If your child tries to run a blocked program, again, a pop-up window appears with the message, "Parental Controls has blocked this program."

> **Windows Parental Controls**
>
> **Parental Controls has blocked this program**
>
> An administrator can allow this program by opening Parental Controls and changing the permissions.
>
> mip.exe
> Path: c:\program files\common files\microsoft shared\ink
>
> [OK]
>
> If you want access to this program, you will need permission.
> Ask an administrator for permission.

Important The tricky part about blocked programs is that Parental Controls will allow some of the Windows-specific programs to run, even if they are not marked as allowed (for example: Calculator and Internet Explorer). However, any third-party applications that are installed on the computer won't be allowed to run on your child's user account unless marked as allowed.

Key Points

- Turning on Parental Controls can be done only if your child has a standard user account.

- You can easily set time limits in addition to restrictions on applications and games.

- Game restrictions can be set using many criteria, including the rating and the types of content they contain.

- Your child is notified each time he tries to log on at a restricted time or run a blocked game or application.

Chapter at a Glance

Network and troubleshoot your computer problems using wizards, **page 482**

Identify and resolve wireless connectivity problems, **page 486**

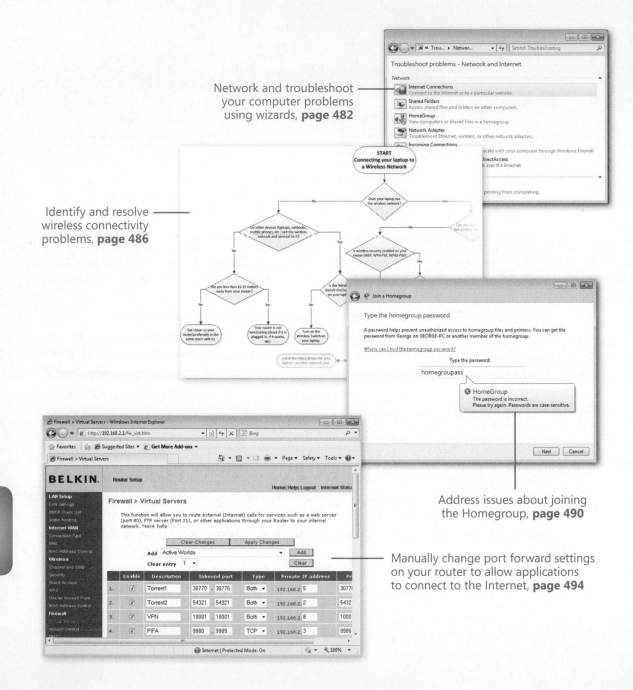

Address issues about joining the Homegroup, **page 490**

Manually change port forward settings on your router to allow applications to connect to the Internet, **page 494**

15 Troubleshooting Network and Internet Problems

In this chapter, you will learn how to

✔ Fix problems using the Network and Internet Troubleshooting wizards.

✔ Change the date and time settings on your computer to resolve joining Homegroup errors.

✔ Manually configure port forwarding settings on your router.

✔ Find troubleshooting help on the Web.

Now that you have your home network set up and secured, everything should function without problems—well, most of the time, anyway. For those times when there are problems, Windows 7 offers a simple way of identifying possible root causes and fixes. With the use of Network and Troubleshooting wizards, anyone can identify the root cause of almost any network issue and fix it in minutes. For those situations when they cannot help you, this chapter has some additional tips.

In this chapter, you will learn about the Network and Troubleshooting wizards, how they work, and how to use them to fix your network problems. Since wizards cannot help with every problem, you will also learn how to troubleshoot problems with your wireless connection. Then, you will learn how to solve problems with joining the Homegroup and how to do manual port forwarding on your router. Last but not least, you will also learn where to find help online, so that you can solve your home networking problems.

> **Practice Files** You won't need any practice files to complete the exercises in this chapter.

Fixing Problems Using the Network and Internet Troubleshooting Wizards

The Network and Internet Troubleshooting wizards are very versatile tools for solving your home networking problems. We highly recommend using them—they are really effective and can help you solve many of the most common problems you might encounter with your home network.

In this exercise, you will learn how to start any of the available Network and Internet Troubleshooting wizards and how to work with them to fix your problems.

SET UP Open the Network And Sharing Center.

1. Click the **Troubleshoot problems** link.

   The Troubleshoot Problems – Network And Internet window opens.

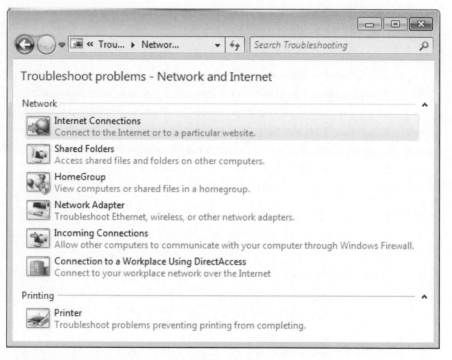

2. Click the appropriate wizard, depending on your problem:

   - **Internet Connections** This wizard can help when you are connected to a network but can't get onto the Internet, or if you have trouble accessing particular Web sites.

- **Shared Folders**   Use this wizard when you are experiencing problems accessing shared files and folders on other computers in your network.

- **Homegroup**   If you have problems viewing computers or shared files and folders in your Homegroup, use this wizard.

- **Network Adapter**   This wizard comes in very handy when problems occur with your wireless or network adapters and anything that seems to be related to your physical connection to the network.

- **Incoming Connections**   This is a useful wizard when other computers have trouble connecting to the shared files and folders on your computer.

- **Connection to a Workplace Using DirectAccess**   This wizard can be used when you're experiencing problems connecting to enterprise network domains.

  Note This wizard works only for Windows 7 Ultimate and Windows 7 Enterprise users.

- **Printer**   When printing problems occur, this a helpful wizard.

The selected troubleshooting wizard starts. For our exercise, we selected the Network Adapter Wizard.

3. Click the **Next** button.

Depending on your computer and the type of wizard you started, you might be asked to select the network adapter you want to diagnose.

4. If you are asked to choose the network adapter that you want to diagnose, choose **Local Area Connection** for diagnosing your cable-based network connection or **Wireless Network Connection** for diagnosing your wireless network connection.

   Windows 7 starts to search for problems.

   ![Network Adapter dialog showing "Detecting problems" with a progress bar and a Close button]

5. If a problem is found, you will see a summary of the problem and the steps you need to follow in order to fix it. Follow the instructions presented by the wizard.

   ![Network Adapter dialog: "Plug an Ethernet cable into this computer." An Ethernet cable looks like a telephone cable but with larger connectors on the ends. Plug this cable into the opening on the back or side of the computer. Make sure the other end of the cable is plugged into the router. If that does not help, try using a different cable. Options: "Check to see if the problem is fixed — Click here after you follow the instructions above." and "Skip this step — Continue trying to fix the problem." Cancel button.]

Note Sometimes, due to the nature of your problem, the wizard will recommend that you contact your Internet service provider because the problem can be fixed only by them.

6. When you have finished carrying out the instructions, click **Check to see if the problem is fixed**.

   Windows 7 determines if the problem was fixed and shows a summary of its findings.

```
┌────────────────────────────────────────────────────────────────┐
│                                                          [─][x]  │
│  (←)  ▣  Network Adapter                                          │
│                                                                  │
│   Troubleshooting has completed                                  │
│                                                                  │
│   The troubleshooter made some changes to your system. Try       │
│   attempting the task you were trying to do before.              │
│                                                                  │
│   ┌ Problems found ─────────────────────────────────────────┐    │
│   │  A network cable is not properly plugged in or may be        │
│   │  broken                                      Fixed      ✓  │  │
│   │                                                          │    │
│   └──────────────────────────────────────────────────────────┘    │
│                                                                  │
│   ┌──────────────────────────────────────────────────────┐      │
│   │  →  Close the troubleshooter                           │      │
│   └──────────────────────────────────────────────────────┘      │
│                                                                  │
│   →  Explore additional options                                  │
│                                                                  │
│   View detailed information                                      │
│                                                                  │
│                                              [   Close   ]        │
└────────────────────────────────────────────────────────────────┘
```

7. If the problem is fixed, click **Close**. If the problem persists, try clicking **Explore additional options** and follow the instructions there.

Important If the Troubleshooting Wizard hasn't detected any faults but you still have problems, it might mean that you have used the wrong wizard. In this case, try another wizard from the list of available options that is more closely related to the issues you are experiencing.

If all went well, your network or Internet problem is fixed. For those times when the wizards cannot help, read the next sections.

✖ **CLEAN UP** Close the Network and Sharing Center.

Starting the Network and Internet Troubleshooting Wizards from the Command Line

In the event that you have problems starting Network and Internet Troubleshooting wizards with the mouse, you can start them from the command line. To do so, open the Command Prompt and type the appropriate command for the wizard you want to start, as detailed in the following list:

- To open the Internet Connections troubleshooter, type **msdt.exe -id NetworkDiagnosticsWeb**.

- To open the Shared Folders troubleshooter, type **msdt.exe -id NetworkDiagnosticsFileShare**.

- To open the HomeGroup troubleshooter, type **msdt.exe -id HomeGroupDiagnostic**.

- To open the Network Adapter troubleshooter, type **msdt.exe -id NetworkDiagnosticsNetworkAdapter**.

- To open the Incoming Connections troubleshooter, type **msdt.exe -id NetworkDiagnosticsInbound**.

Identifying and Resolving Wireless Connectivity Problems

The most commonly reported networking problems are related to wireless connectivity. Many people have difficulty with older routers that don't work well with newer operating systems such as Windows 7 and Windows Vista. Other problems might be the result of incorrect wireless network card drivers installed on the operating systems. The list of possible problems is almost endless. In order to help, we've created some flowcharts that should help you identify what is wrong when wireless connection problems occur.

To understand the flowcharts, start at the top. Each chart asks you several questions (within the diamond objects), which provide a Yes or No answer. Depending on the answer, follow the appropriate path in the flowchart until you arrive at one of the possible answers that are contained inside the ellipses.

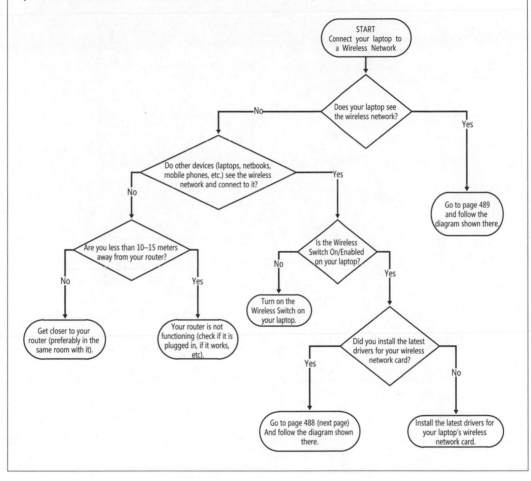

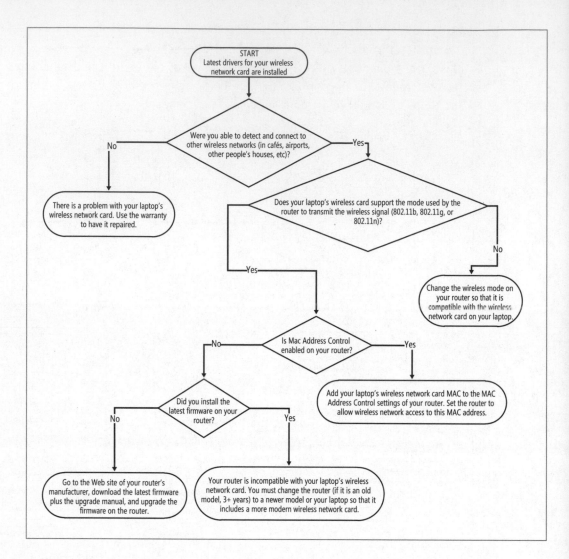

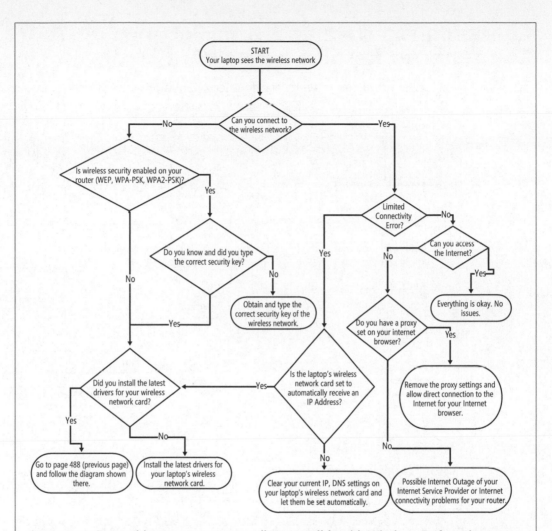

Important Some older routers are not really compatible with Windows 7. If you have a model older than three to four years, you probably need upgraded firmware for it, or you need to replace it with a newer model. To learn if your router is compatible with Windows 7, you can check the Windows 7 Compatibility Center Web site, which you can find at *http://www.microsoft.com/windows/compatibility/windows-7/en-us/default.aspx*.

Changing the Date and Time Settings on Your Computer to Resolve a Password Error

One of the problems you might encounter when joining the Homegroup is receiving a "The password is incorrect" error, even if you have typed the correct Homegroup password.

This error is actually not related to the password you typed; it is the result of the date and time settings not being synchronized between your computer and the computer that created the Homegroup in the first place. In order to resolve it, you need to set the date and time correctly on both computers or simply change it on your computer to match the settings on the computer that created the Homegroup, even if those settings are not correct.

In this exercise, you will learn how to change the date and time settings on your computer.

SET UP Go to the notification area of your computer's taskbar and click the time.

1. Click the **Change date and time settings** link.

   The Date And Time window opens, in which you will make all the necessary changes.

Note Alternatively, you can search for the word date in the Start search box, then click Date And Time.

2. Click the **Change date and time** button.

   The Date And Time Settings window opens. This is the window in which you actually change the date and time.

3. Change the date in the **Date** box and the time in the **Time** box to match the corresponding settings on the computer that created the Homegroup.

4. Click **OK**.

   You are returned to the Date And Time window.

5. Click **Change time zone**.

   The Time Zone Settings window opens.

7. In the **Time zone** drop-down list, select the time zone so that it matches with the computer that created the Homegroup.

8. Click **OK**.

   You are returned to the Date And Time window.

9. Click **OK**.

   The date and time settings on your computer are now synchronized with the computer that created the Homegroup.

 **CLEAN UP** Restart the procedure to join the Homegroup.

Important If you are running Windows 7 in a virtual machine and this error occurs, even though the date and time of the virtual machine and the computer that created the Homegroup are synchronized, the problem is likely the result of having incorrect network connection settings for your virtual machine. You are probably using Network Address Translation (NAT). In order for the joining to be successful, you need to use the Bridged connection.

Configuring Port Forwarding Settings on Your Router

In a typical home networking setup, the router is the center of your home's Internet connection. All traffic goes through it and is filtered by it. By default, your router will block traffic through the ports that are considered nonstandard use. For example, games that can be played online (for instance, FIFA 11), applications such as BitTorrent clients (uTorrent, Blizzard Downloader, BitComet), Windows Media Player, or VPN (Virtual Private Network) applications need to use specific ports that may be blocked by your router, depending on how it is configured. In such a scenario, the games or applications you use won't be able to fully connect to the Internet and function correctly.

Therefore, you need to establish which ports are used by these games or applications and "unblock" them in the router's settings by performing what is called manual **port forwarding**.

What is port forwarding?

First, you need to understand that every Internet Protocol (IP) Address (the address used by your computer to be identified on the network) is divided into thousands of ports. When your computer sends data to another computer, it sends it from a port on its IP Address to a port on the other computer's IP Address. A port can be used only by one program at a time. If the router blocks a port used by a game or an application, it cannot communicate and send data to the computer where it needs to send it. Port forwarding is when you configure your router to allow communication through a certain port for a certain IP Address that is used by a computer on your network. For example, you would use this with a computer on which you have set up Windows Media Player 12 to do media streaming over the Internet. This way, you can connect to another computer from work or a friend's house and exchange media with it. If Windows Media Player 12 doesn't show the remote computers in the Other Libraries section, even if the configuration you've done is correct, it means the ports used by the application to do media streaming over the Internet are blocked. The ports used by Windows Media Player 12 for remote media streaming are TCP 44442 and 443. You need to map them both to port 10245.

See Also For more information about IP Addresses and what this concept is, check out the Glossary and the "Installing and Configuring Your Router" section, in Chapter 1 "Setting Up Your Router and Devices."

In this exercise, you will learn how to set up manual port forwarding. For the purposes of this exercise, we use a Belkin N+ Wireless router.

SET UP Open your router's administration page.

1. Type the administrator password to access your router's settings.

2. Go to the **Port Forwarding** configuration page.

   Depending on your router, the path might be very different. For example, on Belkin routers it is found in the **Firewall -> Virtual Servers** section. On Linksys routers it is found in the **Applications & Gaming -> Port Range Forwarding** section. On D-Link routers it is found in the **Advanced -> Port Forwarding Rules** section.

   In this page, you can see the current ports that are forwarded and for which of the computers in your home network.

3. Go to an empty entry and select the **Enabled** check box.

4. Type a description for the port forwarding you are about to do.

   To make things easier, it is best to type the name of the application that uses the ports you are about to forward. For our exercise, you could type **WMP12**.

5. Type the inbound port used by the application. In our example of Windows Media Player 12, it is 44442. Type **44442** in both fields in the **Inbound port** column.

Note If you need to open a range of ports—let's say from 44442 to 44445—you could type 44442 in the first field and 44445 in the second. This would open all the ports between the start and end port.

6. Select the type of traffic that is allowed through this port. Your choices are TCP (Transmission Control Protocol), UDP (User Datagram Protocol), or Both (TCP and UDP). Windows Media Player 12 uses TCP. Therefore, select **TCP**.

7. In the next column, type the IP Address of the computer for which you want to open the specified port.

8. In the next column (Private Port on Belkin routers), you need to specify to which port you want to map the specified inbound port you typed at step 5. Most times, this is identical to the inbound port. However, Windows Media Player 12 needs you to map port 44442 to 10245. Therefore type **10245** in both fields.

   Note You can also specify a range of ports, if needed, as described in the Note in step 5.

9. Click **Apply Changes** (or **Save Settings** on other routers).

   Now inbound port 44442 is mapped to 10245, and the router permits TCP traffic for your computer for this combination of ports.

CLEAN UP Repeat the procedure and map all the ports as you need. For Windows Media Player 12, you also need to map port 443 to 10245 so that remote streaming via the Internet functions correctly. In the case of remote media streaming, you should also repeat this procedure on the router that filters the traffic of the network where the other computer is located.

Important A port forwarding rule on your router is applied only to the computer with the specified IP Address. Other computers are still blocked from using the rule. If you want a port forwarding rule to be applied to all computers on your home network, you need to create a rule for each computer.

See Also If your router's configuration pages are very different than the ones described in this exercise, it is best to consult your router's manual and learn how to implement port forwarding on your specific model.

Finding Troubleshooting Help on the Web

In case the troubleshooting wizards and the tips that are found in this chapter do not help, you should definitely search for help online. We recommend the following Web sites:

- **Windows 7 Compatibility Center** (*http://www.microsoft.com/windows/compatibility/windows-7/en-us/default.aspx*) When specific software or hardware devices do not work on Windows 7, you should check if they are compatible with Windows 7 in the first place. This Web site has a very thorough list of software and hardware you can use to quickly see whether your software or hardware truly is compatible with Windows 7.

- **Port Forward** (*http://portforward.com*)   If you need help understanding how to forward ports manually on your router, this is the place you must visit. This Web site has an extensive list of support documentation that shows how to implement port forwarding for almost any router model ever manufactured. It also provides free software downloads to help you test your port forwarding.

- **Microsoft Answers** (*http://answers.microsoft.com/en-us/default.aspx*)   This is a very active community of experts and normal computer users who share their experiences with Microsoft products. If you have a problem, you should definitely report it to this community and you will be able to find help from real people.

- **Super User** (*http://superuser.com*)   This is a very active community where people share their questions and problems about computing. You can post a summary of your problems, receive answers in a very short time, and also rate the quality of the feedback you receive. This community prides itself on the quality of their responses.

- **How-To Geek** (*http://www.howtogeek.com*)   This is one of the best how-to Web sites on the Internet. It features an incredibly long list of tutorials and also has a very active community that can help you solve your problems.

- **The Windows Club** (*http://forum.thewindowsclub.com*)   This is a very friendly community, populated by many Microsoft Most Valuable Professionals who have lots of knowledge about Microsoft products.

- **7 Tutorials** (*http://www.7tutorials.com*)   This Web site is operated by the authors of this book. It features lots of tutorials and also troubleshooting guides on how to fix problems with your network or your operating system.

Key Points

- The Network and Internet Troubleshooting wizards can help you fix most network and Internet problems.

- Manual port forwarding on your router allows applications to use nonstandard ports to communicate over the Internet so that they function correctly.

- If you cannot fix your problem using the Network and Internet Troubleshooting wizards and the advice found in this chapter, check out the Web sites that we recommend.

Glossary

32-bit In Windows, this refers to the way memory is accessed. 32-bit applications access memory in 32-bit "chunks" (4-bytes). A processor with 32-bit memory addresses can directly access 4 GB of byte-addressable memory.

64-bit In Windows, this refers to the way memory is accessed. 64-bit applications access memory in 64-bit "chunks" (8-bytes). Many new applications (such as graphics and multimedia programs) work best with 64-bit or higher access memory. A processor with 64-bit memory addresses can directly access more than 4 GB of byte-addressable memory.

802.11a A wireless protocol that operates in the 5-gigahertz (GHz) range. The 802.11a standard offers an enhanced data speed up to 54 megabits per second (Mbps) and became available after 802.11b.

802.11b A wireless protocol that is capable of data speeds up to 11 megabits per second (Mbps) and works in the frequency range of about 2.4 gigahertz (GHz).

802.11g A wireless protocol that operates in the 2.4-gigahertz (GHz) band, is compatible with 802.11b devices, and operates at up to 54 megabits per second (Mbps).

802.11n A higher-speed wireless network protocol that improves the throughput over previous standards. It operates at up to 600 megabits per second (Mbps) in the frequency range of about 40 megahertz (MHz).

ActiveX controls Small program building blocks used to create distributed applications that work over the Internet through Web browsers. Examples include customized applications for gathering data, viewing certain kinds of files, and displaying animation. This technology was first used in Internet Explorer 3.0 (1996).

Ad hoc network Temporary network that allows wireless devices within range of each other to locate and communicate without involving central access points.

ADSL (Asymmetric Digital Subscriber Line) High-speed digital network connection that is generally used to connect a home and an Internet service provider (ISP).

Anti-spyware An application designed to protect against, identify, and remove known or potential spyware on your computer.

Antivirus An application designed to protect against, identify, and remove known or potential viruses on your computer or your smartphone.

Authentication The process of establishing and confirming with some degree of confidence the identity of the user requesting authorization to perform a certain computing task, such as logging on to a computer.

Bandwidth A measurement of how much data can be sent through a connection. It can be expressed in bits per second or multiples of it (kilobits/s, megabits/s, and so on).

Bluetooth A technology created by Ericsson in 1994 that uses radio communications to wirelessly link devices over short distances. Applications include mobile phones, personal digital assistants (PDAs), and wireless headsets. It can cover only short distances, about 30 feet (10 meters).

Command Prompt A Windows program that acts as a DOS-like command line interpreter. The command prompt can be used to run advanced commands in text mode.

Direct connection A permanent connection between a computer and a network.

Domain Name System (DNS) The system that translates Internet domain names (Web site names such as *www.google.com* or *www.7tutorials.com*) into Internet Protocol (IP) numbers. This system allows you to type a friendly, human-recognizable name such as a Web address instead of actually typing its IP address. The DNS server performs this conversion function.

Driver (or device driver) A computer program that allows other programs to interact with a hardware device. For example, the driver for your computer's video card allows games to interact with it and generate the advanced graphics shown on your screen. Drivers are hardware dependent and are specific to each operating system.

Dynamic Host Configuration Protocol (DHCP) A networking protocol used by computers to obtain Internet Protocol (IP) numbers and other network information. The IP is obtained from a DHCP server on the local network or from an advanced networking device such as a router that can automatically assign addresses.

Dynamic IP Address A temporary IP address given to a computer or network device for the duration of the network session.

Ethernet A technology that allows users to physically connect computers using Ethernet cables. Ethernet is the most used standard for local area networks (LAN), and it generally transmits data at speeds of 10 or 100 megabits per second (Mbps).

Ethernet cable A generic name for cables that are used in cabling computer networks such as Ethernet. The most common types of Ethernet cables are Category 5 (Cat5) and Ethernet crossover cable.

Encryption The process of transforming information to make it unreadable to all except those who are authorized and possess the required information to decipher it (usually referred to as encryption key).

Entertainment Software Rating Board (ESRB) A self-regulatory organization that assigns age and content ratings for computer and video games and other types of entertainment software in North America.

Extranet A computer network that allows controlled access from the outside of the network. Extranets are typically used by businesses or educational institutions.

File Sharing A networking feature that allows more than one person to access the same file at the same time, from different computers.

File Transfer Protocol (FTP) A network protocol optimized and used to copy files from one host to another over a TCP/IP-based network, such as the Internet.

Firewall A hardware or software solution that is designed to block unauthorized access while permitting authorized communications, based upon a set of rules and other criteria. They are designed to prevent unauthorized Internet users from accessing private networks connected to the Internet. All messages entering or leaving an intranet pass through the firewall, which inspects each message and blocks those that do not meet the specified security criteria.

Firmware Small programs that control the very basic low-level internal operations for various electronic devices such as routers, digital cameras, hard disks, motherboards, and so on. Without firmware, a device would be completely non-functional.

Gateway A network node equipped for interfacing with another network that uses different protocols (also called protocol converters). Gateways are important network points that act as the entrance to other networks, translating between the different protocols used in communication.

Hotspot A location where a wireless network is available to the public. They are generally found in airports, hotels, coffee shops, restaurants, and so forth.

Hypertext Transfer Protocol (HTTP) A networking protocol that is the foundation of data communication for the World Wide Web (WWW). HTTP functions as a request-response protocol that facilitates the moving of the files across the Internet

Internet Protocol (IP) The principal communication protocol used for dispatching data across a large computer network. It is the primary protocol that establishes the Internet.

Internet Protocol (IP) Address A unique number consisting of four parts separated by dots. Every device on the Internet (and on any network) must have a unique IP address to participate and be part of it. An example of an IP address is: 192.168.0.1.

Internet The global system of interconnected computer networks that use the standard Internet Protocol Suite (TCP/IP) to serve all the users worldwide. The Internet carries a vast range of information resources and services, such as the inter-linked hypertext documents of the World Wide Web (WWW) and the infrastructure to support electronic mail.

Intranet A private network that is contained in a larger one. The main purpose of an Intranet is to share information and resources among a restricted group of people, such as the employees of a company.

Local Area Network (LAN) A computer network limited to a small physical area, usually in the same building or floor of a building. Home networks are very good examples of LANs.

Logon The process of connecting to a computer or a network by inputting a specific username and password.

Line Printer Daemon (LPD)/Line Printer Remote (LPR) A network protocol used for submitting print jobs to a remote printer. This is used mostly for Unix-based operating systems (Ubuntu Linux, Mac OS X).

Media Access Control (MAC) address A unique identifier that is assigned to network interfaces for communications. Most often, a MAC address is assigned by the manufacturer of a network interface card (NIC) and stored in its hardware (the card's read-only memory). It is stored as six groups of two hexadecimal digits, separated by hyphens (-). For example: 01-2c-45-6e-89-ab.

Modem A device that modulates an analog carrier signal to encode digital information. It also demodulates a carrier signal to decode the transmitted information. These signals can be transmitted over telephone lines and demodulated by another modem at the receiver side to recover the digital data.

Nautilus The official file manager of the GNOME desktop that is included in Linux distributions such as Ubuntu Linux.

Network A collection of computers and devices (such as printers, smartphones, etc.) interconnected by communication channels that facilitates communications among users and allows them to share information and resources.

Network Adapter Synonym for Network Interface Card (NIC)—A hardware network card installed into the computer that is used to connect the computer to a network.

Network Address A unique identifier for a computer on a network. The network address is most times used as another name for an Internet Protocol (IP) address.

Network Address Translation (NAT) A technology that allows a local area network (LAN) to use one set of Internet Protocol (IP) addresses for internal traffic and a second set for external traffic.

Network Discovery A network setting in Windows that determines whether your computer can see other computers and devices on the network and whether they can see your computer.

Network Interface Card (NIC) A hardware network card installed into the computer that is used to connect the computer to a network.

Pairing Used for establishing communications over Bluetooth. Pairing occurs when two Bluetooth devices agree to communicate with each other and establish a connection.

Point-to-Point Protocol over Ethernet (PPPoE) A network protocol used with many Digital Subscriber Line (DSL) services where individual users connect to the DSL modem to have access to the Internet. Mainly used by telephone companies to connect their clients to the Internet.

Point-to-Point Tunneling Protocol (PPTP) A method for implementing virtual private networks (VPN), which is used by companies to connect employees to the company Intranet from external networks.

Port Is an application-specific or process-specific software construct serving as a communications endpoint. A specific port is identified by its number, commonly known as the port number, the Internet Protocol (IP) address with which it is associated, and the protocol used for communication.

PostScript Printer Description (PPD) Files that contain PostScript code used to invoke features for printing jobs. PPDs function as drivers for PostScript printers.

Protocol A formal set of rules that must be followed for computers and networks to exchange information.

Proxy server A computer that is between a user's computer and a computer or network that the user wants to access. When a proxy server is established, the user's computer makes all of its requests for data from the proxy server; the proxy server then makes requests from the computer that contains the data. This adds an extra layer of security to the network and is often used in corporate local area networks (LANs).

Router A piece of hardware that handles data being sent between two networks. Routers look at the source and destination addresses of the data packets passing through and decide which route to use to send them. In home networking, a router is usually a hardware device that routes data from the local area network (LAN) to the Internet.

Samba A Unix-specific software that provides file and printer services for Windows clients. It is used by nearly all distributions of Linux, including Ubuntu Linux, to facilitate networking interactions with Windows computers.

Service Set Identifier (SSID) A name that identifies a wireless network. It can be up to 32 characters long.

Server This is most often a computer that provides a specific kind of service to client computers. For instance, there are mail servers, print servers, Internet servers, and data servers, all of which provide a service to users on a network. Servers are most often used in domains, but workgroups can have servers as well (such as Windows Home Server).

Server Message Block (SMB) A protocol used to provide shared access to files, folders, and printers between the nodes of a network. This protocol is used mostly by Windows operating systems.

Spyware Software that is installed on a user's computer without the user's knowledge. Spyware often monitors the use of the computer without the user's knowledge or consent and can acquire personal information or copy keystrokes.

Static Internet Protocol (IP) Address An Internet Protocol (IP) address that never changes.

Subnet Mask Used to determine what subnet an Internet Protocol (IP) address belongs to. It has the same format as the IP address.

Transmission Control Protocol/Internet Protocol (TCP/IP) The set of protocols that transfers data on the Internet. TCP/IP software is included with every major kind of computer operating system and is required to obtain direct access to the Internet.

Universal Serial Bus (USB) A specification for establishing communication between devices and personal computers. USB can connect computer peripherals such as memory sticks, digital cameras, mice, keyboards, printers, flash drives, external hard disk drives, and so on.

User Datagram Protocol (UDP) A simple protocol used to transfer data over the Internet.

Uniform Resource Locator (URL) The address of a web page on the World Wide Web. For example: http://www.7tutorials.com.

Virtual machine A software implementation of a computer. It literally simulates a computer and executes instructions as it if were a physical machine.

Virtual Private Network (VPN) A network that uses the Internet to provide remote offices or individual users with secure access to their organization's network. Generally used by businesses to connect their employees to the organization's Intranet.

Virus Auto-replicating and harmful computer software. A virus will copy itself and may display messages, delete files, rename files, change Web browser home pages, steal data, and so forth.

Wide Area Network (WAN) A computer network that covers a large area—for example, a city, region, or country. WANs are used to connect local area networks (LANs) together.

Wi-Fi Protected Access Pre-shared key (WPA-PSK and WPA2-PSK) A protocol for securing wireless networks that encrypts all network traffic using a 256-bit key. The WPA2 protocol is an improved version of WPA.

Windows Internet Name Service (WINS) A Microsoft networking protocol that allows legacy computer applications to be used on modern TCP/IP networks.

Wired Equivalent Privacy (WEP) A deprecated security protocol for wireless networks. Compared to WPA and WP2, this protocol can be easily hacked.

Wireless The transfer of information without the use of wires.

World Wide Web (WWW) A term used to describe the Internet.

Worm A virus that does not infect other programs but instead makes copies of itself and infects other network computers. A worm might also harm files and programs.

Index

Numbers

A

V

W

About the Authors

Ciprian Rusen

 Ciprian Rusen is a Romania-based IT project manager for a major consumer goods corporation. During work hours, he manages complex rollouts of enterprise IT solutions, while in his spare time, he loves to experiment with the latest technologies, learn how best to use them, and share his knowledge with others. This book is the result of his work and experience in the field, in addition to the contributions that were made by the 7 Tutorials Team. Ciprian coordinates the team at *www.7tutorials.com*. Together, they write tutorials for Windows 7 users, helping them to obtain the best possible computing experience out of the operating system. The team also worked together on writing this book, each member contributing to its creation.

7 Tutorials Team

Florina Muntenescu is a computer science graduate and a programmer with a passion for Artificial Intelligence and mobile devices. She believes that anyone can approach and use computers in a familiar and casual manner, if they overcome their reluctance or fear of technology. She contributed to the chapters about user accounts and parental controls. Florina is based in Cluj-Napoca, Romania.

Jack Busch is a freelance writer and editor from Pittsburgh, Pennsylvania. Jack works with bloggers, Internet marketing firms, and web developers from around the world to craft compelling content for the Web. Technology plays a large role in making Jack's collaborative work possible, and he enjoys sharing tips that help both professional and personal users get the most out of Windows 7. He contributed to the chapters about Windows Media Player and the interoperability between Mac OS X and Windows 7.

George Grigorita is Editor-in-Chief of the Romanian edition of *PC World* computer magazine, which is published in 51 countries. A journalist with a major passion for technology, he does his best to share his knowledge of all things tech with everyday users. George contributed to the chapters about Ubuntu Linux and Windows 7 interoperability as well as the chapter about sharing and working with devices. He is based in Bucharest, Romania.

Chuck Houghton has been an IT professional for more than a dozen years, supporting businesses with as few as 3 employees as well as organizations as large as 2,000 employees. He has a passion for technology and maybe a greater passion for communicating its benefits and pitfalls. He acted as the book's technical reviewer and contributed to the step-by-step exercises in the book. Chuck is based in the U.S.